FUNCTIONING LOCAL GOVERNMENT IN SOUTH INDIA

FUNCTIONING LOCAL GOVERNMENT IN SOUTH INDIA

U.B. Singh

GYAN PUBLISHING HOUSE
NEW DELHI-110 002

FUNCTIONING LOCAL GOVERNMENT IN SOUTH INDIA

ISBN: 81-212-0715-0

Published in 2000 in India by
Gyan Publishing House
5, Ansari Road,
New Delhi-110 002
Phone : 3282060, 3261060
Fax : 3285914
E-mail: gyanbook@del2.vsnl.del.in

Laser Typesetting at: Power Photocomposers
Printed at: Chawla Offset Printers

Contents

Preface

The urban local government in India owes its origin to the British rule in the country. The history of modern municipal administration in the country starts with the establishment of first municipality in 1687 in Madras by the British. Thus, the modern structure of local self-government in India is a British creation. The local self-governing institutions—as they exist today—do not represent a process of continuous growth but are the product of convenience, which was found necessary by the British government in the interest of administration. The local government witnessed a number of reforms during the British rule. When the popularly elected ministries came to the power in 1937, the problems of local self-government were studied afresh and various committees were constituted in order to improve the structure and working of local bodies. But the recommendations of those committees could not be implemented due to the resignation of popular ministries and the Second World War hampered the growth and development of local self-government in India.

The advent of Independence opened a new chapter in the socio-economic reforms embodied in the Constitution of India. The local self - government has now become an integral part of the national administration playing the same vital role that is assigned to the local self-government in other independent democratic countries. The multi-dimensional decline in urban local government, however, highlighted the importance and urgency of reform in the system. As a result, post-independence era has witnessed numerous impressive attempts for reforms at the level of urban government. The National Commission of Urbanisation (1985) gave detailed recommendations about the measures required for strengthening the management and administration of urban local government institutions in the country. At the time of the recommendations made by the Commission, a number of Panchayat and

Palika Sammelans as well as Workshops were organised. As a consequence of this extraneous exercise, the attempts were made to amend the Constitution of the country. As a result, the 74th Amendment to the Constitution was enacted in 1992. The detailed historical development of local self-government in India is discussed in my another book *Urban Local Government* (1996).

The Constitution 74th Amendment Act (CAA) is a landmark in the historical development of urban local government in the country. It provides for two types of provisions—mandatory as well as discretionary. Mandatory provisions were to be adopted compulsorily throughout the country while optional ones were left to the State Government in view of the subject having been placed in the State List. All the states have enacted, modified or amended their respective municipal laws to commensurate to the provisions of the Constitution.

The southern states of the country enjoy special status in view of having been blessed with the first unit of urban local self-government in the country. The urbanisation characteristics in the region are also unique and noteworthy. The comparatively higher level of literacy in the region helps make the countrymen more aware and rightful. The demographic specialities cast their shadow on the administration as well.

In southern states, during 1981-91, Kerala registered the highest urbanisation growth of 1589.84 per cent followed by Andhra Pradesh with 872.26 per cent. Karnataka was in third place with 748.09 per cent and Tamil Nadu emerged the last with 600.15 per cent. Karnataka recorded the highest growth of 50.65 per cent during 1971-81 in the post-independent period. In this decade, Karnataka stood first. On the other hand, Kerala experienced the highest growth of 61 per cent during 1981-91 whereas other states experienced a decline. One important point worth mentioning is that urbanisation in Karnataka has not been as high as in Kerala or Andhra Pradesh during the last one or two decades. This, however, does not mean that Karnataka is less urbanised. In fact, it is next only to Tamil Nadu among the southern states. What is relevant to note is that Karnataka's urbanisation reached a plateau earlier to Andhra Pradesh or Tamil Nadu on account of which the subsequent increases have not been as high as in those two states.

Decadal Variations

(Percentage)

	All India	*Karnataka*	*Andhra Pradesh*	*Tamil Nadu*	*Kerala*
1901-11	0.35	4.64	17.68	15.57	15.44
1911-21	8.27	17.76	1.03	8.86	29.78
1921-31	19.12	21.65	23.17	23.40	34.58
1931-41	31.97	22.99	36.07	22.30	30.47
1941-51	41.43	61.71	47.86	41.75	52.72
1951-61	26.41	18.26	15.76	22.59	39.89
1961-71	38.23	32.22	33.92	38.64	35.72
1971-81	46.14	50.65	48.62	27.98	37.64
1981-91	36.47	29.62	43.24	19.59	60.97
1901-91	741.76	758.89	872.26	600.65	1589.84

In this context, the present volume, attempts earnestly to discuss the municipal administration in the southern states of the country in post-74th-CAA era. It highlights the legal structural framework of urban governance in four major developed states in the country. It may, probably, prove to be a pioneering work on the subject. The book will be of immense help to the academicians, researchers and students in the field of administration in general and urban administration in particular.

Separate sections have been devoted to the urban local bodies in the transitional, smaller and larger urban areas. The mandatory provisions enshrined in the Constitution regarding the Wards Committees, District and Metropolitan Planning Committees, Finance Commission and State Election Commission are discussed separately. The consolidated picture in all the four states at a glance is depicted in Annexures appended at the end.

In completing the book, I received cooperation and assistance from many individuals and institutions. I express my sincere gratitude to all the concerned. I would like to place on record the efforts of Sri K.D. Pandey for the neat typing of the manuscript. I am extremely thankful to Gyan Publishing House, New Delhi for publishing the volume in record time.

U.B. Singh

1
Urban Local Government in India

Local self-government is a system under which the people of a locality possess certain responsibility of public local affairs, and the raising of money to meet their expenses (Jha, 1953). Thus, the goal of this system to be aimed at is the betterment or welfare of every citizen. Local self-government also involves distribution of work on a territorial basis. Such a government is necessary precisely because some public requirements are local in their intensity, character and scope. It provides an extensive range of services to the people and performs functions of great variety and magnitude. Local self-government ensures two way communication between the state government, and plans and programmes of the state and central governments flow in the reverse direction. Thus, it can be said that local self-government contributes to resilience, strength and richness of democracy by promoting diversification of political experience and by setting itself up as yet another centre of creative activity through democratic action (Singh, 1997). The present day local self-government is concerned principally with the provision of public services (Jackson, 1945). Thus, local government is a local self-government in the field of administration rather than in the field of legislation. Local authorities do not pass laws, they administer the laws passed by some higher authority. Their business is primarily administrative. They are administrative rather than legislative bodies.

Historical Perspective

The emergence of local self-government as a distinct government unit is the result of the interplay of several factors—historical, ideological and administrative. Historically, local self-government had obviously preceded national government. Administratively, civic services are needed by a community for a planned, programmed and integrated development in terms of region or area inhabited by them.

There was no such conception like that of local self-government in ancient India, although it is said that the origin of local self-government has very deep roots in ancient India. On the basis of historical records , excavations and archaeological investigations, it is believed that some form of local government did exist in the remote past (Mukherjee, 1958). The *Ramayana* and the *Mahabharata* also point to the existence of several forms of local self-government such as Paura, Nigama, Pauga and Gana, performing various administrative and legislative functions and raising levies from different sources. Local self-government continued during the succeeding period of Hindu rule in the form of town committees, known as Gosthis and Mahajan Samitis. The representative character of these Samitis was represented by the rulers (Sharma, 1965).

Kautilya gives a vivid account of urban administration dominated by central organisation of the monarchy, which as a matter of fact, has been so nicely reflected and confirmed by the accounts of Megasthenes. The urban life was equally regulated. The direct control and participation of the state officials was felt in town administration under a Nagaraka, who was also called Puramukhya. Kautilya has mentioned that Nagaraka was responsible for the city administration with the assistance of Gopa or Sthanika. Kautilya mentions different types of committees and specialists which appear fully relevant in modern times (Singh, 1998). According to Strabo, many of the duties of Nagaraka were discharged by Boards of Five (Panchayats). He enumerates six such boards.

As regards rural administration, village in India has been the pivot of administration since time immemorial. Ancient India was built upon the basis of decentralisation in principle and government from the sovereign at the top extended through all grades and strata of society down to the lowest classes in the villages. Every village was self-governing and there was union of villages and self-governing federations. Kautilya, despite of being a staunch supporter of strong and absolute monarchy, allowed these village communities to have freedom from central control. For effective and smooth administration, the rural collective life was promoted by organising every village into a number of common administrative units known as Sangrahana, Kharwatika and Mahagram or Sthaniya. The Chief Executive Officer of the village administration was called Gramani or Gramika, who was appointed by the king. He carried on the village administration with the help of village elders (Singh, 1998).

In the Mauryan period, followed by Gupta era and subsequently in the medieval period, the system of local self-government continued to be more or less the same. However, the system was quite different in the Mughal period. In managing the affairs of the village, the members acted as a body, their agents being the headman chosen from among themselves, according to the custom of the locality. The headmen could let to tenants the land not required by the members of the brotherhood, and they represented the village in its dealings with the administration. The extent of their powers varied in different regions, but they were important everywhere. Each village had a hereditary registrar or accountant who maintained the records of cultivation, receipts and payments and assisted the headmen in the performance of his duties.

The Mughal administration was concentrated in the provincial capital. It was a city government living and working in cities and concerning itself mainly with the inhabitants of the city and their immediate neighbourhood (Singh, 1998). The representative character was abolished and whole administration of the city was placed in the charge of a nominated government official known as Kotwal. The Kotwal not only controlled the various municipal activities but also performed certain magisterial functions, including the control over police and intelligence. In the later Mughal period, the system suffered a marked decline; not only were the urban areas maladministered, but most of them lay unhealthy and unclear till the time British came and assumed the authority (Humes and Martin, 1961).

Thus from time immemorial, ideas of local self-government in India existed to a far greater extent than anywhere else in the world. These ideas and their beginnings were a landmark in the community life of the pre-historic civilisations. These communities were, in fact, the earliest form of social organisations (Venkatarangalaya, 1960). Although, local self-government existed in India in ancient times, in its present structure and style of functioning it owes existence to the British rule in India. The ancient village committees were constituted on a narrow basis of hereditary privileges or castes, restricted closely in the scope of their duties—collection of revenue and protection of life and property were their main functions and were neither conscious instruments of political education nor important parts of administrative system.

Evolution of Modern Local Government

A beginning of modern local self-government in India may be said to have been made in 1687 when the first local self-government body was set up for the city of Madras (now Chennai). The long history of more than three centuries is rather chequered and even exotic. For our purpose, it may be divided into following phases as under:

1. First Phase (upto 1882)
2. Second Phase (1882–1919)
3. Third Phase (1919–1947)
4. Fourth Phase (1947–1992)
5. Fifth Phase (1992 onwards)

(The detailed history of urban local government in India may be seen in my other books entitled *Urban Local Government*, Rawat, 1997 and *Administrative System in India (Vedic Age to 1947),* APH, 1998).

First Phase (Upto 1882)

The local self-governing institutions—as they exist today—do not represent a process of continuous growth but are the product of convenience, which was found necessary by the British Government in the interest of administration.

As far back as 1687, Directors of the British Company ordered that a corporation consisting of European and Indian members be formed at Madras for the purpose of local taxation. The council was formed because the Company believed that the people of India would pay willingly "five shillings for the public good being taxes by themselves than six pence raised by our despotical power" (Maheshwari, 1971). This corporation had a Mayor, twelve aldermen and sixty burgesses. In 1726, the Madras Municipal Council was replaced by a Mayor's Court which was, by and large, a judicial organisation. The system of voluntary taxation perhaps dictated the expediency of popular concurrence for the arrangement made by Hastings in 1773. Accordingly, the town of Calcutta was divided into a number of wards and each ward was placed under a Kotwal appointed with the general approval of the people. The Governor-General-in-Council enacted a set of regulations in 1780. The object of these reforms was to perfect the municipal administration for the town of Calcutta. Provisions were made to establish a body of thirteen Commissioners chosen by the Governor-General-in-Council. The Commissioners were authorised to assess the annual rent of every holding in the town, and separate Collectors were appointed to realise municipal taxes. They were also authorised to take cognisance of any offence committed against municipal law. The municipal administration was established in the district towns in Bengal in 1842. The Act of 1847 vested the collection and disbursement of assessment in a Board of Seven Commissioners to be called the Board of Conservancy for the city of Bombay (now Mumbai).

The Royal Army Sanitary Commission presented its report in 1863 which again speeded up the growth of the local bodies. As a result, several Acts were passed in different provinces and several new municipalities were established in order to perform the functions of public health. The Act of 1869 authorised the Bombay Government to make provisions for expenditure on matters of local public utility and to form committees for administration of such funds. The Madras Act of 1867 divided the city into eight wards to each of which, the local government appointed four Commissioners. In addition, a President was also appointed by the Government. The executive functions vested in him.

Lord Mayo's decentralisation scheme of 1870 was a significant step in the direction of local self-government. In the next year, Acts were passed in the different provinces providing for the levy of rates and the constitution of local committees to administer the funds. The Act of 1872 constituted two representative bodies in Bombay. The first was the Municipal Corporation of the city of Bombay consisting of sixty-four persons. Their term was two years. They elected chairman for a year. The second body was the Town Council. It consisted of twelve members. They also held office for two years. The Government appointed one of its members as Chairman. The function of the Corporation was to exercise a general control over all municipal affairs. The council was to secure due administration of the municipal fund. It was a sort of finance committee of the corporation whose duty was to control expenditure and prepare annual budgets. The Calcutta Municipal Corporation Act, 1876 established corporation of the town of Calcutta. The Madras Act of 1878 empowered the rate payers to elect half of the 32 Commissioners.

Thus, the Mayo's plan for decentralisation desired that the central government should be relieved of its responsibility for providing funds for local purposes but its operative provisions made it necessary to develop municipal institutions. Furthermore, the main object of the Lord Mayo's resolution was to promote education, public health, sanitation, medical relief and local civic services and also give facilities to self-government for strengthening municipal institutions. However, it can be said that the representative local self-government in India was established by the British rulers with two main considerations. Firstly, to provide on the spot solution to the administrative problems faced due to the large size of the country and secondly, to provide finances to imperial authority. The purpose of Mayo's reform was to lessen the burden on imperial finances.

Second Phase (1882–1919)

The effect of local self-government of the policy inaugurated by Lord Mayo was reviewed in 1882. It was found that till 1882, the local self-government in India was functioning without the participation of Indian people and, therefore, it was neither the 'local' nor the 'self-government'. Lord Ripon's resolution of 1882 provided for the introduction of principles of local self-government in the municipalities. The resolution of 1882 is regarded as the Magna Carta of local self-government in India. According to Lord Ripon, local self-government was "an instrument of political and popular education". The Taxation Enquiry Committee observed, "it was Lord Ripon's resolution of 1882 that paved the way for the development of local self-government".

Lord Ripon's resolution introduced a new era in the constitution, powers and functions of the municipal bodies which were changed greatly. According to it, the actual municipal administration was to be transferred to the elected representatives of the people working under a non-official Chairman, though the ultimate supervision, control and superintendence remained with the government. It was proposed further that the charges for the maintenance of the town police, hitherto paid out of municipal revenues, should be met by the government, and municipalities should spend equivalents sums on education, medical relief and local works of public utility. The system of election for the municipal bodies was introduced with a limited franchise.

The mechanical objectives of the policy laid down in the Ripon's resolution were two-fold. In the first place, it was desired that provincial governments should apply the principle of financial decentralisation. Secondly, it became necessary to consider the steps that were necessary to render the existing local bodies more efficient and better-suited conditions to discharge the duties with which it was proposed to entrust them.

The most remarkable innovation proposed by Lord Ripon, was a network of rural local bodies. The provincial legislations of 1883–85 had one common feature, creation of a two-tier system, with district boards and sub-district boards based upon the sub-division or the tehsil. The innovation did not, however, bear much fruit. It had organisation and control but lacked the vital spirit of democracy.

Thus, through various measures municipal administration in the presidency towns had developed a few important features, e.g. a limited electorate, a strong executive in the hands of a Government official, certain safeguards for control over finance and auditing of accounts, and statutory provisions for such works as sanitation, water supply etc. The Government had the right to interfere in cases of mismanagement or negligence. There was no real self-government in the municipalities and Government control was maintained over them in many respects. The reforms inaugurated by Lord Ripon failed in almost every direction to evolve as he had desired. In the words of the British, "if we return to local self-government, we shall find everywhere stagnation and inefficiency with local variations in favour of section animosity". There was, however, a growing consciousness in the country for making municipalities self-governing and efficient.

In 1907, the subject of local self-government was considered by the Royal Commission on Decentralisation as an aspect of administrative devolution. The Commission attributed the failure to factors like artificial character of local areas, absence of general elections, lack of finance, excessive control of the government and inadequate control of local bodies over services. The recommendations of the Commission were conservative in terms of administrative improvement rather than national, political aspirations. They had a slightly unreal approach and did not recognise the fundamental changes that were taking place into the Indian public-opinion. They were an echo of Lord Ripon's resolution of 1882.

Third Phase (1919–1947)

The Government of India Act, 1919, established a responsible government in provinces by introducing the system of dyarchy. The Act laid down a schedule of taxes, which could be levied only by or for the local bodies. This not only enhanced the effective share of taxation but also enabled the local bodies to feel relatively independent. In 1930, the Simon Commission made a thorough study of the problems of local self-government in India. The Commission came to the conclusion that the efficiency of the local self-government depended upon the control or pressure which was exercised by the provincial government. It concluded that the financial resources of the local bodies were too inadequate to produce trained personnel for the local bodies. During this period, local self-government units to the smallest unit of the rural areas were established. The progress in the development of local self-government was, however, relatively slow. According to the report of the Rural Urban Relationship Committee, "The central control for the approach was the negative issue of directions to prohibit certain acts and suppression of the local bodies in the extreme cases. No attempt was made to strengthen the administrative machinery of local bodies".

The inauguration of provincial autonomy under the Government of India Act, 1935 is very important in the evolution of the local self-government in India. Under this Act, a fully responsible government of the British Parliamentary type was provided for each province with certain restrictions. While the functions of the local bodies were increased, their financial powers were curtailed actually. When the popularly elected ministries came into power in 1937, the problems of local self government were studied afresh and various committees were constituted in order to improve the structure and working of local bodies.

Most of the legislations enacted during the period were to democratise the municipal government in country. Moreover, local self-government had not taken the roots before it was overwhelmed by anti-imperialist and communal politics. There would have been an element of continuity and some substance of self-government if the traditional panchayat system, which was rooted in the community and based on custom, had received statutory recognition. Modern municipalities did not grow from below. They came in primarily as a source of taxation. The distance between them and the community remained.

Fourth Phase (1947–1992)

The advent of Independence opened a new chapter in the socio-economic reforms embodied in the Directive Principles of the State Policy incorporated in Part IV of the Constitution of India. India, as a "union of states" adopted a federal–unitary system of public administration, and the acceptance of the objective of a welfare state, to secure to all the citizens social, economic, political equality, and opportunity. With the end of the British rule, there was self-government at all the levels—union, state and local.

With the advent of democracy in 1947, local self-government, institutions attained remarkable status and importance. The post-Independence era has witnessed momentous development in the field of local self-government. The planning and implementation work based upon democratic pattern and popular initiative was provided in the Constitution. However, great importance was attached to laying down a smooth and strong system of local self-government in the rural areas. Article 40 of the Constitution clearly lays down, "The state shall take steps to organise village panchayats and to endow them ... to function as a unit of self-government". The Constitution allots the local government to the state list of functions. Since Independence, much important legislations for reshaping the local self-government were passed. The Constitution of local bodies was democratised by the introduction of adult suffrage and the abolition of communal representation.

Although, there was a growth in the number of local self-government bodies and appreciation of their plan in the system of administration, there was no corresponding development of the usefulness and effectiveness of local bodies. The main factor for this state of affairs was the inadequacy of financial resources available to them. The multi-dimensional decline in the urban local government highlighted the importance and urgency of reforms in the system. As a result, post-Independence era has witnessed numerous impressive attempts for reform at the level of urban government. Yet, most of the thinking on municipal reforms remained confined to augmenting the financial resources only. Unfortunately, the decline led them to lose their legitimacy to a great extent. As a consequence, they have failed miserably to deal with the dynamic growth created by the process of steady urbanisation and urban growth. Simultaneously, most of their functions, especially developmental, growth. Simultaneously, most of their functions, especially developmental, were transformed to the specialised agencies created for the purpose.

As a consequence of this and the complexities arisen of the increasing urban population and the growing demand of qualitative efficient civic services, setting up of a National Commission on Urbanisation in 1985 was a welcome step. The Commission gave detailed recommendations about the measures required for strengthening the management and administration of urban local government institutions in the country. The need for according an independent status to urban local government institutions had also been considered. Based on the recommendations of the Commission, the then Prime Minister organised and addressed a number of Nagar Palika and Panchayat Sammelans where officials and non-officials were invited to discuss the subject thoroughly. As a result of these deliberations, it was aimed to take the government to the people, to make the administration accountable to the people and to ensure people's participation in the administration.

With a purpose to achieve these three main objectives, the Union Government introduced in the Lok Sabha the Constitution (65th Amendment) Bill in 1989 which could not be passed and lapsed due to dissolution of Lok Sabha. Another Bill (72nd Amendment) was introduced by the succeeding Janata Party Government and met the same fate. Again, in 1991, another Bill (73rd Amendment) was introduced and passed in 1992. It was ratified by majority of the states and, after the Presidential assent, came into force with effect from April 24, 1993 as the Constitution (74th Amendment) Act (CAA).

The 74th CCA is a landmark in the history of urban local government in the country. The Act places urban local bodies in the Indian Constitution by inserting a new part IX. The Act consolidates the democratic decentralisation in the country. The local institutions are favoured with a fixed tenure. The representative character of local bodies is ensured. The Act provides for two types of provisions—mandatory as well as discretionary. Mandatory provisions were to be adopted compulsorily throughout the country. Such provisions included the uniform structuring, stability, representation, ward committees, district/metropolitan planning committees, finance commission, state election commission etc. Local Government being a state subject, the discretionary provisions were left to the states to enact according to their needs and local situations. Thus, urban local government in the country has been given a face lift by the Constitution itself. This opens a new broader spectrum before these grassroots institutions in an unitary–federal system of governance.

Fifth Phase (1992 onwards)

The State governments have modified/amended their municipal laws in conformity with the 74th CAA. The decentralisation phase has started. The provisions of the Central Act are being implemented in letter and spirit. Still a much more is left in many states to be operationalised. Despite a uniform structural framework having been enunciated by the 74th CAA, urban governance is not uniform all over the country. The regional socio-politico-economic situations differentiate local grassroot governance pattern and diversity characterises uniformity.

References and Suggested Readings

1. Jha, C., Indian Local Self Government, Novelty, Patna, 1953.
2. Jackson, W.E., Local Government in England and Wales, Hunt. Sylesbuory, 1945.
3. Humes, S. and Martin E.N., The Structure of Local Government Throughout the World, 1961.
4. Maheshwari, S.R., Local Government in India, Orient, Delhi, 1971.
5. Sharma, M.P., Local Self Government in India, Kitab, Allahabad, 1965.
6. Venkatarangalaya, H.M.V., Local Self Government in India, Journal of AIILSA, 10(2), 1960.
7. Singh, U.B., Urban Local Government, Rawat, New Delhi, 1997.
8. Singh, U.B., Administrative System in India (Vedic Age to 1947), APH, New Delhi, 1998.
9. Rural–Urban Relationship Committee Report (1966).
10. National Commission on Urbanisation Report (1988).
11. Taxation Enquiry Committee's Report (1953).
12. Singh, U.B., Urban Governance in North Eastern Region, Gyan, New Delhi, 1999.

2
Andhra Pradesh

The word 'Andhra' is used to denote a distinct linguistic region, the people of that region and the language spoken by them. It is also used synonymously with 'Telugu or Tenugu'. Andhra Desa is also known as Trilinga Desa, which means the land covered by the three famous seats of Lord Siva namely Srisailam, Kaleswaram and Draksharama.

The regular history of Andhra Desa begins with 236 B.C., the year of Ashoka's death. During the following centuries, Satavahanas, Sakas, Ikshvakus, Eastern Chalukyas and Kakatiyas ruled the Telugu country. Other dynasties which ruled over the area in succession were the dynastics of kingdom of Vijayanagar and Qutab Shahi dynasty followed by Mir Qumruddin and his successors, known as Nizams. Slowly and gradually from the 17th century onwards, the British annexed territories of the Nizam and constituted a single province of Madras. After Independence, Telugu speaking areas were separated from the composite Madras state and a new Andhra state came into being on 1st October, 1953. The area in the state is divided politically, geographically and historically into three regions, the coastal districts (Coastal Andhra or the circars), Rayalseema and Telangana. The first two parts were in the Madras Presidency until October 1, 1953. The third region was in the erstwhile state of Hyderabad. With the passing of the States Reorganisation Act, 1956, there was a merger of Hyderabad State and Andhra State and Andhra Pradesh came into being on 1st November, 1956. Before merger, Kurnool was the capital and, afterwards, Hyderabad was made the capital of Andhra Pradesh. Telugu is the predominant language and the next important language is Urdu. Telugu is spoken by eighty per cent of the population, whereas Urdu is spoken by about seven per cent.

Andhra Pradesh is bounded on north by Orissa and Madhya Pradesh, on west by Maharashtra and Karnataka, on south by Tamil Nadu and on east by the Bay of Bengal. The total area of the state is about 275,068 sq. km. and sea coast is about 974 km. in length. The state is divided into 23 districts.

Agriculture is the main occupation of about 70 per cent of the people in Andhra Pradesh. About 40 percent of cultivated area is irrigated. The state is surplus in foodgrains, particularly rice. Forest covers about 23 percent of the state's area. Several major industries are in operation around Hyderabad and Vishakapatnam. They manufacture machinetools, synthetic, drugs, pharmaceuticals, ships, fertilisers etc. Andhra Pradesh has virtual monopoly of quality chrysolite asbestos in the country. It accounts for about 93 percent of India's total production of barytes.

Urban Status

Urbanisation in the state is increasing consistently. The state accounted for more than eight per cent urban population to the country's urban population in 1991, whereas the proportion was less than eight (7.83) per cent in 1981. However, the decennial growth rate of urban population decreased from 48.62 per cent in 1981 to 42.64 per cent in 1991, whereas proportion of urban population to total population was contrary. It increased from 23.32 per cent in 1981 to 26.84 per cent in 1991. The total number of towns in the state was found decreasing, whereas number of class one towns increased over the decades. The population inhabiting class one towns is alarming. About two-thirds (66.88 per cent) of urban population lives in these big towns, according to 1991 census. The proportion was a little more than half (53.76 per cent) in 1981, less than half (48.36 per cent) in 1971 and still less in previous decades.

Out of 23 districts in the state, Hyderabad district is an urban district accounting for about 4.5 per cent of total population in the state. Rangareddy is another district having 47.1 per cent urban population and sharing 3.7 per cent of the total population. Two districts have urbanisation between 30–40 per cent accounting for about more than one-tenth of the total urban population. About half of the districts (11) have level of urbanisation between 20–30, inhabiting more than half of the urban population. The eight districts are less urbanised (10–20 per cent) and account for a little less than one third (31.3 percent) of the urban population. Cuddapah and Ramagundam are two towns which show maximum growth rates (109 and 158 per cent, respectively) in 1981–91; Hindupur (87.18 per cent), Vishakhapatnam (74.3), Karimnagar (72.25), Hyderabad (67), Chittoor (54.5), Tirupati (52.57), Khammam (50.52) and Ongole (50.21) are other class one towns having recorded rapid urbanisation in 1991, while Ramagundam (159.7), Nellore (77.5), Karimnagar (76.1), Khammam (73.5), Tirupati (72.1), Mahabubnagar (69.1), Chirala (67.1), Vishakhapatnam (66.11), Warangal (61.5), Ongole (60.1), Beemavaram (59.8), Nizamabad (58.3), Cuddapah (55.8), Vijayawada (55.3), Proddutur (51.2) and Kurnool (51.0) were the towns which showed tremendous increase in 1981. Kothagudem town recorded lowest growth (7.55) in 1991 while Tenali (15.9) was less urbanised in 1981. Surprisingly, the towns of Vijayanagaram (1010), Eluru (1008), Chirala (1004), Kothagudem (1003) and Kakinada (1001) have maximum sex ratio, while Hyderabad has the minimum of 924.

As regarded urban literacy, the State commands appreciable position with 56.8 per cent in female population. Chittoor is the most literate district (62.9 per cent), while Nizamabad is lowest with 50.1 per cent. In male literacy Chittoor (71.2), Warangal (71.0) and Vishakhapatnam (70.4) top the list, while nine other districts have more literacy in male population than the state. In females, Chittoor occupies the top position with 54.2 followed by Vishakhapatnam (52.5), West Godavari (52.6), Krishna (53.8), Nellore (52), Hyderabad (50.2), Khammam (50.1) and Nalgonda (50.1). In urban centres, Tirupati occupies the top place with 68.84 per cent literacy, followed by Karimnagar (67.48), Chittoor (66.95), Mahbubnagar (64.05), Khammam (64), Ongole (63.74), Visakhapatnam (63.22), Machilipatnam (62.32), Anantapur (61.82), Warangal (61.43), Vijayawada (60.60), Nellore (60.15) and Tenali (60.26). The details of demographic characteristics of the state are shown in Table I.

There are two Acts dealing with municipal affairs in the State, i.e., The Municipal Corporations Act, 1956 and Municipalities Act, 1965.

TABLE I

Demographic Characteristics

	1971	*1981*	*1991*
Total population (lakh)	–	535.50	663.55
Decadal growth (%)	–	–	23.91
Urban population (lakh)	84.03	124.88	178.13
Decadal growth (%)	33.92	48.62	43.24
Proportion of urban population (%)	–	23.32	26.84
Number of towns	206	234	213
No. of Class I towns	13	20	32
Population covered under class I	48.36	53.76	66.88
Towns (%)	–	975 (948)	973 (957)
Sex ratio	–	29.94 (51.99)	37.59 (56.89)
Literacy	–	275068 (4045.9)	275045 (–)
Area (km²)	–	104.22 (23.07)	134.75 (34.71)
No. of occupied residential houses (lakh)			
No. of households (lakh)	–	108.85 (24.58)	139.37 (36.10)
Total main workers (lakh)	–	226.29 (37.96)	284.45 (54.19)
Marginal workers (lakh)	–	18.77 (1.00)	15.18 (0.94)
Non-workers	–	290.44 (85.91)	365.44 (123.74)

Figures given in parentheses denote urban areas.

I. Constitution of Municipalities

The State Government by notification in the Official Gazette can constitute a Municipality in a local area with a population of not less than 25,000.

Municipal Authorities

The Municipal Authorities consist of :

(a) a Council,

(b) a Chairperson,

(c) a Commissioner, and

(d) the Wards Committees.

Municipal Council

The Municipal Council consists of:

(i) Elected Councillors: Number of elected Councillors is notified by the State Government from time to time.

(ii) Ex-Officio Councillors:

(a) every member of the Legislative Assembly whose constituency forms whole or part of the municipal area;

(b) every Member of Lok Sabha representing the constituency of which a Municipality or a portion thereof forms part; and

(c) every Member of the Rajya Sabha registered as elector within the Municipality.

(iii) Co-opted Members:

(a) Persons having special knowledge or experience in Municipal Administration co-opted by the Municipal Council:

(1) Nagar Panchayat—One

(2) Municipality having population of less than three lakhs—Two, and

(3) Municipality having population of more than three lakhs—Three.

(b) One person belonging to minorities to be co-opted by the members from among the persons who are registered as voters in the Municipality and who are not less than 21 years of age. Such a co-opted member has the right to speak in and to take part in the meetings, with the right to vote.

The Ex-Officio Members can participate in the meetings of the council. A person who becomes member of more than one Council has to by notice in writing to the Commissioner within fifteen days from the date of his becoming a member, intimate his wish to serve the particular Council. In case of default, his membership acquired later will be valid. Likewise, the Co-opted Members also have right to speak in meetings but not to vote.

Constituting New Municipality

In case of constituting a municipality for the first time, the Government may appoint a special officer to exercise the powers, discharge the duties and perform the functions of the Council, its Chair-person, its Committees and the Commissioner. He makes the arrangement for electing the Councillors on the date specified by the Government but in no case later than one year.

Reservation

In every Municipality out of the total elected members the seat would be reserved for:

(i) the Scheduled Castes and Scheduled Tribes in proportion to their shares in total population;

(ii) one-third of the total number of seats to the Backward Classes;

(iii) one-third of the seats are reserved for the Scheduled Castes, Scheduled Tribes and Backward Classes are reserved for the women belonging to these classes; and

(iv) not less than one-third of the total seats to be filled by the direct election reserved for women.

Deciding Disqualification of Councillors

Where an allegation is made by any voter or authority to the Commissioner in writing that any councillor has not qualified or has become disqualified and the Commissioner has given intimation of such allegation to the councillor and the councillor disputes it, such councillor or any other councillor may, within a period of two months from the date of intimation, by the Commissioner can either on the direction of the Council or with the approval of the Government, if no such direction is given, within the two months from the date of placing the matter by the Commissioner before the Council, apply for the decision to the District Judge of the district in which the municipality is situated. The District Judge after making inquiry determines the disqualification and his decision is final. Pending such decision, the Councillor is entitled to act as if he was not disqualified.

Disqualifications for Candidate/Councillor

A person can be disqualified for election or for holding office as Councillor if he holds an office of profit under a municipality or the Central or the State Government, OR has been sentenced by the criminal court to imprisonment for an offence under the Untouchability (offences) Act, 1995, OR sentenced to imprisonment for a period of not less than one year for any offence other than an offence of political character, OR is of unsound mind, a deaf-mute or is suffering from leprosy, OR is an applicant to be adjudicated an insolvent or undischarged insolvent, OR is interested in a subsisting lease or except as a shareholder, other than a Director in a company, OR is employed as a paid legal practitioner on behalf of the Council or as a legal practitioner against the Council, OR is an honorary magistrate for the municipal town, OR is already a Councillor whose term of office as such will not expire before the fresh election can take effect, OR is the employee or employer or the official subordinate or official superior of Council or holding office on the said date, OR is in arrears of any kind due by him to the municipality upto and inclusive of previous year in respect of which a bill or notice has been duly served upon him and the time for payment has expired, OR is dismissed from service of Central or State Government or any Municipality or any local authority for misconduct, OR absents himself from the meetings of the Council for a period of three consecutive months.

A person having more than two children is disqualified for election or for continuing as member.

Election of Chairperson

In every municipality, a Chairperson is elected directly by the persons. In case of any vacancy in the office of the Chairperson, the Commissioner intimates the fact to the election authority and the election is arranged. During the vacancy, the Vice-Chairperson performs all the functions of the Chairperson where there is either vacancy in the office of the Vice-Chairperson or the Vice-Chairperson has been continuously absent for more than 15 days, the District Collector, in the case of a special grade municipality, exercises the powers and performs the functions of the Chairperson until a new Chairperson or Vice-Chairperson is elected or the Vice-Chairperson returns to jurisdiction or recovers from incapacity.

The Chairperson, by virtue of his office, becomes a Councillor and has all rights and privileges of an elected Councillor and he is entitled to vote at all the meetings of the Council.

Election of Vice-Chairperson

Every Council elects one of its elected councillors to be its Vice-chairperson within 15 days from the date of election of the Chairperson. The ex-officio members are entitled to participate in the meeting convened for the election of the Vice-Chairperson.

Motion of No-confidence in Vice-Chairperson

A written notice of intention to make motion of No-confidence in the Vice-Chairperson can be moved by not less than one-half of the sanctioned strength of Council. Such a notice, alongwith a copy of the proposed motion, is delivered in person by any two of the elected Councillors signing the notice to the District Collector, in the case of special or selection grade municipality, or to the Revenue Divisional Officer, in case of any other municipality. The District Collector or the Revenue Divisional Officer convenes the meeting for considering the motion not later than 30 days from the date of delivery of notice. He gives to the Councillors, including ex-officio ones, notice of not less than 15 clear days of such meeting. The District Collector or the Revenue Divisional Officer presides over the meeting. If he does not present himself to preside within half an hour of the appointed time, the meeting stands adjourned. If the District Collector or the Revenue Divisional Officer is unable to preside over the meeting, he adjourns the meeting after recording his reasons, for the date not later than 15 days from the date of meeting. A notice of not less than three clear days is given by him to the Councillors of the adjourned meeting. Such a meeting can not be adjourned again.

As soon as the meeting commences, the District Collector or the Revenue Divisional Officer reads to the Council the motion for the consideration and declares it to be open for debate. Such a debate automatically terminates after two hours from the time appointed for the meeting and the motion is put to vote. A copy of the minutes of the meeting together with a copy of the motion and the result of the voting is forwarded immediately on the termination of the meeting by the District Collector or Revenue Divisional Officer to the Government.

If the motion is carried with the support of majority of the strength of the Councillors as on the date of the meeting, the District Collector or Revenue Divisional Officer publishes the result on the notice-board at the municipal office. On such publication, the Vice-Chairperson is deemed to have been removed with immediate effect. Any such result is final and cannot be questioned in any court of law.

If the motion is not carried by a majority or if the meeting could not be held for want of quorum, no notice of any subsequent motion in the same Vice-Chairperson can be made until after the expiry of one year from the date of meeting. No notice of a motion can be made within one year of the assumption of office by a Vice-Chairperson.

Powers and Functions of Chairperson

The Chairperson exercises all powers and performs all the functions imposed by the Act. He makes the arrangements for the election of the Vice-Chairperson and convenes and presides at the meetings of the Council. He can refer any resolution of the Council for its reconsideration. All official correspondence is made in the name of the Chairperson.

The Chairperson may incur contingent expenditure in the case of second or third grade municipality for an amount not exceeding Rs. 1500 and in case of first or special or selection grade municipality, a sum not exceeding Rs. 3000 The Chairperson has to report the expenditure so incurred and the reason to the Council at its next meeting.

The Chairperson enjoys certain emergency powers as well. He may direct the execution of any work or doing of any act for the safety of public and may direct the expense to be paid out of the municipal fund.

The Chairperson may, by an order in writing, delegate any of his function to the Vice-Chairperson and any of his administrative functions to the Commissioner. If the Chairperson has been absent from jurisdiction continuously or incapacitated for more than ten days, his functions are devolved on the Vice-Chairperson. If the Vice-Chairperson has continuously been absent or is incapacitated for more than ten days or if the office of the Vice-Chairperson is vacant, the Chairperson may, by an order in writing, delegate any of his functions to any elected Councillor. No delegation, however without the special sanction of the Council can be made for any period exceeding 90 days in any year and every such order has to be communicated to the Council and the Regional Director. The exercise of all such powers and performance of functions is subject to control and revision of the Chairperson.

Duties and Powers of Councillors

Any Councillor may call the attention of the Chairperson to any neglect in the execution of any municipal works, to any waste of municipal property or to the wants of any locality and may suggest any improvements. Every Councillor has the right to move resolution and to interpellate the Chairperson on matters connected with the municipal administration. Every Councillor has access to the records of the municipality after giving a reasonable notice to the Chairperson.

Resignation of Chairperson or Vice-Chairperson or Councillor

The Chairperson or the Vice-Chairperson or any Councillor, by writing under his hand addressed to the Commissioner, may resign his office. The Commissioner on receipt of such resignation places it before the next meeting of the Council, which may accept the resignation and the resignation so accepted takes effect from the date of acceptance. If the Council is not satisfied as to its genuineness, the notice of resignation lapses. Before the resignation is accepted, the person concerned can withdraw his resignation by writing under his hand addressed to the Commissioner.

Committees

The Council may constitute committees consisting of the Chairperson, the Commissioner and not less than three but not more than seven Councillors chosen in this behalf by the Council in respect of matters pertaining to formulation, review and general superintendence of development programmes relating to:

(a) education,
(b) health,
(c) sanitation,
(d) water supply,
(e) drainage,
(f) welfare of the SCs, STs, OBCs, women and children.

The term of the members of the committees is one year and the retiring members are eligible for re-election to such committees.

The Council may also, by a resolution supported by not less than one-half of the sanctioned strength of the Council, appoint as members of any committee any persons who are not Councillors but possess special qualifications for serving on such committee. The number of such members, however, should not exceed one-third of the total number of members of such committee.

Powers and Functions of the Council

The municipal administration vests in the Council, however, the Council cannot exercise the powers assigned to the Chairperson or the Commissioner. The Council may, at any time, require the Chairperson to produce any document which is in his custody. The Council may constitute committees or may appoint individual councillors to inquire into the report or advise on any matters.

Every year after the first day of April, the Commissioner prepares a report on administration of the municipality during the preceding year and submits to the Council. The Council considers the report and the Government through the District Collector. The report and the resolutions are published. The Council also furnishes to the Zilla Parishad information relating to the plan schemes of the municipality as required by the Zilla Parishad from time to time.

No act of the Council or of any person acting as the Chairperson, Vice-Chairperson or Councillor be invalid by reason only of a defect in the constitution of municipality on the ground that the Chairperson, or Vice-Chairperson or the Councillor was not entitled to continue in office by reason of any disqualification or by reason of any irregularity or illegality in his election or by reason of such acts having been done during the period of any vacancy or in the office of the Chairperson, Vice-Chairperson or Councillor.

The Council may accept any donation, endowments or trust for the furtherance of any purpose for which the Municipal Fund may be applied.

Duties

(1) The Council, so far as the funds at its disposal permit, causes the public streets to be lighted and for that purpose provides such lamps and works.
(2) The Council provides and maintains a sufficient system of drains.
(3) The Council has to make adequate arrangements for the regular sweeping and cleaning of streets and removal of sweepings therefrom.
(4) The Council causes the public streets and bridges to be maintained and repaired.
(5) The Council gives names to all public streets/roads.
(6) The Council causes a number to be affixed or painted to the side or outdoor of any building or to some place at the entrance of the premises.
(7) The Council may, with the sanction of the Government, direct the construction of water-works and may cause existing works

for the supply of water to be maintained and supplied with water.

(8) The Council registers all births and deaths occuring in the municipality.

Transaction of Business

Every meeting of the Council is presided over by the Chairperson and in his absence, by the Vice-Chairperson, and in the absence of both, by a Councillor included in the panel. Where no such temporary Chairman is present and if there is no quorum, one of its Councillors may be chosen by the meeting to preside for the occasion.

Every year at the first meeting of the Council, the Chairperson may nominate from amongst the elected Councillors a panel of not more than four temporary Chairmen to preside over the meetings in absence of the Chairperson or the Vice-Chairperson.

The Chairperson preserves order and decides all points of order arising at or in connection with meetings. There can be no discussion on any point of order. Where the conduct of any Councillor is disorderly, the Chairperson may direct him to withdraw from the meeting and the Councillor cannot be allowed to attend the remainder of the day's meeting. The Chairperson may, in case of grave disorder, suspend the meeting for a period not exceeding three days. In case of disregarding the authority of the chair by the Councillor, the Chairperson puts the name before the Council for his suspension and the Council may suspend him for a period not exceeding three consecutive months reckoned from the date of that meeting. Such a suspended Councillor forthwith withdraws from the precincts of the Council.

Commissioner

The State Government appoints a Commissioner for every municipality. The Commissioner is the executive authority of the municipality. Where it is considered necessary, the Government may appoint a Deputy Commissioner to assist the Commissioner. The salaries, allowances, pensions etc. to these officers are paid out of the Consolidated Fund of the State.

The Commissioner can bring into effect all the resolutions of the Council and furnishes to the Council periodical reports regarding the progress made in carrying out the resolutions. The Commissioner exercises the executive powers for the purpose of carrying out the provisions of the Act, and is directly responsible for its due fulfilment, exercises all powers in relation to the collection of taxes and fees, the licenses and the removal of encroachments. He is in charge of the office of the municipality and has custody of the municipal records, and can exercise all the powers and perform all the functions imposed on him. He can inspect the places of entertainment for the purpose of verification of the sale of the tickets.

The Commissioner may, by order in writing, delegate any of his powers or functions to any officer or other employee of the Council or to any employee of the Government. He works under the administrative control of the Chairperson.

The Commissioner may incur contingent expenditure in the case of a second or third grade municipality not exceeding Rs. 1000; in the case of first grade, Rs. 1500; and in special or selection grade municipality, not exceeding Rs. 2000. He reports the expenditure so incurred to the Council.

The Commissioner can attend the meetings of the Council and has the right to speak in the meetings and of any of its committees but is not entitled to make any resolution or to vote at any meeting.

Municipal Officers

The State Government may sanction a post of Municipal Health Officer, Municipal Engineer, Education Officer and Town Planning Officer. However, in the case of a municipality, which has an annual income of less than Rs. Three lakh from ordinary receipt, the Government may, without sanctioning the posts, appoint any officer of the Public Health Department, Public Works Department, Education Department or the Town Planning Department to exercise the powers and discharge the functions. If there is no such Officer, the Commissioner exercises the powers and discharges the functions of such officer. All the appointments to posts sanctioned are made by the Government. The salaries, allowances etc. of every officer are paid out of the Consolidated Fund of the State. The Government may withdraw any such officer if such withdrawal is recommended by a resolution passed at a special meeting called for the purpose and supported by the votes not less than three-fifths of the sanctioned strength of the Council. However, such a resolution cannot be moved within one year of the assumption of charge by such officers.

The Government may, on the application of any Council, place the service of any Government employee at the disposal of the Council. Such an employee cannot be dismissed or removed without the consent of the Government in case of a Medical Officer and, in any other case, without the consent or until three months' notice in writing is given to the chief controlling authority of the Government department concerned. No such employee can be withdrawn without the consent of the Council or until the Government gives three months notice to the Council to that effect or unless some other Government employee is deputed to replace the withdrawn one.

The State Government may, after consulting all the Councils, constitute any class of officers or employees of Councils a municipal service for the State.

The Government has the power to make rules to regulate the classification and methods of recruitment, conditions of service, pay and allowances and disciplinary conduct of the officers and to recover from the Council the whole or a proportion of salary and allowances paid to officers by general or special order.

All proposals for fixing or altering the number, designation and grades of the officers and employees and the salaries, fees and allowances payable to them are placed before the Council by the Commissioner for its consideration and sanction. The proposal adversely affecting any officer or employee who has been in permanent service for more than five years and is drawing a salary of not less than Rs. 50 per mensum can be considered at a special meeting convened for the purpose and be given effect when assisted by at least one-half of the members on the Council. The appointments on these posts are made by the Commissioner. The appointments to the post of a headmaster or headmistress of a high school and all other posts are made from a panel prepared by a committee constituted for the purpose by the Government.

The State Government has power to transfer any officer or employee of a municipality to the service of any other municipality or any other local authority.

The Commissioner may censure, fine, withhold increment, withhold promotion, suspend or reduce in rank, remove or dismiss any officer or employee from service except the one appointed by the Government. A fine is imposed only on Bill Collector.

Municipal Property

All public streets with the pavements, stones and other materials thereof and all works, materials and other things provided for such streets, all sewers, drains, drainage works, tunnels and culverts, whether made at the cost of the Municipal Fund or otherwise in, alongside or under any street, whether public or private and all works, materials and things appertaining thereof vest in the Council. All rubbish and filth and other matters collected by or on behalf of the Council belong to the Council.

Contracts

The Commissioner of the second or third grade Municipality can enter into contract valued upto not exceeding Rs. 5000, while the Commissioner, in first grade Municipality has the power upto Rs. 10,000. The Committee consisting of the Chairperson, Commissioner and not less than three but not more than seven councillors, chosen in this behalf by the Council, has power to enter into contracts amounting to exceeding Rs. 5000 but not more than Rs. 20,000 in the case of second or third grade Municipality and Rs. 10,000 to 50,000 in first grade Municipality. As regards Special or Selection Grade Municipality, the Commissioner enjoys the power upto Rs. 25,000 and the Committee between Rs. 25,000 and Rs. 75,000.

Every contract of the value of amount exceeding Rs. 1000 is made in writing and is signed by the Commissioner.

In addition, the State Government may appoint any person to carry any work into execution on behalf of a Council to make necessary contracts. Such a person works under the control of the Government and the Council pays to the person required sums for the purpose.

Mandatory Taxes

Every Council can, by resolution, levy the following taxes:

(i) a property tax,

(ii) a tax on carriages and carts, and

(iii) a tax on animals.

Optional Taxes

The Council may, by resolution and with the previous sanction of the Government, also levy:

(i) a tax on Advertisement, and
(ii) duty on transfer of property.

Imposition of Taxes

Before passing a resolution imposing a tax for the first time or increasing the rate of an existing tax, the Council has to publish a notice in at least one newspaper published in the language of the district having circulation in the municipality on the notice-board of the municipal office and in other specified places and by beat of drums, of its intention, fix a reasonable period not less than one month for submission of objections and consider them within the period specified in this respect. Any resolution determining to levy a tax should specify the rate at which and the date from which such tax should be levied. A notification to this effect is published by the Commissioner.

Alteration in Taxes

Any resolution abolishing an existing tax or reducing the rate is reported immediately to the Government. In municipalities, which have an outstanding loan such abolition or reduction cannot be brought into effect without the sanction of the Government.

Property Taxes

The property tax is levied on all buildings and lands within the municipal limits. It comprises:

(a) a tax for general purpose,
(b) a water and drainage tax,
(c) a lighting tax, and
(d) a scavenging tax.

These taxes are levied at such percentage of the annual rental value of lands or buildings or both as may be fixed by the Council. However, the incidence of property tax together with the education tax and library cess should not exceed 25 per cent of the annual rental value in the case of residential buildings and 33 per cent in the case of non-residential buildings.

The tax on lands not used for agricultural purposes and not occupied by or adjacent and appurtenant to building is levied on capital values of lands. In the case of lands used exclusively for agricultural purposes, the Council may levy these taxes at such proportions of land revenue payable thereon as is fixed with the approval of the Government.

The Government may, after consultation with the Council, by order published in the Gazette, direct the levying of property tax.

Every building is assessed together with its site and other adjacent premises occupied as an appurtenance thereto unless the owner of the building is different from the owner of such sites or premises. The annual rental value is deemed to be the gross annual rent at which they may reasonably be expected to be let from month to month or from year to year with reference to its location, type of construction, plinth area, age of the building, nature of use to which it is put and such other criteria as may be prescribed.

In case of any Government or railway building or any building not ordinarily let, the gross annual rent of which cannot in the opinion of the Commissioner, be estimated, the annual rental value of the premises is deemed to be nine per cent of the estimated value of the land and the present cost of erecting the building after deducting a depreciation amount which should, in no case, be less than ten per cent of such cost. The depreciation amount in case of lands and buildings upto the age of 25 years is ten per cent and above the age of 25 years is twenty per cent of the annual rental value.

A rebate of 40 per cent of the annual rental value is allowed in respect of residential buildings occupied by the owner. The rebate amount is inclusive of the depreciation value.

An area not exceeding three times the plinth area of the building including its site or a vacant land upto 1000 sq. metres, whichever is less, is deemed to be adjacent land appurtenant to the building. Area of land in excess of the limit is assessed on capital value.

General exemptions are granted to the places for public worship, choultries rent charged for which is used exclusively for charitable purpose, recognised educational institutions including hostels, public buildings and places used for charitable purpose of sheltering destitutes or animals and libraries and playgrounds which are open to public, protected ancient monuments, charitable hospitals and dispensaries, hospitals and dispensaries maintained by railway administration, burial and burning grounds, buildings and lands belonging to the Council and any irrigation work vesting in the Government. and all other Government property.

The exemptions are not granted to residential quarters attached to schools and colleges not being hostels or to residential quarters attached to hospitals, dispensaries and libraries.

The water and drainage taxes are not levied on any land used exclusively for agricultural purposes and not deriving any benefit from the water and drainage works. The Council may, with the previous sanction of the government, exempt any particular part of a municipality from the payment of the whole or a portion of water and drainage taxes or lighting tax on the ground that such area is not deriving full benefit from the water supply and drainage or from the lighting system. The Council may exempt any building or land from whole or portion of scavenging tax if it is satisfied that the owner or occupier has made sufficient arrangements for the daily removal of rubbish, filth and carcasses of animals. The owner-occupied residential buildings, annual rental value of which does not exceed Rs. 300 are exempted from property tax. In respect of houses constructed for urban poor, the municipality can collect one rupee for every half year towards property tax. A person to be assessed does not own any other buildings or lands assessed to the property tax and is not liable to profession tax may be given exemption.

The property tax is levied every half year and is paid within 30 days after the commencement of the half year. A simple interest at the rate of two per cent can be imposed in case of any failure to pay property tax within due dates. If the tax is not paid within the due dates, the Commissioner can, after giving the notice, disconnect all the essential services.

A building or land having remained vacant for 30 days or more consecutive days in the half year deserves remission on tax. The remission is granted in case of construction, reconstruction or demolition of building. The remission can be sought in current or following half year and not afterwards. If the notice of intention is given by the owner to the Commissioner within the last two months of the half year, the remission is granted for the half year. If the notice is given within first four months, the remission is granted to the extent of half of the tax payable for that half-year.

The Valuation Officers are appointed by the Government who exercise the powers, discharge the duties and perform the functions of the Commissioner in connection with assessment work for the property tax. The Government can sanction the required establishment for the purposes of enabling the Valuation Officers to carry out their duties. The Government pays out of the Consolidated Fund of the State the salaries, allowances to the Valuation Officers and their establishment. The Commissioner maintains the assessment books relating to the property tax in accordance with the valuation fixed by Valuation Officer.

The assessment books are completely revised by the Commissioner ones in every five year. When assessment books are prepared for the first time and when general revision has been completed, the Commissioner gives public notice stating that the petitions will be considered if they reach the municipal office within sixty days from date of notice, in case of the Government or railway administration or a company and, of thirty days in other cases. The notice can be affixed to the notice-board of the municipality office and, on the same day, be published in the newspaper, and be published by the municipality by beat of drum.

Any person may, at any time not being less than 30 days before the end of a half year, move the Commissioner by revision petition to reduce the tax to which he is liable for the forthcoming half year on the ground that the capital value or the annual rental value has decreased since the last revision.

Tax on Carriages and Carts

The rate of tax is determined by the Council and cannot exceed the maximum as determined in respect of carriages and, in respect of carts, such rate should not exceed eight rupees per cart per year.

Every person having possession, custody or control of any taxable carriage is liable for tax if the carriage period is not less than 120 days in the year. If the period does not exceed 30 days, no tax is levied. If the period is more than 30 days but less than 120 days, a moiety (half) of the yearly tax is charged.

Every owner of any such carts has to register it once in every year in the municipal office, and a number is affixed to every registered cart.

A carriage or cart tax cannot be levied on carts belonging to the Government and used for defence purposes, carts belonging to the Council, carts kept solely for sale or repair, children perambulators and tricycles, carts kept solely to be used for the conveyance of the sick, the injured or the dead, free of charge and private bicycle and owner-driven rickshaws.

If a number is not affixed to a cart, the Commissioner may seize and detain the vehicle. If the seized cart is not claimed and the tax is not paid within ten days from the date of seizure, the Commissioner may direct that the vehicle or animal should be sold through public auction.

Tax on Animals

If the Council by a resolution determines that a tax on animals has to be levied, the Commissioner takes steps to levy tax yearly on the animals which are kept or used within the municipality. The rates are determined by the Council.

Tax on Advertisements

Every person who erects, exhibits, fixes or retains upon or over any land, building, wall, hoarding or structure, any advertisement or who displays any advertisement to public view in any manner in any place whether public or private, has to pay on every such advertisement.

Duty on Transfer of Property

The duty on transfer of property is charged in the form of a surcharge on the duty imposed on every instrument in respect of whole or part of the immovable property. The rate is fixed by the State Government but not exceeding five per cent of the amount.

Budget

The Council, in each year, frames a budget showing the probable receipt and the proposed expenditure during the following year. A copy of the budget is submitted to the Government. The budget contains provisions adequate in the opinion of the Government for due discharge of all liabilities, for the maintenance for a working balance, and for the execution of works. If the budget fails to make those provisions, the Government may modify any part of the budget to ensure that provisions are made.

If in the course of a year the Council thinks it necessary to modify the figures shown in the budget, it may submit a supplemented or revised budget provided no alteration can be made without the consent of the Government in the amount allotted for the service of debt or in the working balance.

Accounts and Audit

The Government can appoint auditors for auditing the accounts of receipts and expenditures of the Municipal Fund.

Rules, Bye-Laws and Regulations

The State Government may, by notification in the Gazette, make rules for carrying out all or any of the purposes of the Act. Every rule is laid before each House of the State Legislature if it is in session, and if it is not in session, in the session immediately following for a total period of 14 days which may be comprised in one session or in two successive sessions, and if before the expiry of the session in which it is laid or the session immediately following, both Houses agree in making any modification in the rule or in the annulment of the rule, shall, from the date on which the modification or annulment is notified in the Gazette, have effect only in such modified form or shall stand annulled.

The Council may make bye-laws to provide for all matters required or allowed by the Act to be provided for. The Council has before making or altering bye-laws, to publish a draft of the proposed bye-laws and alteration together with a notice specifying a date at or after which such draft is taken into consideration, and receives and considers any objection or suggestion before the specified date. No bye-law or cancellation or alteration of bye-law has effect until the same is approved and confirmed by the Government. Any bye-law duly confirmed is published in English and in the main language of the district and comes into operation three months after its publication.

Regulations made by the municipal authorities are published in such manner as the Council may determine.

Control

The State Government may either *suo motu* or on representation of any Councillor, the Chairperson or the Commissioner, by order in writing, cancel any resolution passed, order issued or license or permission granted or prohibit the doing of any act. The Government may suspend the resolution, order, license, permission or act for such period as it thinks fit. The Govenrment may, by notification in the Gazette, remove any Chairperson or Vice-Chairperson, who in their opinion, wilfully omits or refuses to carry out or disobeys the provisions of the Act or any rules, bye-laws or lawful orders issued or abuses his position or the power vested in him. While proposing to remove a person the Government has to give him an opportunity for explanation and the notification should contain a statement of the action taken. Such a removed Chairperson or Vice-Chairperson is not eligible to office until the date on which notice of the next ordinary elections to the Council is published.

If, at any time, it appears to the Government that default in performing any duty is made, they may, by order in writing, fix a period for the performance of such duty. If the duty is not performed within the period fixed, the Government may appoint some person to perform it and may direct the expenses to be paid by the Council.

The State Government may appoint a Director of Municipal Administration and a number of Deputy and Regional Directors and other officers for inspecting or superintending the operations of the Councils. All schools, hospitals, dispensaries, vaccine station, choultries and other institutions and all documents are open to the inspection of officers appointed by the Government.

The Government may, with the consent of the Council, undertake on its behalf the construction of water supply, drainage or other works, appoint person to carry out construction of such works and direct the expenses to be paid from the Municipal Fund. The State Government may, after consultation with Council, constitute planning committees for any municipality for the purpose of preparing plans in respect of development works for execution within the municipality.

If it appears to the District Collector that the Chairperson has made default in carrying out any resolution, he asks for any explanation and sends the report together with the explanation to the Government for taking necessary actions. A copy of such report is sent by the Collector to the Council also. The District Collector can enter on and inspect any immovable property or work in progress under the control of the municipality. He may call for any report, document, statement, accounts, record etc. The District Collector enjoys certain emergency powers also. He can direct or provide for execution of any work or doing of any act necessary for the safety of the public and may direct to pay the expenses incurred on it, Every such case has to be reported by the District Collector with the reason in full for the exercise of such powers. A copy of the letter is sent to the Council for information. The District Collector may suspend the resolution, order, license, permission or act and report to the Government who may either rescind the Collector's order or after giving the reasonable opportunity of explanation, direct to continue in force with or without modification permanently or for such period as they think fit.

Dissolution

The State Government can dissolve the Council if it finds that the Council is not competent to perform or persistently makes default in performing the duties or exceeds or abuses its position or powers or a situation exists in which the municipal administration cannot be carried on or the financial stability or credit of the Council is threatened. Before publishing a notification in the Gazette, the Government communicates to the Council the grounds for proposed dissolution, fixes a reasonable period to show cause against the proposal and considers its objections. The Chairperson is also given a reasonable opportunity of being heard.

After dissolution, all powers and functions of the Council, Chairperson and Wards Committees are to be exercised and performed by a person appointed by the Government. Any person who is not a District Collector or Revenue Divisional Officer receives payment for his services from the Municipal Fund. The Government may direct the Commissioner to exercise and perform any powers and duties in addition to his own.

Such a resolution can be done for six months only within which the Council has to be reconstituted. The newly constituted Council can continue only for the remainder of the term of the previous Council. If the remainder period is less than six months, it is not necessary to hold any election.

II. Municipal Corporation

Municipal Authorities

The Municipal Authorities charged with the responsibility of carrying out the Act are:

(a) a Corporation,
(b) a Standing Committee,
(c) a Commissioner, and
(d) the Wards Committee.

Constitution of Corporation

The Corporation consists of:

(i) Elected Members

(a) In the city of Hyderabad 66 Councillors.

(b) In the city of Secunderabad 28 Councillors.

(c) In the case of establishment of corporation in other cities the number of Councillors is fixed by the Government. The total number of Councillors shall not exceed one hundred at any time,

(ii) Ex-Officio Members

(d) Every member of the State Legislative Assembly elected from any constituency which forms part, wholly or partly of the corporation,

(e) Every member of the Lok Sabha elected from any constituency which forms part wholly or partly of the corporation,

(f) Every member of Council of State registered as an elector within the area of the municipal corporation,

(iii) Co-opted Members:

(g) Five persons having special knowledge or experience in Municipal Administration are co-opted by the Corporation.

(h) Two persons belonging to minorities to be co-opted from among the persons who are registered voters in the Corporation and who are not less than 21 years of age.

The Co-opted Members under category (g) have the right to speak in and otherwise to take part in the meetings of the Corporation but no right to vote, but the Co-opted Members under Category (h) have the right to vote also.

Reservation of Seats

In the Corporation, out of the total elected members, the Government make reservations:

(i) to the Scheduled Castes and Scheduled Tribes in proportion to their share in the total population,

(ii) one-third of the seats for the Other Backward Classes,

(iii) not less than one-third of the seats reserved for Scheduled Castes, Scheduled Tribes and Backward Classes for the women belonging to these categories, and

(iv) not less than one-third of the total number of seats for women.

Disqualification

A person is disqualified for being elected as a Councillor if such person is at the date of election:

(i) has been sentenced by any court to imprionment or for an offence involving moral turpitude and punishable with imprisonment for a term exceeding six months or to transportation.

(ii) is of unsound mind and stands so declared by a competent court, a deaf, mute or a leper;

(iii) holds any office or place of profit under Government or under the Corporation or under any local authority;

(iv) is an undischarged insolvent;

(v) holds any judicial office with jurisdiction within the limits of the city;

(vi) is employed as paid legal practitioner on behalf of the corporation, or accepts employment as legal practitioner against the Corporation;

(vii) having been a legal practitioner he has been dismissed or is under suspension by order of the High Court on the ground

(a) a criminal offence implying a moral defect of character, and

(b) being guilty of fraudulent conduct;

(viii) has directly or indirectly, by himself or his partner any share or interest in any contract or has employment with, by or on behalf of the Corporation;

(ix) has been dismissed from the service of the Government, Corporation or any local authority for misconduct or has been declared by a competent authority to be not eligible for further employment in the public service;

(x) having contested the election as a candidate, has failed to lodge a return of election expenses within the time and in the manner prescribed unless five years have elapsed from the date by which it ought to have been lodged or the Government has removed the disqualification;

(xi) had been disqualified for voting, unless such period has elapsed for which he was disqualified for voting;

(xii) is disqualified otherwise by or under any law for the time being in force for the purposes of elections to the State Legislature; and

(xiii) has more than two children.

A Councillor is disqualified for continuing as Councillor if he :

(i) ceases to reside in the city;

(ii) is or becomes disqualified to be elected as Councillor;

(iii) fails to pay arrears of any kind of due by him to the Corporation within three months from the date of service of a notice requiring payment thereof issued by the commissioner;

(iv) absent himself at more than three consecutive meetings of the Corporation unless leave so to absent, which shall not exceed six months, has been granted by the Corporation or absents himself for over six consecutive months from meetings of the Corporation.

When a Councillor ceases to be a Councillor on this count, the Commissioner shall, at once, intimate the fact in writing to such Councillor and report the same to the Corporation at its next meeting. If such councillor applied for restoration of office to the Corporation on or before the date of its next meeting, or within fifteen days of the receipt by him of such intimation, whichever is later, the Corporation may at the meeting next after the receipt of such application, or *suo motu* at the said meeting, restore him to his office as Councillor. A Councillor, however, shall not be so restored more than twice during his term of office.

A Councillor or Mayor is disqualified on the ground of defection. The Mayor or Councillor belonging to any political party ceases to be such Mayor or Councillor:

(a) if he has voluntarily given up his membership of such political party, or

(b) if he votes or abstains from voting contrary to any direction issued by the political party he is a member of,

(c) if he has been expelled from such political party in accordance with the procedure established by the constitution, rules or regulations of such political party.

Election of Mayor and Deputy Mayor

The Mayor of the Corporation is elected directly by the persons from amongst themselves. The term of office of the Mayor is five years from the date of the first meeting and expires on the day before the date of next such meeting. But he continues in office beyond the said period until a new Mayor is elected and enters upon his office. In case of any casual vacancy, a person elected as Mayor holds office only so long as the person in whose place he is elected would have been entitled to hold that office. No casual vacancy in the office of the Mayor is filled within three months before the date on which the ordinary election of the Mayor is due.

The Councillors elect one of its elected councillors to be its Deputy Mayor. The Deputy Mayor is elected at the first meeting of the Corporation after the ordinary election. The ex-officio councillors, except the co-opted expert members, are entitled to participate in the meeting convened for the election of the Deputy Mayor. He holds his office for a period of five years from the date he assumes the office. A person elected in the casual vacancy holds office only so long as the person in whose place he is elected would have been entitled to hold that office.

When the office of the Mayor is vacant, his functions are devolved on the Deputy Mayor until a new Mayor is elected. If the Mayor leaves the city for more than fifteen days or is incapacitated, his functions are devolved on the Deputy Mayor until the Mayor returns to the city or recovers from his incapacity.

Resignation

The Mayor may resign his office by giving a notice in writing to the Corporation. The Deputy Mayor may resign by giving the notice in writing to the Mayor. Such resignation takes effect in the case of Mayor, from the date of its acceptance by the Corporation and in the case of the Deputy Mayor, by the Mayor.

A Councillor may resign his office at any time by notice in writing to the Mayor. Such resignation takes effect from the date on which it is accepted by the Mayor.

Election Petition

No election can be called in question except by an election petition presented in the manner prescribed. An election petition can be presented to the Election Tribunal by any candidate or any voter within two months. An election can be questioned on the following grounds:

(i) the election was not free by reason that bribery, undue influence or group intimidation had prevailed extensively at the election,

(ii) the election was affected materially by any corrupt or illegal practice,

(iii) any corrupt practice was committed by a returned candidate or his agent or by any other person with the connivance of a returned candidate or his agents,

(iv) the result of the election was affected materially by the improper reception or refusal of a vote or by the reception of any vote which is void or by non-compliance with the provision of the Constitution or of the Act or of any rules, and

(v) that on the date of his election, a returned candidate was disqualified to be elected as a Councillor.

An election petition shall contain a concise statement of the material facts on which the petitioner relies and full particulars of any corrupt or illegal practice that the petitioner alleges. The petition shall be signed by the petitioner and is duly verified.

The Government can appoint any person who is or has been or is eligible to be appointed as Judge of the High Court as an Election Tribunal for trial of election petitions. The Tribunal has the powers which vest in the court.

An appeal from an order passed by the Tribunal can lie to the High Court and is heard by a bench consisting of not less than two judges. No such appeal is heard by the High Court unless it is filed within thirty days from the date of the order of the Tribunal. The Tribunal sends a copy of its orders, unless a appeal is preferred therefrom, in which case, a copy of the order of the High Court, alongwith the records of the case, to the Commissioner. Every order of the Tribunal, unless an appeal is preferred to the High Court, is final and conclusive. An order of the

Tribunal takes effect immediately after the expiry of the period of appeal unless an appeal is preferred as soon as it is pronounced.

Whenever it is alleged that any person who has been elected as a Councillor is disqualified, such Councillor or any other Councillor and the Commissioner can in accordance with the directions of the Corporation, apply to the Tribunal for a decision. The Tribunal, after making necessary inquiry, determines the case and its decision is final.

Standing Committee

A Standing Committee is constituted for every Corporation. It consists of the Chairpersons of the Wards Committees in the Corporation. The Chairman of the Standing Committee is elected by the members from amongst themselves. He holds office for a period of one year from the date of his election and is eligible for re-election. The Chairman ceases to hold office if he ceases to be a member of the Standing Committee. Any casual vacancy in the office of the Chairman is filled by election from amongst the members of the Standing Committee.

The Committee is constituted to exercise the powers and to perform the functions entrusted to it under the Act.

The Committee meets at least once a week. The first meeting is held on a day and at a time fixed by the Commissioner. If meeting is not held on that day, it is held on some subsequent day to be fixed by the Commissioner. The Chairman of the Standing Committee can call a special meeting of the Committee upon a written requisition signed by Commissioner within twenty four hours for the transaction of any business which in his opinion, cannot be delayed until the next ordinary meeting. No business can be transacted at a meeting of the Committee unless at least half of the total number of the members are present from the beginning to the end of such meeting. Every meeting is presided over by the Chairman. If the Chairman is absent, one of the members present is chosen by the meeting to be the Chairman for the occasion. Every question is decided by a majority of votes of the members of the Committee present and voting.

The presiding authority has a second vote when there is an equality of votes.

The Committee may delegate its powers or duties by a specific resolution in this behalf to sub-committees. If no Chairman is elected or, if he is absent, the members of the sub-committee present choose one of them to be the Chairman of the meeting. A sub-committee may meet and adjourn as it thinks proper. The Chairman of the Standing Committee may, whenever he thinks fit and can, upon the written request by not less than two members of a sub-committee, call a special meeting of such sub-committee. Questions at meeting are decided by a majority of votes of the members present. In case of an equality of votes, the Chairman of the meeting has a casting vote. No business is transacted at any meeting unless at least two-thirds of the members of the sub-committee are present from the beginning to the end thereof.

A minute is kept by the Municipal Secretary of the names of the members present and of the proceeding at each meeting of the Standing Committee and of the Sub-Committees in a book. It is signed at by the presiding authority of the next meeting.

A member of the Standing Committees cannot vote or take part in the discussions on any matter in which he is directly, by himself or by his partner, professionally interested. The Commissioner can be present and take part in the discussion as a member but he cannot vote upon or make proposition at meeting. The Standing Committee may require any officer of the Corporation to attend any meeting. He may be called upon to make a statement or explanation or facts or supply such information as may be in his possession relating to any matter dealt with by him.

Special Committees

The Corporation may appoint, out of their own body, the Special Committees. It may, by specific resolution carried by a vote of at least two-thirds of the members of the Corporation present at the meeting delegate any of its powers and duties to such committees. The corporation may define the sphere of business of Special Committees and direct that all matters and questions included in any such sphere can, in the first instance, be placed before the appropriate special committees and be submitted to the corporation with its recommendations.

Every Special Committee appoints two of its members to be the Chairman and Deputy Chairman. A member cannot be the Chairman of more than one Special Committees at a time. In the absence of the Chairman or Deputy Chairman, the members of the Special Committee present can choose one of them to preside over the meeting.

All the proceedings of every Special Committee are subject to confirmation by Corporation. However, a Special Committee may, by a resolution supported by at least one-half of the total number of members, direct to take action in accordance with its decision without waiting for confirmation by the Corporation.

The Standing Committee may, by a resolution carried by a vote of at least two-thirds of its members present at the meeting, delegate to any Special Committee any of its powers and duties or refer any matter for disposal or report. Every Special Committee has to conform to any instructions given by the Standing Committee.

A member of a Special Committee who absents himself during two successive months from the meetings of the Committee, except by reason of temporary illness or other cause to be approved by Committee, or absents himself from, or is unable to attend the meetings during four successive months from any cause whether approved or not,ceases to be a member of such Committee and his seat falls vacant.

The Corporation makes bye-laws for regulating the constitution and the conduct of business and for the keeping of minutes and the submission of reports.

Ad-hoc Committee

The Corporation may appoint from amongst the councillors such Ad-hoc Committees consisting of such councillors as it thinks fit. It may refer for inquiry and report or for opinion any special subjects and direct that the report of any such committee should be submitted through the Standing Committee or a Special Committee.

An Ad-hoc Committee with the previous sanction of the Corporation may co-opt not more than two persons who are not councillors but who possess special qualifications for serving thereon.

Joint Committee

The corporation may join a local authority in appointing a Joint Committee for any purpose in which they are jointly interested.

Conduct of Business

The ordinary meeting of the Corporation is held not later than the 20th day of the preceding month. The first meeting after general election is held within a month of the publication of the declaration of the result at the time and place as fixed by the Commissioner. The day, time and place of every other meeting is fixed by the Mayor, in his absence by the Deputy Mayor and in absence of both, by the Chairman of the Standing Committee. A meeting can be called upon a written requisition signed by not less than one-sixth of the total number of Councillors or by not less than four members of the Standing Committee.

Every meeting is presided over by the Mayor and in his absence, by the Deputy Mayor or in the absence of both, by one of the Councillors present or chosen by the meeting to be the Chairman at the occasion.

A minimum seven days notice is ordinarily given of every meeting other than adjourned meeting. In case of urgency, except for the purpose of considering an annual budget estimate, in pursuance of a written requisition signed by not less than four members of the Standing Committee, a notice of not less than three clear days is required. In case of adjourned meetings, previous notice is given as is practicable having regard to the period of adjournment. Every notice of a meeting should specify the time and place and the business to be transacted. The notice is given by the Municipal Secretary. Any Councillor who desires at any meeting to bring forward any business or to make any substantive proposition, which is not specified in the notice can give notice to the Municipal Secretary at least three clear days before the day fixed for the meeting. A supplementary announcement of the business of propositions is given by the Municipal Secretary not later than the day previous to the meeting. Except at a meeting called on a requisition of urgency or at the discussion at any meeting of a budget estimate, no business can be transacted other than the business specified in the notice. An urgent business can be brought before any meeting if at least three-fourths of the councillors present at meeting assent to its being brought forward. The three-fourths of such members should not be less than one-sixth of the whole number of the councillors.

Every question is decided by a majority of votes of the councillors present and voting on that question. The presiding authority has a second vote in case of equality of votes.

The Commissioner has the right of being present at a meeting and of taking part in the discussions as a Councillor. He, with the consent of the presiding authority may make a statement or explanation of facts but he cannot vote upon or make any proposition. The Corporation may require any officer to attend any meeting. He may be called upon to make a statement or explanation of facts or supply such information in his possession as the Corporation may require.

Every meeting shall be open to the public, unless a majority of the councillors present there at decide by a resolution otherwise.

If any time during a meeting it is brought to the notice of the presiding authority that the number of councillors present inclusive of the presiding authority, falls short of one-fourth of the whole number of councillors, the presiding authority can adjourn the meeting.

A minute of the proceedings at every meeting and showing the names of the councillors present, on the day following the meeting is drawn up and entered fairly by the Municipal Secretary in a book. It is signed by the presiding authority of the next ensuing meeting. The minute book at all reasonable times be open at the Chief Municipal Office to inspection by any councillor free of charge and by any other person, on payment of a fee of eight annas.

The presiding authority has preserving order and may direct any councillor whose conduct is grossly disorderly to withdraw immediately from the meeting. If any councillor is ordered to withdraw second time within 15 days, the presiding authority may suspend the councillor from attending the meetings for any period not exceeding 15 days. The presiding authority may remit the period of suspension of apology being made to his satisfaction by the councillor under suspension. The presiding authority may, in the case of grave disorder arising in the meeting, suspend the meeting for a period not exceeding three days.

Municipal Commissioner and Deputy Commissioner

The Commissioner is a whole time officer of the Corporation. He is appointed by the Government. He is liable to be removed from his office if at a meeting of the Corporation, not less than two-thirds of the total number of councillors vote for his removal. Such a resolution cannot be passed if he makes default in performing the duties imposed or exceeds the powers conferred upon him or neglects or refuses to implement the decisions of the Corporation or Standing Committee or any other Committee of the Corporation or acts in a manner prejudicial to the interests of the Corporation. If it appears to the Government that he is incapable of performing the duties of his office or has been guilty of misconduct and neglect, the Commissioner is removed.

The Government can appoint Additional or Deputy Commissioner. Every person so appointed is subject to the same liabilities, restrictions and conditions to which the Commissioner is subjected. The Deputy Commissioner is subordinate to the Commissioner. He exercises such of the powers and performs such of the duties as the Commissioner confers on him. The Commissioner informs the Corporation to the powers and duties deputed by him to the Deputy Commissioner.

Leave of the Commissioner is granted by the Government in consultation with the Standing Committee.

During the absence of the Commissioner or the Deputy Commissioner, the Government may appoint a person to act as a Commissioner or Deputy Commissioner. Every person appointed so to act can exercise the powers and performs the duties conferred and imposed on the Commissioner or the Deputy Commissioner.

A person who has, directly or indirectly or by himself or his partner or as a member of a Joint Hindu Family, a share or interest in any contract or employment cannot be appointed as the Commissioner or Additional or Deputy Commissioner.

Local Government Service

A Local Government Service consisting of officers and servants of a Corporation is constituted. The Government has the power to appoint, dismiss and transfer and to take disciplinary action against officers belonging to this service and prescribes conditions of their service. To meet the expenditure in respect of salaries, allowances, pensions etc. payable to the officers and servants of this service, a Local Government Service Fund is constituted. The Corporation contributes 12.5 per cent of its revenue towards the Fund.

In addition to the officers and servants enumerated in Schedule C, the Government may appoint Superintending Engineer, Chief Town Planner, Divisional Engineers, Assistant Engineers, Assistant Town Planning Officers, Architects, Inspecting Officers or other officers for the whole or any part of the State. They also belong to the Local Government Service and their expenses are defrayed from the Local Government Service Fund. The powers and duties of these officers are determined by the Government.

Municipal Corporation Service

The Government may, after consulting all the municipal corporations in the State, by notification in the Gazette, constitute any class of officers or employees of the Corporation of the category of Upper Division Clerks and above into a Municipal Corporation Service for the State. The Government has power to make rules to regulate the classification, methods of recruitment, conditions of service, pay and allowances and discipline and conduct of the Service.

City Engineer and Medical Officer of Health

The Government can appoint persons fit to be City Engineer, Medical Officer of Health, Municipal Examiner of Accounts and Municipal Secretary for the efficient functioning of the Corporation.

The City Engineer and Medical Officer of Health can perform such duties as they are directed to or as may be required by the Commissioner or the Standing Committee.

Municipal Examiner of Accounts

He has to perform such duties as he is directed with regard to the audit of the Accounts of the Municipal Fund by the Corporation or by the Standing Committee. He specifies the duties and powers of the Auditors, Assistant Auditors, Clerks and servants under him subject to directions of the Standing Committee, and subject to the orders of the Standing Committee, exercises supervision and control over their acts and proceedings.

Municipal Secretary

He is the Secretary of the Corporation and also of the Standing Committee. He performs such duties as he is directed and such other duties with regard to the Corporation and the Standing Committee. He has the custody of all papers and documents connected with the proceedings of the Corporation, the Standing Committee, other Committees and Sub-committees. He specifies subject to the directions of the Standing Committee the duties of the officers and servants subordinate to him and exercises supervision and control over their acts and proceedings subject to the orders of the Standing Committee.

Municipal Officers and Servants

The Standing Committee may determine the number, designations, grades, fees, allowances of officers and servants under the Municipal Examiner of Accounts and the Municipal Secretary. The Commissioner prepares and brings before the Standing Committee statements setting forth the numbers, designations, grades, fees, and allowances of the officers and servants. A new post, whether permanent or temporary cannot be created without the sanction of the Standing Committee in respect of the posts upto and inclusive of an Upper Division Clerk or any equivalent post carrying the same or similar scale of pay, and without the sanction of the Corporation in respect of the posts upto and inclusive of a Superintendent or any equivalent post carrying the same or similar scale of pay without the sanction of the Government in respect of all other posts.

The Commissioner may impose any penalty on any Municipal officer or servant appointed by the Corporation or by the Standing Committee except the officers and servants subordinate to the Municipal Examiner of Accounts and Municipal Secretary. The Municipal Examiner of Accounts and Municipal Secretary may impose any penalty on any officer or servant subordinate to them and drawing a minimum monthly salary not exceeding rupees hundred exclusive of allowances subject to a right of appeal to the Standing Committee. Any Municipal officer or servant on whom any penalty is imposed by any authority other than the Corporation, may, within three months of the Communication to him the order of imposition of the penalty, appeal to the authority, immediately superior to the authority imposing the penalty and the appellate authority after obtaining the remarks of the authority imposing the penalty passes the appropriate order which is conclusive.

The Commissioner can grant leave of absence to any Municipal officer or servant whom he has power to appoint and for a period not exceeding one month to any Municipal officer or servant subordinate to the Municipal Examiner of Accounts and the Municipal Secretary.

Duties and Powers of Municipal Authorities

The Corporation has to make adequate provisions for:

(i) erection of substantial boundary marks;

(ii) the watering, scavenging and cleansing of all public streets and places in the city and the removal of all sweepings therefrom;

(iii) the collection, removal, treatment and disposal of sewage; offensive matter and rubbish and the preparation of compost manure from such sewage, offensive matter and rubbish;

(iv) construction of drains and drainage works after collecting the fees prescribed by the Commissioner;

(v) the maintenance and cleansing of drains, drainage works and the construction, maintenance and cleansing of public latrines, water-closets, urinals and similar conveniences;

(vi) the lighting of public buildings vested in the Corporation, public streets and municipal markets;

(vii) the maintenance of a municipal office and of all public monuments and open spaces and other property vesting in the Corporation;

(viii) the naming or numbering of streets and of public places in the Corporation in the numbering of premises;

(ix) the maintenance, change and regulation of places for the disposal of dead and the provision of new places for the purpose and disposal of unclaimed dead bodies;

(x) the construction or acquisition and maintenance of public markets and slaughter houses and the regulation of all markets and slaughter houses;

(xi) the construction or acquisition and maintenance of cattle pounds;

(xii) public vaccination;

(xiii) the reclamation of unhealthy localities, the removal of noxious vegetation and generally the abatement of all nuisances;

(xiv) the registration of births and deaths;

(xv) the construction, maintenance, alteration and improvement of streets, bridges, subways, culverts, causeways or the like;

(xvi) the removal of obstructions and projections in or upon streets, bridges and other public places;

(xvii) the management and maintenance of all municipal water works and the construction or acquisition of new works necessary for a sufficient supply of water for public and private purposes;

(xviii) preventing the spread of infectious deceases;

(xix) the securing or removal of dangerous buildings and places;

(xx) the improvement of the city,

(xxi) the provisions of public parks, gardens, playground and recreation grounds;

(xxii) the fulfilment of any obligation imposed upon it;

(xxiii) the provisions of relief to destitute persons in the city in times of famine and security and the establishment and maintenance of relief works in such times;

(xxiv) make payments for the maintenance and treatment in any institute suitable for anti-rabic treatment; and

(xxv) make payments for the maintenance and treatment at any asylum, hospital or house suitable for lunatics.

Discretionary Duties

The Corporation, at its discretion may provide wholly or partly for all or any of the following matters:

(i) the organisation, maintenance or management of institutions within or without the city for the care of persons who are infirm, sick or incurable or for the care and training of blind, deaf, mute, or otherwise disabled persons or of handicapped children;

(ii) the organisation, maintenance or management of maternity and infant welfare homes or centres;

(iii) the provisions of milk to expectant or nursing mothers, infants or school children;

(iv) the organisation, maintenance or management of chemical or bacteriological laboratories for the examination or analysis of water, food and drugs, for the detection of disease or for researches connected with public health;

(v) swimming pools, public wash-houses, bathing places and other institutions designed for improvement of public health;

(vi) dairies or farms for the supply, distribution and processing of milk products for the benefit of the residents;

(vii) the construction and maintenance in public streets or places of drinking fountains for human beings and water troughs for animals;

(viii) the planting and maintenance of trees on road sides and elsewhere;

(ix) providing the entertainment at public places or public resorts;

(x) the holding of exhibitions, athletics or games;

(xi) the regulation of lodging houses, camping grounds, and rest-houses in the city;

(xii) the maintenance of an ambulance service;

(xiii) the construction, establishment and maintenance of theatres, places of entertainment, rest-houses and other public buildings;

(xiv) the organisation or maintenance of shops or stalls in times of scarcity for the sale of necessaries of life;

(xv) the building or purchase and maintenance of dwellings for municipal officers and servants;

(xvi) the grant of loans to the municipal officers and servants for construction of houses and purchase of house sites and vehicles;

(xvii) the organisation, maintenance or management of transport facilities for the conveyance of the public of goods;

(xviii) the furtherance of educational objects, and the making of grants to educational institutions;

(xix) the establishment and maintenance or the aiding of libraries, museums and art galleries, botanical or zoological collections and the purchase or construction of buildings thereof;

(xx) the destruction of vermins, birds or animals causing a danger or nuisance and the confinement of destruction of stray dogs;

(xxi) contributions towards any public fund raised for the relief of human suffering without the city;

(xxii) granting the rewards for information for correct registrations of vital statistics;

(xxiii) the acquisition and the maintenance of grazing grounds and the establishment and maintenance of a stud farm;

(xxiv) establishing and maintaing a farm or factory for the disposal of sewage;

(xxv) supplying, constructing and maintaining receptacles, fittings, pipes and other appliances on or for the use of premises receiving and conducting the sewage thereof into drains under the control of the Corporation;

(xxvi) granting rewards for information regarding the infringement of any provisions of the Act, rules, laws, orders etc.,

(xxvii) laying out new street and acquiring land for that purpose or for the construction of buildings or cartilages thereof to abut on such streets;

(xxviii) the building or purchase and maintenance of suitable dwellings for the poor and working classes;

(xxix) the provision of shelter to destitute or homeless persons and any form of poor relief;

(xxx) the building or purchase and maintenance of sanitary stables or byres for horses, ponies, cattle used for hackney carriages or carts or for milchkine;

(xxxi) the surveying of buildings or lands;

(xxxii) taking measures to meet any calamity affecting the public in the city;

(xxxiii) the making of a contribution towards any public ceremony or entertainment in the city;

(xxxiv) the construction, purchase, organisation, maintenance, extension and management of tramways, trackless trains, mechanically propelled transport facilities for the conveyance of the public;

(xxxv) the purchase, maintenance, management and conduct of any undertaking for the supply of electricity or gas to the public or the subsidising of any such undertaking;

(xxxvi) the acquisition of immovable or movable property for any purpose including payment of the cost of investigation, surveys or examinations in relation to or the construction or adaptation of buildings necessary for such purposes;

(xxxvii) preparation and presentation of address to persons of distinctions;

(xxxviii) maintaining, aiding and suitably accommodating schools for primary education;

xxxix) provide parking places, public landing spaces, halting places for vehicles including motor vehicles and levy fees for their use; and

xl) the taking of any measure likely to promote public safety, health, convenience or instruction.

Municipal Property

The Corporation has the power to acquire and hold movable and immovable property or interest therein whether within or without the limits of the city. The Commissioner may, by sale or exchange, dispose of any movable property belonging to the Corporation the value of which does not exceed Rs. 500 in each instance, or grant for any term not exceeding twelve months, a lease of any immovable property belonging to the Corporation. With the sanction of the Standing Committee, the Commissioner may, by sale or exchange, dispose of any movable property the value of which does not exceed Rs. 5000 in each instance, or grant for any term not exceeding three years lease of any immovable property. With the sanction of the Corporation, the Commissioner may lease, sell or, otherwise, dispose of any movable or immovable property belonging to the Corporation.

Municipal Fund

All moneys received by or on behalf of the Corporation, all proceeds of the disposal of property, all rents accruing from the property, all moneys raised by any tax levied, all fees and fines payable and levied, all moneys received by way of compensation or for compounding offences, all moneys received from the Government or public bodies, private bodies or private individuals by way of grant, or gift or deposit and all interest and profits arising from any investment of or from any transaction are credited to the Municipal Fund. It includes the accumulated balanced at the credit of the Corporation.

The payments out of the Municipal Fund can be made through cheque signed by the two persons, i.e. by either the Commissioner or Deputy Commissioner or in the absence of both, by the Assistant Commissioner, and either by the Examiner of Accounts or in his absence, by the officer immediately subordinate to him. No payment of any sum can be made by the Commissioner unless the expenditure is covered by a current budget grant and sufficient balance of such budget grant is available.

The moneys credited to the Municipal Fund can be applied in payment of all sums, charges and costs inclusive of the expenses of every election, the contribution made, the salaries and other allowances of all municipal officers and servants, all expenses and cost incurred by the Commissioner in the exercise of any power or the discharge of any duty conferred upon him and conveyance allowance to Mayor and the Councillors for attending any meeting of the Committee or Corporation.

Expenditure by the Corporation out of the Municipal Fund can be made within the city only, but may, by a resolution supported by not less than half of the total number of councillors be made outside the city. On the written requisition of a Secretary to the Government, the

Commissioner may undertake the execution of any work certified by the Secretary to be required urgently in the public service and, for this purpose, may temporarily make payments from the Municipal Fund. The cost of all work so executed and of the establishment engaged is paid by the Government and credited to the Municipal Fund.

The Corporation may constitute special funds. Surplus moneys at the credit of the Municipal Fund which cannot be immediately or at an early date be applied or any loan raised may be deposited at interest or be invested in public securities. All such deposits and investments are made by the Commissioner on behalf of the Corporation with the sanction of the Standing Committee. The loss arising from any deposit or investment is debited to the Municipal Fund.

Municipal Taxation

The Corporation can impose the following taxes :

(i) taxes on lands and buildings,
(ii) octroi,
(iii) taxes on vehicles,
(iv) taxes on animals and boats,
(v) taxes on advertisements, and
(vi) a tax on transfer or immovable property.

Optional Taxes

In addition to above ones, the Corporation may also impose any of the following taxes :

(i) tax on entertainments, and
(ii) any other tax subject to the previous sanction of the Government.

Property Taxes

The following taxes are levied on buildings and lands and are known as property taxes :

(a) a general tax,
(b) a water tax,
(c) a drainage tax,
(d) a lighting tax, and
(e) a conservancy tax.

The aggregate of the percentages should not be less than 5 or more than 30 per cent.

The General Tax is levied in respect of all buildings and lands except buildings and lands solely used for purposes connected with the disposal of dead; solely occupied and used for public worships or for a charitable or educational purpose and vesting in the Central Government or the Corporation. The buildings and lands vesting in the State Government used solely for public purposes and not used or intended to be used for purposes of profit the tax is leviable from the State Government.

Water Tax is levied only in respect of premises to which private water supply is furnished from or which are connected by means of communication pipes with any Board Water Works or which are situated in a portion of the city in which the Commissioner has given public notice that sufficient water is available from Board Water Works for furnishing a reasonable supply to all premises in the said portion.

The Conservancy Tax is levied only in respect of premises situated in any portion of the city in which public notice has been given by the Commissioner that the collection, removal and disposal of all excrementitious and polluted matter from privies, urinals and cesspool is undertaken by Municipal agency and in which there is a privy, water closet, cesspool, urinal, bathing place or cooking place connecting by a drain with a Board sewer.

Imposition of Taxes

Before the Corporation passes a resolution imposing a tax, it directs the Commissioner to publish a notice in the Gazette and in the local newspaper to this effect. He fixes a reasonable period not being less than one month, from the date of publication of such notice of submission of objections. The Corporation after considering the objections determines by resolution to levy the tax. Such resolution specifies the rate, the date and the period of levy.

Collection of Taxes

The property taxes are payable in half-yearly or quarterly instalments, while tax on vehicles and animals is paid quarterly. When any tax is due, the Commissioner causes to be served upon the person liable for the payment thereof a bill for the sum due. If the tax is not paid within fifteen days, the Commissioner may cause to be served upon the person liable for payment a notice of demand. If the person liable for the payment of tax does not pay the tax within fifteen days or show sufficient cause for non-payment to the satisfaction of the Commissioner and if no appeal is preferred against the said tax, such sum with all costs of the recovery is levied under a warrant, to be issued by the Commissioner, by distress and sale of goods and chattels of the defaulter, or if the defaulter be the occupier of any premises, goods found on the premises or if the tax due in respect of any vehicle or animal, by distress and sale of such vehicle or animal.

Appeal Against Valuation and Taxes

Appeals against any rateable value or tax are heard and determined by the Judge. An appeal can be heard if it is brought within fifteen days after the accrual of the cause of complaint, a complaint has previously been made to the Commissioner and disposed of, a complaint has been made by the person aggrieved within fifteen days after the first received notice of any amendment made in the assessment book and his complaint has been disposed of and in the case of an appeal against the tax, the amount claimed from the appellant has been deposited by him with the Commissioner. If before or on the hearing of an appeal any question of law or usage having the force of law arises, the Judge may either on his own motion or on the application of the party to the appeal refer it with his opinion for the decision of the High Court.

An appeal may lie to the High Court from any decision of the Judge in an appeal by which a rateable value in excess of Rs. 2000 is fixed and upon a question of law or usage or the construction of a document.

Contracts

Every contract on behalf of the Corporation is made by the Commissioner, who carries it out with the approval or sanction of municipal authority. A contract other than a contract relating to the acquisition of immovable property, involving an expenditure exceeding Rs. 2 lakh is made by the Commissioner with the previous approval of the Standing Committee. Every such contract involving an expenditure exceeding Rs. 5000 and not exceeding Rs. 2 lakh is reported by the Commissioner within 15 days to the Standing Committee. Every contract is sealed with the common seal of the Corporation. Every contract involving a sum exceeding Rs. 5000 is made in writing and sealed. The common seal is affixed in the presence of the Commissioner and two members of the Standing Committee. They have to sign the seal. The signature of the Commissioner or the members should be distinct from the signature of any witness to the execution of any such contract.

The Commissioner, at least seven days before entering into contract for the execution of any work involving an expenditure exceeding Rs. 2 lakh, gives notice by advertisement in the local newspapers inviting tenders for such contract. Where a project is framed for the execution of any work the estimated cost of which exceed Rs. 10 lakh, the Commissioner causes a detailed report and the Standing Committee lays the same before the Corporation. After approval of the Corporation, the report is submitted to the Government, which after technical scrutiny, sanctions the project. The project sanctioned with modification is returned to the Corporation for its reconsideration. If after reconsideration, the Corporation resubmits the project, the Government may sanction it subject to such modifications as it may deem fit to make and such sanction of the Government is final.

In respect of any work with the estimated cost exceeding Rs. 50 lakh, the Commissioner gives notice by advertisement in the newspapers, inviting tenders. The Government may appoint or authorise the Corporation to appoint a committee for the purposes of scrutinising and evaluating the tenders and for making its recommendations to the Commissioner. The Commissioner, after considering the recommendations of the committee and with the prior approval of the Government, accepts any tender so recommended which appears to him the most advantageous, and thereupon issues the tender schedules in respect of work to the concerned person. The Government may, by notification in the Gazette, make rules for carrying out the work.

Accounts and Audit

Accounts of the receipts and expenditure of the Corporation is kept in the manner and form specified by the Standing Committee. The Commissioner, as soon as after first day of April, causes to be prepared a detailed report of the previous financial year, together with a statement showing the amounts of the receipts and disbursements credited to the Municipal Fund during the said year and the balance at the credit of the Fund at the close of the year and submits the same to the Standing Committee. After examination and review of the report and statement by the Standing Committee, a printed copy of such report and statement together with a copy of the Commissioner's review is forwarded to each Councillor by the date specified by the Standing Committee and copies are placed for sale at the Chief Municipal Office at such price as the Commissioner may fix. The Commissioner forwards a copy of each report and statement together with a copy each of the report and statement together with a copy of the Committee's review to the Local Administration Department for the purpose of being laid before the Legislative Assembly. On receipt of such report and statement, the Secretary with his comments takes steps to cause the report and statement to be laid without delay before the Legislative Assembly.

The Municipal Examiner of Accounts conducts a weekly examination and audit of the municipal accounts and reports thereon to the Standing Committee, which may conduct independently an examination and audit of the municipal accounts. The Standing Committee places the report to the Corporation together with the orders having been passed by the Standing Committee and the Corporation takes the necessary actions. As soon as after the commencement of each financial year of the Municipal Examiner of Accounts delivers to the Standing Committee a report upon the whole of the municipal accounts for the previous financial year. The Commissioner causes the report to be printed and a copy thereof is forwarded to each councillor alongwith the printed copy of Administrative Report and Statement of Accounts.

The Government may appoint an auditor for the purpose of making special audit of the municipal accounts and of reporting thereon to the Government. An auditor so appointed exercises any power as exercised by the Municipal Examiner of Accounts.

Budget

The Commissioner, on or before each tenth, day of November, causes to be prepared and lays before the Standing Committee an estimate of the expenditure to be incurred by the Corporation in the next financial year, an estimate of all balances available for reappropriation or expenditure at the commencement of the next ensuing financial year, an estimate of the Corporation's receipt and income for the next ensuing financial year other than from taxation and a statement of proposals as to the taxation which will be necessary or expedient to impose in the next financial year.

The Standing Committee, as soon as may be after each tenth day of the November, considers the estimates and proposals of the Commissioner after having obtained from the Commissioner detailed information. The budget estimate of a Standing Committee proposes the levy of municipal tax. The Commissioner causes the budget estimates as finally approved by the Standing Committee to be printed and forwards not later than the 15th day of the December a printed copy thereof to each councillor. At a meeting of Corporation called for some day in January, not later than the tenth, the budget estimate, prepared by the Standing Committee with the report of the Committee is laid before the Corporation for consideration. The Corporation on or before the 20th day of February, after considering the Standing Committee's proposal in this behalf, determines the rate at which municipal taxes are to be levied in the next financial year. The Corporation may refer the budget estimate back to the Standing Committee for further consideration, or adopts the budget estimates or any revised budget estimates submitted to it.

On the recommendation of the Standing Committee, the Corporation may, during the financial year, increases the amount of any budget grant or make an additional grant for the purpose of meeting any special or unforeseen requirement arising during the year.

The Standing Committee, during the financial year, may reduce the amount of budget grant from one minor head to another or sanction the transfer of any amount exceeding Rs. 5000 within a minor head from one subordinate head to another.

The Commissioner may, during a financial year, sanction the transfer of any amount not exceeding Rs. 5000 within a minor head from one subordinate head to another. Every such sanction of amount exceeding Rs. 500 is reported by the Commissioner to the Standing Committee.

Rules and Bye-laws

The Government may, by notification in the Gazette, make rules. Every rule made is laid immediately before each House of the Legislature if it is in session and if it is not in session, in the session following immediately, for a total period of fourteen days.

The Corporation may make the bye-laws. It is the duty of the Commissioner either suo motu or at the instance of the Standing Committee to lay before the Corporation for its consideration a draft of any bye-law. No bye-law is approved finally by the Corporation unless notice of the intention of the Corporation has been given by advertisement in the Gazette and in the local newspapers six weeks at least before the day of the meeting at which the Corporation finally considers such bye-laws. The Corporation, before approving any bye-law, receives and considers any objection or suggestion which is made in writing not less than ten days before the day of meeting on giving notice to the Commissioner. The person is heard by the Corporation at the meeting. Every bye-law comes into force only after sanction by the Government and publication in the Gazette.

The Commissioner may make standing orders consistent with the rules and bye-laws.

Control

The Government may require the Corporation or Commissioner to produce any extract from any proceeding of the Corporation, the Standing Committee or any other Committee, record, correspondence, plan or other document; to furnish any return, plan, estimate, statement of accounts or statistics; and to furnish or obtain any report and the Corporation or the Commissioner has to furnish the same without unreasonable delay. The Government may depute any officer to inspect or examine any Municipal Department, office, service, work or thing and to report thereon. If on receipt of any report, the Government is of opinion that any duty has not been performed or has been performed in an imperfect, inefficient or unsuitable manner or that adequate financial provision has not been made for the performance of any duty, the Government may direct the Corporation or the Commissioner the performance of the act within stipulated period of time or to make financial provisions for the performance of the duty to the satisfaction of the Government. If the orders of the Government is not complied with, the Government may, by order, appoint some person to take action, fix the remuneration to be paid to him and direct that such remuneration and the cost be defrayed out of the Municipal Fund. The Government may, at any time for the purpose of satisfying itself as to the correctness, legality, propriety or regularity of any proceedings of or order passed by the Commissioner or any officer, call for and examine the record and pass such order as it thinks fit. A copy of such order is sent to the Corporation by the Government. The Government may, either suo motu or on representation of any councillor, the Mayor or the Commissioner, by order in writing, cancel any resolution passed, order issued or license or permission granted or prohibit the doing of any act. The Government may, by notification in the Gazette, remove the Mayor or the Deputy Mayor who omits wilfully or refuses to carry out or disobeys the rules, bye-laws, regulations or lawful orders or abuses his position or the powers vested in him. However, before removal, they are given an opportunity of explanation, if in the opinion of the Government Standing Committee is not competent to perform or persistently makes default in performing its duties or exceed or abuses its position or powers, the Government may and can, if the dissolution is recommended by a resolution of the Corporation passed at a special meeting called for the purpose and supported by votes of not less than two-thirds of the strength of the Corporation by notification in the Gazette, dissolve the Standing Committee. In case of the Government proposing the action, the Standing Committee is given an opportunity to show cause against the dissolution giving reason therefor.

On the dissolution, the Corporation takes steps for the reconstitution of the Standing Committee within fifteen days, but the members of the dissolved committee are not eligible for re-election to the committee for a period of one year. During the interval between the dissolution and the reconstitution of the Standing Committee, all or any of the powers and functions of the Committee may be exercised by the Mayor under the control of the Corporation.

Dissolution

If, in the opinion of the Government, the Corporation is not competent to perform or persistently makes default in performing the duties or exceeds or abuses its position or powers or a situation exists in which the municipal administration cannot be carried on in accordance with the Act or the financial stability or credit of the Corporation is threatened, the Government may, by notification in the Gazette, direct that the Corporation be dissolved with effect from a specified date not later than six months from the date of dissolution. The notification, is laid before the Legislative Assembly. Before publishing the notification, the government has to communicate to the Corporation the grounds on which they propose to do so, fix a reasonable period for the Corporation to show cause against the proposal, and consider its explanation or objections. The Mayor of the Corporation is also given a reasonable opportunity of being heard.

During the interval between the dissolution and reconstitution of the Corporation, all or any of the powers of the Corporation, and of its Mayor and of the Standing Committee are performed by a person appointed by the Government in that behalf. The Government may determine the relations of such person with the District Controlling Officers and with themselves and the Government may direct the Commissioner to exercise and perform any powers and duties in addition to his own.

The Members including the ex-officio members of the reconstituted Corporation enter upon their offices on the date fixed for its reconstitution and the term of the office of the elected members continues only for the remainder of the period for which the dissolved Corporation would have continued had it not been dissolved. The Government may reconstitute the Corporation before the expiry of period. However, where the remainder of the period is less than six months, it is not necessary to hold any elections.

III. Wards Committee

In respect of a Municipality having population of three lakhs or more, there are constituted by the Commissioner and Director of Municipal Administration by order, such Wards Committees as may be determined by them. In case of Corporation towns, the order of constituting the Committees is passed by the Government. In Municipality, Wards Committee should consist of not less than five wards and in Corporation not less than ten wards. The Commissioner and the Director of Municipal Administration may constitute Wards Committees even in the municipalities having population of less than three lakhs.

Each Wards Committee consists of the members elected from the wards. The Commissioner may specify the officers of the Municipality to attend the meeting of the Committee. They have the right to speak and participate in the meetings but no right to vote.

The Chairperson is elected by and from amongst the members in the prescribed manner. He can hold office for one year from the date of his election and be eligible for re-election. The Chairperson ceases to hold office if he ceases to be a member of the Wards Committee. Any casual vacancy in the office is filled by election.

The powers and functions of the Wards Committee and the manner of conduct of business are prescribed under rules.

Finance Commission

The Municipal Acts in the State make provisions for setting up of a Finance Commission in pursuance of the Art. 243 I of the Constitution. The details are not given. The A.P. Panchayati Raj Act, 1994 incorporates the constitution of a Commission by the Governor on the recommendation of the Government. The Commission consists of a chairman and other members. The chairman is to be selected from amongst persons who have experience in public affairs, and the other members are selected from amongst the persons who have special knowledge of finance and accounts of Government, or have had wide experience in financial matters and in administration or have special knowledge of economics.

Every member can hold office for such periods as may be specified in the order and are eligible for re-appointment.

State Election Commission

Both the Acts make mention that the preparation of electoral rolls, and the conduct of elections to all urban local bodies in the State be under the Commission. The Commission consists of a Commissioner. The Governor, on the recommendation of the Government, appoints a person who is holding or who had held an office not less than that of a Principal Secretary of Government in rank as the State Election Commissioner.

District Planning Committee

There is no mention in Act regarding the constitution of the District Planning Committee in the State.

Metropolitan Planning Committee

Despite being a mandatory provision, the provisions regarding the Metropolitan Planning Committee are not inserted in municipal laws.

3
Karnataka

Karnataka has a written history of more than 2000 years. Apart from being subject to the rule of the Nandas, Mauryas and the Satavahanas, Karnataka came to have indigenous dynasties like the Kadambas of Banavasi and the Gangas from the middle of the 4th century AD. The Chalukyas of Badami ruled over a wider area from Narmada to Kaveri from the days of Pulkeshi II (609–642 AD). After the fall of the Peshwa (1818) and Tipu (1799), Karnataka came under the British. Mysore dynasty helped industrialisation and cultural growth. Freedom Movement was followed by the movement for the unification of Karnataka. After Independence, the new united Mysore State was created in 1956 and was renamed Karnataka in 1973.

Karnataka lies to the south of Goa and Maharashtra, to the west of Andhra Pradesh, to the north-west of Tamil Nadu and to the north of Kerala. It has a sea coast of nearly 260 km and an area of 191,791 sq. km with 20 districts.

Karnataka is predominantly rural and agrarian. Agriculture and allied activities account for nearly 65 per cent of the workforce in the state. The State stands fifth in oilseeds production in the country. Karnataka has the largest area planted under coffee (39.31 per cent) in the country and accounts for a major portion of the coffee produced. The area under forests covers about 16 per cent of the total geographical area. Karnataka occupies seventh position with five per cent of the total forest area in the country.

Karnataka is one of the leading industrialised states contributing four per cent of the national production in the industrial sector and 20 per cent to the state income.

Urban Scenario

The state is divided into 20 districts. Although there is an increase in urban population, the share of urban population of the state to the country's urban population is found decreasing. The state accounted for 6.73 per cent of total urban population in 1981, while it reduced to 6.38 per cent in 1991. The decennial growth in 1981–91 also reduced from 50.65 in previous decade to 29.09 per cent. The number of towns is found increasing over the decades. So is the case with class one towns, whose number and population both recorded an increase. The proportion of population contained by class one towns was 51.32 per cent in 1971, increased to 58.66 per cent in 1981, and further to 64.60 per cent in 1991. However, the growth rate of population in these towns decreased to 42.1 in 1991 from 72.2 in 1981 and 67.7 in 1971.

Among twenty districts Bangalore is the most urbanised district with 85.82 per cent of urban population, followed by Dharnad containing only 34.95 per cent of the urban population. All other districts have less than one-third of their population inhabiting in urban areas. Four districts have no class one towns. Three districts of Bangalore, Dharvad and Bellary have urban population more than thirty per cent. Thus, level of urbanisation in the state is not uniform. One district with 10.7 per cent of total population has urbanisation level more than 30 per cent, while another one containing 7.8 per cent population records level between 30 and 40 per cent. The highest number of eleven districts with majority of the population (59.3 per cent) fall between 20 and 30 per cent and the remaining seven, with 22.2 per cent population, come into 10–20 per cent urbanisation.

As regards cities, Bangalore is the most populous one. It experienced a tremendous growth of 75.58 per cent in 1971–81. The cities of Dangers and Bellary had more than 60 per cent growth. The city of Udupi with 12.30 per cent growth was at the bottom. In 1981–91, Harem Udupi faced the highest growth of 252.39 per cent. Bidar (65.88) and Tumkur (65.18) followed the suit. Hassan recorded 51.62 per cent, and Gulbarga and Devangare had more than 40 per cent. Bangalore (39.87), Mysore (36.15), Mangalore (39.11), Belgaum (33.71), Bijapur (31.04), Raichur (36.66), and Chitradurga (38.57) were the towns having a growth rate of more than thirty per cent. Kolar Gold Fields was at the bottom with 8.32 per cent, preceded by Gadg Batigeri (14.10), Bhadravati (14.18), and Mandya (19.63).

In respect of urban literacy, Dakshin Kannad topped with 74.2 per cent followed by Koddagu (71.81), Uttar Kannad (69.7), Bangalore

(68.9), Chikmagalur (67.8), Shimoga (67.2), Hassan (67.0), and Tumkur (65.5). The literacy rate in the state was 63.6 per cent. All other districts recorded less literacy with Raichur (46.3) at bottom, preceded by Bellary (52), Gulbarga (53.3), Bidar (56.6), Bijapur (57.6) and Bangalore Rural (57.7). Dakshin Kannad (79.6), Kodugu (76.3), and Uttar Kannad (75.7) had maximum male literacy, while Bangalore (74.4), Belgaum (71.1), Chikmagalur (73.2), Hassan (72.6), Shimoga (72.7), and Tumkur (71.8) recorded male literacy more than that of the state (70.5). The female literacy in the state was 56.3 per cent. Dakshin Kannad (68.8) was at the top followed by Kodagu (67.1), Uttar Kannad (63.4), Bangalore (62.8), Chikmangalur (62.1), Shimoga (61.3), and Hassan (61.2). Raichur was the lowest with 35.8 per cent preceded by Ballary (42.1), Gulbarga (43.1), Bidar (46.5) and Bijapur (46.8). The demographic profile of the state is given in Table 1.

The evolution of urban local bodies in the state was patterned on the experience of the British Provinces. In the princely state of Mysore, the first municipal organisation was created in 1897 for Bangalore Cantonment area where the British army was stationed. Subsequently, the Mysore City Municipalities Act of 1937 established the elected municipalities in Mysore and Bangalore. The other towns were governed by different legislations depending upon their location in the Bombay and Madras Provinces. After the reorganisation of the state, a comprehensive Municipal Act was passed in 1964 to create municipal bodies, and to empower them to perform civic functions. Likewise, in 1976 a separate Act was passed, creating City Corporations. Today there are six Municipal Corporations, twenty Town Municipal Councils, one hundred thirty-five Town Municipal Councils, forty-eight Town Panchayats, a few Notified Area Committees, and two Sanitary Boards. The total number of statutorily constituted urban local bodies in Karnataka today is two hundred and ten. Among the City Corporations Belgaum, Gulbarga and Hubli-Dharwad experienced much higher rate of population growth than others. Mangalore City Corporation had lowest rate of 4.51 per cent only. In the case of City Municipal Councils, though the overall increase was 23.64 per cent, Chikmangalore experienced less than one per cent increase whereas Shimoga experienced 46 per cent followed by Bidar with 37 per cent. Among the Town Municipal Councils, Sindhanur experienced the highest population growth by almost doubling between

1981—91, and only a few Town Municipal Councils experienced single digit population growth. The negative growth rate was experienced by only four towns viz. Konnur, Terdal, Suratkal, and Arasikere, Bangalore City Corporation accounted for about 19 per cent of the urban population and six per cent of total population of the state. Out of every five persons living in urban areas, one is a Bangalorean. Out of 100 people living in urban areas, 18 lives in City Municipal Councils, 27 in Town Municipal Councils, 34 in City Corporations, and the remaining 21 live in other urban areas including Town Panchayats.

There are presently two Municipal Acts to govern the urban affairs in the state. The Karnataka Municipalities Act, 1964 regulates the management of municipal affairs in towns and cities. The municipal corporations in the state are managed by the Karnataka Municipal Corporations Act of 1976.

Table 1

Demographic Profile

	1971	1981	1991
Total population (Lakhs)	—	371.36	449.71
Decedal growth (per cent)	—	—	21.11
Urban population (Lakhs)	—	107.30	139.08
Decedal Growth (per cent)	33.23	50.65	29.62
Proportion of urban population to total population	—	28.89	30.92
Number of towns	227	250	254
No. of class I cities	12	17	21
Proportion of population	51.32	58.66	64.60
Literacy (urban)	—	—	63.60
Area (km^2)	—	191791.00 (3682.80)	191791.00 (4270.15)
No. of households (Lakh)		64.02 (18.46)	81.44 (25.91)
No. of occupied residential Households (Lakhs)		62.64 (18.02)	79.63 (25.37)
Total main workers (Lakh)	—	101.99 (26.67)	172.92 (43.72)
Marginal workers	—	12.93 (0.95)	15.95 (0.83)
Non-workers	—	221.92 (74.24)	260.90 (94.53)

Figures in parentheses denote urban.

I. Transitional Area

The Governor may specify any areas as a transitional area if it contains a population of not less than ten thousand but less than twenty thousand, the density of population is not less than four hundred inhabitants to one square kilometre and the percentage of employment in non-agricultural activities is not less than fifty per cent of the total employment.

Town Panchayat

For every transitional area, a Town Panchayat is constituted. It is a body corporate and has perpetual succession and a common seal with power to acquire and dispose of property and to contract and may be sued and may sue.

Constitution

A Town Panchayat consists of not less than eleven and not more than twenty councillors.

Municipal Area

The Governor may specify by notification, such area to be Smaller Urban Area if the population of such area is not less than 20,000 and not more than three lakhs; the density of population is not less than 1500 inhabitants to one square kilometre; the revenue generated for local administration from tax and non-tax sources is not less than rupees nine lakhs per annum or as calculated at the rate of Rs. 45 per capita per annum, whichever is higher and the percentage of employment in non-agricultural activities is not less than fifty per cent of the total employment.

The Governor may also specify such area to be a City Municipal Area, in case the population is not less than 50,000 or a Town Municipal Area, if the population is not less than 20,000 but less than 50,000.

Municipal Council

In every municipal area, a municipal council is constituted. It may be the City Municipal Council or the Town Municipal Council. It is a body corporate and has perpetual succession and a common seal with power to acquire, hold, and dispose of property and to contract and may sue and be sued through its Chief Officer or Municipal Commissioner.

Constitution

The municipal council consists of the following types of members.

1. Elected Councillors:

   The number of directly elected councillors is as under:

   (a) for a municipal area with a population of not less than 20,000 but less than 40,000—23;

   (b) for a municipal area with a population of not less than 40,000 but less than 50,000—27;

   (c) for a municipal area with a population of not less than 50,000 but less than 1 lakh—31; and

   (d) for a municipal area with a population of not less than 1 lakh but less than 3 lakhs—35.

2. Nominated Members:

Not more than five persons and nominated by the Government amongst the residents of the municipal area and who are :

   (a) persons having special knowledge or experience in municipal administration or matters related to health, town planning or education; or

   (b) social workers.

3. Ex-Officio Members:

   (a) the members of the House of the People and the members of the State Legislative Assembly, representing a part or whole of the municipal area whose constituencies lie within the municipal area and who are registered as electors within the area; and

   b. the members of the Council of States and members of the State Legislative Council registered as electors within the municipal area.

The nominated members have no right to vote in the meetings of the municipal council.

Reservation

Seats are reserved in a municipal council:

(a) for the Scheduled Castes and the Scheduled Tribes in proportion of their population in the total population of the municipal area;

(b) one-third of the total number of seats to be filled directly by the persons belonging to the Other Backward Classes (Eighty per cent seats are reserved for the persons falling under category 'A' and the remaining twenty per cent for the persons belonging to category B);

(c) not less than one-third of the seats for women belonging to the Scheduled Castes, Scheduled Tribes, Other Backward Classes and non-reserved seats to be filled by direct election.

The allotment of seats is done by rotation.

Disqualifications

A person is disqualified for being chosen as, and for being a councillor:

(a) if he has been sentenced by a Criminal Court to imprisonment for an offence which involves moral turpitude, and which is punishable with imprisonment for a term exceeding six months or for an offence punishable under the Karnataka Marriage Act, 1976; or

(b) if he is convicted of an offence under the provisions of the Untouchability Offences Act, 1955 or the Prevention of Food Adulteration Act, 1954; or

(c) if he holds any office of the profit under the Government of India or the Government of any state or of any local or other authority; or

(d) if he has been dismissed from service under a local authority or Government service; or

(e) if, having been a legal practitioner, he has been dismissed or suspended from practice by order of a competent authority; or

(f) if he has been removed from office; or

(g) if he is of unsound mind and stands so declared by a competent court; or

(h) if he is an undischarged insolvement; or

(i) if he is not a citizen of India, or has voluntarily acquired the citizenship of a foreign state or is under any acknowledgement of allegiance or adherence to a foreign state; or

(j) if he is disqualified by or under any law for the purpose of election to the State Legislature; or

(k) if he has directly or indirectly, by himself or his partner, any share or interest in any work done by order of the municipal council, or in any contract or employment with or under or by or on behalf of the municipal council; or

(l) if he is employed as a paid legal practitioner on behalf of the municipal council or accepts employment as legal practitioner against the municipal council; or

(m) if he is a licensed surveyor, or plumber or water supply contractor of the municipal council or he is a partner of a firm of which any such licensed person is a partner; or

(n) if he fails to pay arrears of any kind due by him to the municipal council within three months after a notice in this behalf has been served upon him; or

(o) if he has in proceedings questioning the validity or regularity of an election been found to have been guilty of any corrupt practice or any offence punishable under the Indian Penal Code.

The disqualifications under (a), (d), and (f) cease to operate after expiry of four years from the date of such sentence, dismissal or removal. The disqualification under (b) ceases after the expiry of the period during which a person is ordered to furnish security, or

(p) if he votes or takes part as a councillor in the discussion of any matter in which he has any interest or is professionally interested or in which he is engaged in any proceedings against the municipal council; or

(q) if he absents from the meetings of the municipal council during three consecutive months except with the leave of the council.

When an application is made by a councillor to the municipal council for leave to absent himself and the municipal council fails to inform the applicant of its decision on the application within a period of one month, the leave applied for is deemed to have been granted. The Deputy Commissioner either suo motu or on a report made to him after inquiry can declare the seat of the person concerned to have become vacant. A person aggrieved by the decision of the Deputy Commissioner may within a period of thirty days from the date of such decision appeal to the Government, if the person affected by the order was a councillor of a City Municipal Council and, to Commissioner, if such person was a councillor of a Town Municipal Council. The orders passed by the

Government or the Commissioner on such appeal are final. However, no order can be passed against any councillor without giving him a reasonable opportunity of being heard.

Removal

The Government, if it thinks fit on the recommendation of the Municipal Council, may remove any councillor elected, if such councillor has been guilty of misconduct in the discharge of his duties, or of any disgraceful conduct, or has become incapable of performing his duties as a councillor. However, no councillor can be removed except after being afforded an opportunity for submitting an explanation.

President and Vice-President

Every Municipal Council has a President and a Vice-President. The councillors at the first meeting of the council after the general election and at a subsequent meeting held immediately before the expiry of the term of office of the President and Vice-President, choose two members from amongst themselves to be the President and the Vice-President.

In case of casual vacancy in either office, they choose accordingly. During a vacancy in the office of the President and when there is no Vice-President to take his place or if a Vice-President fails to assume charge of the office of the President, the Deputy Commissioner or the person performing the duties of the Deputy Commissioner for the time being, in the case of City Municipal Council and, in the case of Town Municipal Council, any officer nominated by him not below the rank of an Assistant Commissioner, in the case of Municipal Council at district headquarters the Tehsildar or the person performing the duties of the Tehsildar or any other person not disqualified for being a Councillor, in the case of other municipal councils can perform the functions of the President.

Every President who, for a period exceeding two months and, every Vice-President, who for a period exceeding one month, absents himself from the municipal areas as to be unable to perform his duties ceases to be President or Vice-President, unless leave for such absence has been granted by the Municipal Council. The question of vacancy arisen is decided by the Deputy Commissioner. Leave cannot be granted for a period exceeding six months. Whenever, leave is granted to a President and the office of the Vice-President is vacant, the vacancy in the office of the President is filled by election from amongst the elected councillors. When leave is granted to a Vice-President or when Vice-President is acting for the President, the vacancy in the office of the Vice-President may be filled by election of some other elected councillor.

Every President and Vice-President is deemed to have vacated his office if a resolution expressing want of confidence in him is passed by a majority of not less than two-thirds of the total number of councillors at a special general meeting convened for the purpose. Such a resolution cannot be moved unless notice of the resolution is signed by not less than one-third of the total number of councillors and at least ten days notice of the intention to move the resolution has been given. If the resolution is negatived, a similar resolution in respect of the same President or Vice-President cannot be given notice of or moved within one year from the date of the decision of the council.

Every President and Vice-President can be removed from his office by the Government for misconduct in the discharge of his duties or for neglect of or incapacity to perform his duties or if he is unable to pay dues he owes to the council or has suffered an order for commitment to civil prison for non-payment of any decretal debt. However, no such order can be made except after the President or the Vice-President has been given an opportunity for submitting explanations.

The President and the Vice-President can hold office for a period of thirty months from the date of their election, provided they do not cease to be councillor. In the event of the non-acceptance of office, death, resignation or removal from office or of his election being void or of his becoming incapable of acting in office or having ceased to be a councillor prior to the expiry of his term of office, is filled by election.

Functions of President

It is the duty of the President to preside at all meetings of the council, to regulate the conduct of business at such meetings, watch over the financial and executive administration of the council, perform all the duties and exercise all the powers imposed, or conferred upon him by, or delegated to him under and in accordance with the Act , furnish within a period of a fortnight to the Commissioner, a copy of resolution passed at any meeting of the council, and furnish any abstract from the minutes of the proceedings of the council or of any committee or other document or things which the Commissioner or other officer calls for.

In case of emergency, the President may direct the execution or stoppage of any work or the doing of any act which requires the sanction of the Council, and the immediate execution of doing of which is necessary for the service or safety of the public and may direct that the expenses of executing such work or doing such act be paid from the municipal fund. However, he cannot act in contravention of any order of the municipal council. He has to report forthwith the action taken and the reason, therefore, to the standing committee at its next meeting.

The President has the following additional powers:

(a) to issue directions to the Municipal Commissioner or the Chief Officer to implement the resolutions of the council or the standing committees;

(b) to require the Administration Report and the Annual Report of the Council prepared and placed before the end of the year;

(c) to issue directions to the officers concerned to comply with the points made out in the audit report;

(d) to undertake inspection and supervision of the works taken up by the council; and

(e) to call for any record by the same to be returned within one month.

The President is ex-officio member of all the standing committees but without the power to vote on any question. The Municipal Commissioner or the Chief Officer has to forward simultaneously the copies of the communications addressed to the Government.

Duties of the Vice-President

It is the duty of the Vice-President to exercise such powers and perform such duties of the President, as the President may delegate to him. It is the duty of the Vice-President to preside, in absence of the President, at the meetings of the council and exercise all the powers of President while doing so and pending the succession, appointment or election of a President, or during the absence of a President for any period exceeding seven days to exercise the powers and perform the duties of the President.

The Vice-President is ex-officio member of all the standing committees but is not entitled to vote on any question.

Allowances

The President and the Vice-President may receive out of the Municipal Fund monthly allowances not exceeding Rs. 200. Different rates may be fixed for different councils. The Municipal Council places at the disposal of the President annually a sum not exceeding Rs. 1,000 by way of sumptuary allowance.

Every councillor may receive a monthly allowance not exceeding Rs. 100. Different rates may be fixed for different councils.

Rights and Privileges

Any councillor may call the attention of the proper authority to any neglect in the execution of municipal work, to any waste of municipal property or the wants of any locality and may suggest any improvements. Every councillor is furnished with the copies of the proceedings of the meetings by the Commissioner or the Chief Officer along with the notice of the next meeting. Every councillor has access to the records of the Council after giving due notice to the Chief Officer or the Municipal Commissioner.

The President has full access to all the records of the council and the Chief Officer or the Municipal Commissioner has to comply without unreasonable delay with any requisition of the President for any information appertaining to the municipal administration. The President may also call for any record of the council from Commissioner, the Chief Officer or any other officer, but any record so made available has to be returned within one month.

If the retiring President or Vice-President or the removed President or Vice-President fails to hand over the charge to his successor, he can be punished with simple imprisonment for a term, which may extend to one month or with fine, which may extend to Rs. 500 or with both.

Election Petition

An election of a councillor can be called in question by an election petition presented to the Election Tribunal within fifteen days from the date of declaration of the result of the election. An election petition may be presented by any candidate at such election or by any voters of the division concerned. In case of equality of votes, the Election Tribunal can decide by lot.

An appeal from an order of the Election Tribunal can lie to the High

Court within a period of thirty days from the date of order of the Tribunal. The decision of the High Court on such appeal is final and conclusive.

Resignation

A councillor may resign his membership or office by giving notice in writing to that effect to the Deputy Commissioner in the case of Town Municipal Council and, to the Commissioner, in the case of a City Municipal Council. The resignation takes effect on the expiry of the tenth day after the receipt of the notice of resignation unless withdrawn in the meanwhile.

Transaction of Business

Ordinary general meeting of the council is held every month. The President may call a special general meeting as and when he thinks fit. He has to convene a meeting upon the written request of not less than one-third of the total number of councillors within not more than fifteen days after the presentation of such request. If the President fails to call such a meeting, the Vice-President or one-third of the councillors may call such meeting for a day not more than thirty days after the presentation of a request and require the Chief Officer or the Municipal Commissioner to give notice to the councillors.

The Chief Officer or the Municipal Commissioner has to give a notice at least seven clear days before an ordinary general meeting and three days notice, or in case of great urgency, notice of shorter reasonable period of a special general meeting. A copy of the notice is posted at the municipal office. The notice should contain any motion or proposition for which a councillor has given notice not less than ten days previous to the meeting, besides specifying the time and place of meeting and the business to be transacted thereat.

Every meeting has to be held at the office of the municipal council. The President or the person presiding over a meeting has a preserving order. He may direct any councillor whose conduct is grossly disorderly to withdraw immediately. Every meeting is open to the public unless a majority of the members present decide to hold any inquiry or deliberation in private.

If less than one-third of the total number of councillors are present at meeting at any time from the beginning to the end, the presiding authority after waiting for thirty minutes, adjourns the meeting to a later date at which original business may be disposed of provided that not less than one-fourth of the total number of councillors are present.

The President or, in his absence, the Vice-President presides at every meeting of the council. In the absence of both, the members present elect one from among themselves to preside. The President or the person presiding over a meeting has a second or casting vote in all cases of equality of votes. All questions are decided by the majority of the votes of the members present and voting. The voting is made by show of hands but the municipal council may resolve that any question can be decided by ballot. Unless voting is demanded by at least four members, a declaration by presiding officer that a resolution has been carried or lost, and an entry to that effect in the minutes of the proceedings is conclusive evidence of the fact without proof of the number or proportion of votes recorded in favour of or against the resolution. No business other than one mentioned in the notice in general meeting and, in case of a general special meeting in the written request, can be discussed. The order of business to be transacted is determined by the presiding authority. In case of any dispute, the proposal is put to the meeting and is guided by the majority of votes.

The minutes of proceedings at each meeting are kept in Kannada and, on a resolution of council, in English, either in lieu or in addition to Kannada. The minutes are signed by the presiding authority. The minutes book is open for inspection by any councillor, and on payment of a fee of twenty paise by any other person.

Any resolution of a municipal council cannot be modified or cancelled within three months after passing thereof, except by a resolution passed by not less than one-half of the total number of councillors at a general meeting set forth fully the resolution which it is proposed to modify or cancel. Every motion or any amendment has to be received in writing and then moved duly. Every motion has to be seconded and until seconded, no debate can take place thereon nor can it be put to vote. An amendment merely negative on original motion can be allowed.

The Executive Engineer of the ward concerned, the principal officer of Health in the district and any other officer approved and notified by the Government may be present at any meeting and, with the consent of the municipal council, may take part in the discussion.

A councillor may ask the Municipal Commissioner or the Chief Officer questions on any matter relating to municipal administration. The councillor has to give to the Municipal Commissioner or the Chief Officer not less than ten clear days notice in writing specifying the question. Not more than two questions can be sent by any councillor for being answered at any ordinary meeting. The presiding officer can disallow any question. Written answers to admitted questions have to be given to the councillors one hour before the meeting. Questions not answered at any meeting for want of time or otherwise lapse.

Standing Committees

In every municipal council standing committees are constituted. They deal with:

(a) taxation, finance and appeals;
(b) public health, education and social justice;
(c) town planning and improvement; and
(d) accounts.

A standing committee consists of councillors not more than eleven or not less than five, as the municipal council determines. The members are elected by the council. The members hold office for a period of one year. The President and the Vice-President are not eligible for being elected as members of the committee. The Chairman of the Standing Committee is elected by the members by the system of single transferable vote.

The committee may meet and adjourn as the members think proper. The Chairman of the Committee may, whenever he thinks fit, and has to, upon the written request of the President of the municipal council or of not less than two members of the committee, within two days, call a special meeting of the committee. A business cannot be transacted unless more than one-third of the members of the committee are present. If the Chairman of any committee has been absent from the municipal area for a period exceeding seven days, the President or Vice-President may, in his absence, call a meeting. The Chairman of the committee may, instead of convening a meeting, circulate a written proposition of his own, or of any other member or of the Municipal Commissioner or Chief Officer or the municipal council for the observation and votes of the members of the committee. The decision on any proposition circulated should be in accordance with the majority of votes of the members of the committee unless a special meeting is convened to consider the same proposition. Every decision arrived at by the committee is recorded in the minute book. Every order passed by a standing committee is subject to revision and open to appeal as may be required or allowed by any rules that may be made by the Government in this behalf.

Joint Committee

The municipal council may join any other municipal council or any Town Panchayat, Cantonment Authority, Taluka Panchayat or Grama Panchayats in appointing a joint committee for any purpose of joint interest and in appointing a Chairman of such Panchayats. The joint body may, subject to sanction by the Government, levy tolls together instead of separately.

Municipal Property

Every municipal council may acquire and hold both movable and immovable property, whether within or without the limits of the municipal area. All public town-walls, gates, markets, slaughter houses, and night soil depots, and public buildings of every description; all public streams, tanks, reservoirs, cisterns, wells, springs, aquaducts, conduits, tunnels, pipes, pumps and other water works and all bridges, buildings, engines, works, materials connected therewith or appertaining thereto, and also any adjacent land not being private property appertaining to any public tank or well, all public sewers and drains, and all sewrs, drains, tunnels, culverts, gutters and water courses, in, alongside or under any street, and all works, materials and things appertaining thereto, as also all dust, dung, ashes, refuse, animal matter or filth or rubbish of any kind collected by the municipal council from the streets, houses, privies, sewers, cesspools or elsewhere, all public lamps, lamp posts and apparatus connected therewith, or appertaining thereto, all lands and buildings transferred to it by the Government, by gift or otherwise, for local public purposes, all public streets and the pavements, stones and other materials thereof and also all trees, erections, materials, implements and things provided for such streets belong to municipal council. The Government can, by notification, take over any municipal property on such terms as the Government may determine.

Municipal Fund

All moneys received by or on behalf of the municipal council, all taxes, tolls and other imposts, fines, fees, penalties paid to or levied by it, all proceeds of land or other property owned by the municipal council. and all rents accruing from its land or property, also all interests, profits and other moneys accruing by gift or transfer from the Government or private individuals or otherwise constitute the municipal fund.

The grant, lease, sale or other transfer of movable or immovable property by the municipal council is subject to Transfer of Property Act, 1882 or any other law.

The President, the Vice-President and every Councillor, the Municipal Commissioner, the Chief Officer or other employees of the municipal council are liable for the loss, waste or misapplication.

Contracts

Any person appointed by the Government to execute any work on behalf of the municipal council may make such contracts as are necessary for executing such works and the municipal council has to pay to the person so appointed the money required.

Any person who has directly or indirectly, by himself or his partner, any share or interest in any contract with, by or on behalf of a municipal council, or any employment with, under, by or on behalf of a municipal council other than as a municipal officer or servant, is disqualified for being an officer or servant of such municipal council. If any municipal officer or servant acquires or has acquired directly or indirectly, by himself or his partner, any share or interest in any contract for employment, he is liable to be transferred or removed from office by an order of the appointing authority. However, such officer or servant is given a reasonable opportunity of showing cause against the proposed action before an order of removal is made. Any councillor, who knowingly has any interest in any contract without being thereby disqualified for being a councillor, be punished with fine, which may extend to Rs. 500.

Every municipal council is competent to lease, sell or, otherwise, transfer any property. No free grant for immovable property whatever may be its value, no grant for an upset price and no lease for a term exceeding five years, and no sale or other transfer of immovable property exceeding Rs. 25,000 in value is valid unless the previous sanction of the Government is obtained. The sanction of the municipal council by a resolution passed at a general meeting is required in the case of a lease for a period exceeding one year or of a sale or other transfer, or contract for the purchase of any immovable property, of every contract which involves expenditure not covered by a budget grant and of every contract, the performance of which cannot be completed within the official year current at the date of the contract. In the case of a contract for the purchase of movable property, if the expenditure involved or the value of the property to be sold as estimated in the municipal accounts exceeds Rs. 1,000, in the case of a town municipal council, and Rs. 2,000, in case of a city municipal council, is required.

For the supply of materials or goods or for the execution of any work involving an expenditure exceeding Rs. 5,000 tenders are invited publicly.

A contract involving an expenditure exceeding Rs. 2,000 cannot be made by the Municipal Commissioner without the approval or sanction of the council. Every contract made by the Municipal Commissioner involving an expenditure exceeding Rs. 250 is reported by him within fifteen days to the council.

Every contract entered into, by or on behalf of municipal council is made in writing and is signed by the President or Vice-President and two other councillors, and is sealed with a common seal of the council. In every contract sanctioned under an authority by a committee, the contract is executed by the Chairman of such committee or by other person empowered in that behalf.

Staff

Every municipal council is entitled to employ such officers and servants as may be necessary for the discharge of its duties.

Municipal Commissioner

The Government may appoint a Municipal Commissioner for any city municipal area. On the appointment of a Municipal Commissioner, the appointment of Chief Officer terminates. The Government may, at any time, discontinue the appointment of a Municipal Commissioner for any municipality. A Municipal Commissioner may be removed from office by the Government if he is incapable of performing the duties of his office or has been guilty of any misconduct or neglect, which renders his removal expedient. He can be transferred by the Government at a specially convened general meeting of the council not less than three-fourths of the total number of councillors vote for such transfer. He receives salary wholly payable by the council or partly by the council and partly by the Government.

Every municipal council has a Chief Officer. He is appointed by the Commissioner from among the persons in the cadre of Chief Officer of the Karnataka Municipal Administrative Service. A Chief Officer can be transferred from office by a resolution of the council at a general meeting passed by a majority of not less than three-fourths of the total number of councillors. The council may recommend disciplinary action against a Chief Officer for abuse of powers, misconduct or neglect of duty. All other officers and servants are subordinate to him.

The Chief Officer has, subject to control of the municipal council, to perform all the duties and exercise all the powers imposed or conferred upon him or delegated to him. Subject to orders of the council or of the standing committee, he has to take prompt steps to remove any irregularity pointed by the Auditor. He has to report to the President, the standing committee and the council all cases of fraud, embezzlement, theft or loss of municipal money or property. He has to supply any return, statement, estimate, statistics, account or report or a copy of any document in his charge, called for by the council or the standing committee and complies with any orders passed by the municipal council or the standing committee thereon. He exercises and controls over the acts and proceedings of all officers and servants and disposes of all questions relating to them and their pay, privileges and allowances.

Subject to the control of the municipal council, the Chief Officer has power to grant, give or issue, under his signature, all licenses and permissions. He may suspend, withheld or withdraw any license. He can receive and recover and credit to municipal fund, all fees payable for licenses, and permissions granted or given by him. He may enter, on behalf of the municipal council, into contracts, which do not involve an expenditure of over Rs. 500, and invite tenders for the execution of any approved work or for the supply of any materials or goods required by the council.

Health Officer

A municipal council may, and, when required by the Government can appoint one or more Health Officer(s) either permanently or temporarily, the officers being officers from the Department of Public Health. Such an officer can be transferred, without the previous sanction of the Government, from office only by the votes of not less than two-thirds of the total number of councillors. The council may recommend disciplinary action against a Health Officer for abuse of powers, misconduct or neglect of duty.

Karnataka Municipal Administration Service

The posts specified by the Government under every local authority are filled by appointment of officers belonging to the Karnataka Municipal Administrative Service. Such officers become the officers of the Government. Every local authority contributed in advance one-fourth percentage of its revenue to the consolidated fund of the state to meet the expenditure in respect of salaries, allowances, pensions, provident fund, gratuities and other necessary expenses payable to the officers of the Karnataka Municipal Administrative Service.

Planning Authority

The municipal council in places where the Planning Authority has not been constituted under the Karnataka Town and Country Planning Act, is required to consult the nearest planning authority in matters affecting town planning.

Directorate of Municipal Administration

The State Government is obliged to establish a Directorate of Municipal Administration. The composition, the powers and the duties of the Directorate are prescribed by the Government. The Government may, by notification, delegate to the Directorate all or any of the powers exercisable by the Commissioner or Deputy Commissioner. There is also a legal cell in the Directorate.

Functions

Every municipal council has to perform certain obligatory as well as discretionary functions:

Obligatory Functions

It is incumbent on every council to make adequate provisions for following matters within the municipal area:

(a) lighting public streets, places, and buildings;

(b) watering public streets and places;

(c) cleaning public streets, places and sewers, and all spaces not being private property, removing noxious vegetation, and abating all public nuisances;

(d) extinguishing fires and protecting life and property when fire occurs;

(e) regulating or abating offensive or dangerous trades or practices;

(f) removing obstructions and projections in public streets, bridges, and other public places;

(g) securing and removing dangerous buildings or places and reclaiming unhealthy locations;

(h) acquiring and maintaining, changing and regulating places for the disposal of dead;

(i) constructing, altering and maintaining public streets, culverts, municipal boundary marks, markets, slaughter houses, latrines, privies, urinals, drains, sewers, drainage works, sewage works, baths, washing places, drinking fountains, tanks, wells, dams, and the like;

(j) obtaining supply of or an additional supply of water, proper and sufficient for preventing damage to the health of the inhabitants;

(k) naming streets and numbering houses;

(l) registering births and deaths;

(m) public vaccination;

(n) providing suitable accommodation for calves, cows, or buffaloes required for the supply of animal lymph;

(o) maintaining schools for pre-primary education;

(p) arranging for the destruction or the detention and preservation of stray dogs;

(q) providing facilities for anti-rabic treatment and treatment of lepers and mental patients and meeting the expenses of indigent persons undergoing anti-rabic treatment within or outside the municipal limit;

(r) providing covered metallic receptacles and covered metallic receptacles mounted on wheels for use by the municipal council for the removal of night-soil and rubbish and disposing of night-soil and rubbish and, if so required by the Government, preparation of compost manure from night-soil and rubbish;

(s) providing accommodation for municipal sweepers and scavengers and granting loans for construction of house;

(t) printing annual report on the municipal administration;

(u) paying salary and the contingent expenditure on account of police or guards required by the council;

(v) vital statistics including registration of births and deaths;

(w) regulation of tanneries;

(x) maintenance of up-to-date record of all buildings and sites; and

(v) planting and maintaining of road-side trees.

Special Functions

Every municipal council has to make reasonable provisions for the following special matters:

(a) providing special medical aid and accommodation for the sick in time of dangerous diseases; and taking measures to prevent the outbreak so as to suppress and prevent the recurrence of the disease; and

(b) giving relief to and establishing and maintaining relief works in times of famine or scarcity for destitute persons within the limits of the municipal area.

Discretionary Functions

Every municipal council may, in its discretion, provide either wholly or in part for all or any of the following matters:

(a) laying out public streets and acquiring the land for that purpose, including the land requisite for the construction of buildings or curtilages thereof to about in such streets;

(b) constructing, establishing or maintaining public parks, gardens;

libraries, museums, mental hospitals, halls, offices, dharamshalas, choultries, musafirkhanas, rest houses, homes for disabled and destitute persons and other public buildings,

(c) providing shelter for destitute women;

(d) constructing and maintaining suitable sanitary houses for the habitation of the poor and granting loans for construction of such houses or for effecting necessary improvements connected therewith;

(e) providing accommodation for any class of servants other than sweepers and scavengers employed by the municipal council or granting loans to such servants for construction of houses;

(f) planting and maintaining roadside and other trees;

(g) taking statistics and granting rewards for information, which may tend to secure the correct registration of vital statistics;

(h) making a survey;

(i) securing or assisting to secure suitable places for carrying on the offensive trades;

(j) supplying, constructing and maintaining receptacles, fittings, pipes and other appliances on or for the use of private premises for receiving and conducting the sewage thereof into a sewer under the control of the council;

(k) providing music or other entertainments in public places or places of public resort;

(l) the promotion of public health or child welfare;

(m) contribution towards any public funds for the relief of human sufferings, within or without the municipal area;

(n) by a resolution passed at a general meeting and supported by one-half of the total number of councillors and with the previous sanction of the Deputy Commissioner, in the case of a town municipal council and, of the Commissioner, in the case of a city municipal council, organising any public reception, ceremony, entertainment or exhibition within the municipal area;

(o) the organisation or maintenance during scarcity, of shops or stalls for the sale of necessaries of life;

(p) housing and maintaining destitute orphans and destitute cripples;

(q) constructing, establishing and maintaining warehouses;
(r) establishment and maintenance of dairy farms and breeding studs;
(s) provision of transport facilities within the municipal area;
(t) maintenance of an ambulance service;
(u) supply of water beyond the limits of the municipal area;
(v) the acquisition and maintenance of grazing grounds;
(w) guaranteeing the payment of interest on money expended for the construction of a telephone line;
(x) promoting the well-being of municipal employees or and class of municipal employees and their dependents;
(y) the construction, purchase, organisation, maintenance, extension and management of mechanically propelled transport facilities for the conveyance of the public;
(z) the construction, maintenance, repairs, purchase of any works for the supply of electrical energy;
(aa) making contributions towards the construction, establishment or maintenance of educational institutions including libraries and museum, any hospital, dispensary or similar institution providing for public medical relief, or any other institution of a charitable nature;
(ab) construction, maintenance and provision of public bathing houses;
(ac) revival or promotion of cottage industries;
(ad) improvement of cattle and livestock including construction and maintenance of veterinary hospitals;
(ae) maintenance of maternity houses and child welfare centres;
(af) maintenance of art galleries;
(ag) slum improvement and upgradation;
(ah) urban forestry, protection of environment and promotion of ecological aspects;
(ai) urban poverty alleviation;
(aj) promotion of cultural, education, and aesthetic aspects;
(ak) promotion, formation, extension or assistance of cooperative societies; and,
(al) any other matter, which is likely to promote education or public health, safety or general welfare or convenience or the advancement of the economic condition of the inhabitants.

Taxation

The municipal council may levy any one or more of the following taxes:

(a) a tax on buildings or lands or both situated within the municipal area;

(b) a toll on vehicles entering the municipal area;

(c) a tax on all or any vehicles, other than motor vehicles, boats used for riding, draught or burden kept within the municipal area;

(d) a water rate for water supplied by the council;

(e) a lighting tax;

(f) a duty on transfer of immovable property in the shape of an additional stamp duty; and

(g) a tax on advertisements erected, exhibited, fixed or retained upon or over any land, building, wall, hoarding, frame, posts or structure or upon or in any vehicle or displayed to public view visible from a public street or public place.

Every municipal council can levy taxes on buildings or lands or both, the aggregate of which is not less than fifteen per cent of the annual rateable value, in the case of Town Municipal Council and, twenty per cent of the annual rateable value in the case of City Municipal Council. In addition, the council can levy a water supply scheme in urban areas and the cess so collected is credited to the Government

Imposition of Tax

Before imposing a tax, the municipal council has to pass a resolution at a general meeting specifying the classes of persons or of property or of both, which the council proposes to make and the amount or rate, at which the municipal council proposes to assess each such class. When such resolution has been passed, the municipal council publishes a notice of resolution in prescribed form. Any inhabitant may, within one month from the date of publication, send his objection in writing to the municipal council. The council takes all objections into consideration or authorises a committee to consider the same and report thereon and, unless it decides to abandon the proposed tax, submits objections with its opinions and any modifications proposed, together with a copy of the notice to the Government. The Government may either refuse to sanction the resolution or may return it to the municipal council for further consideration, or if no objection, or objection which is not sufficient, was made to the proposed tax within one month from the publication of the notice, may sanction the resolution either without modification or, subject to such modifications, not involving an increase of the amount to be imposed or to such conditions as to the application within the municipal area to any proposed of the whole or any part of the proceeds of such tax, as it deems fit. All such resolutions with all modifications are published by the municipal council in the prescribed manner and in the municipal area together with a notice reciting the sanction and the date and number and the tax as prescribed from a date, which is specified in the notice but not less than one month from the publication of such notice. The publication of the notice is conclusive evidence that the tax has been imposed.

A municipal council may, at any time for any sufficient reason, suspend, modify or abolish any existing tax. Suspension, modification or abolition of a tax cannot take effect unless approved by the Government.

Duty on Transfer of Immovable Properties

The duty on transfers of immovable property is levied in the form of a surcharge on instruments of sale, gift, mortgage, exchange and lease in perpetuity of immovable property at a rate not exceeding two per centum on the market value of the property or the value of the rents for the first ten years in the case of a lease. No duty is, however, leviable in respect of a mortgage where the amount secured does not exceed Rs. 2500.

Assessment of Tax

Every building is assessed together with its site and other adjacent premises occupied as appurtenances thereto. The annual rateable value of a building is the gross rent, less a deduction of sixteen and two-thirds per cent of such annual rent. The deduction is in lieu of all allowances for repairs or any other account. For assessing taxes, the Government appoints an assessor. The municipal council has to afford all clerical and other necessary help to the assessor to discharge his duties and bears all expenditure incidental thereto.

The assessor causes an assessment list of all buildings or lands, or buildings and lands in the municipal area to be prepared. It contains the name of the ward and street in which the property is situated, the designation of the property sufficient for identification, names of the owner and occupier, the annual rateable value or other basis, on which the property is assessed and the amount of tax assessed thereon. On the requisition of the assessor, the owner or the occupier is bound to furnish a true return under his signature as to the names and places of abode of the owner or occupier or of both and as to the dimensions of buildings or land and the annual rateable value of the building. When the assessment list has been completed, the assessor gives public notice thereof, and of the place where the list may be inspected. Every person is at liberty to inspect the list and to make extracts therefrom without charge. The assessor, at the time of the publication of assessment list, gives public notice of a time not less than thirty days when the revising authority proceeds to revise the valuation and assessment.

In a municipal area where there is a Municipal Commissioner, the Municipal Commissioner and, elsewhere, any Government officer, not below the rank of an Assistant Commissioner specially appointed by the Government and, where no such officer is appointed, the Assistant Commissioner having jurisdiction over the Revenue Sub-Division in which the municipal area is situated, is the revising authority to whom objections are made. All objections to the valuation and assessment are made to the assessor by the application in writing stating the grounds disputing the valuation and assessment. All applications are registered in a book by the assessor. The revising authority, after allowing the applicant an opportunity of being heard, investigates and disposes of the objections, causes the result thereof to be noted in the book and causes any amendment necessary in accordance with such result to be made in the assessment list. Such an amendment list is authenticated by the revising authority. The authenticated list is kept open for inspection to all owners and occupiers.

The Chief Officer or the Municipal Commissioner may, at any time, alter the assessment list. In respect of any building constructed, altered, added to or reconstructed after the preparation of the assessment list, an alteration in the list may be made after giving notice, not less than one month from the date of notice. Where the alteration is made by the Municipal Commissioner, the revising authority is the Commissioner. The assessment list is revised completely not less than once in every four years. The revised assessment list is authenticated at any time not later than the thirty-first day of July of the official year, to which the list relates.

Whenever the title of any person liable primarily for the payment of a tax is transferred, the person whose title is transferred and the person to whom the same is transferred, have to give notice of such transfer in writing to the municipal council within three months after the execution of the instrument of transfer. In the event of the death of any person liable primarily, the person on whom the title of the deceased devolves, has to give notice of such devolution to the council within six months from the date of death of the deceased. Until such a notice is given, the person primarily responsible for payment of tax has to continue to be liable for the payment.

Where a building or land has been vacant and unproductive of rent for any period of not less than ninety consecutive days or consists of separate tenements, one or more of which has been vacant and unproductive of rent or is wholly or in great part demolished or destroyed by fire or otherwise deprived of value, the municipal council may remit or refund the equitable tax. Such a remittance or refund is granted only on notice.

Fees on Jatra, Urus etc.

A municipal council may impose, by resolution and with the previous sanction of the Government, a fee not exceeding fifty paise per head over twelve years of age resorting to Shrine, Jatra or Urus etc., if it feels necessary to make special arrangements for the health and comfort of persons resorting.

Whenever it appears to the Government that additional funds are necessary to enable the council to discharge its obligatory functions or that the balance of the municipal fund is insufficient for meeting the expenditure or for the performance of any duties, the Government may, by notification, require the municipal council to impose any tax specified in the notification, if no such tax is at that time imposed or, to enhance any existing tax and the council has to forthwith proceed accordingly.

Recovery of Claims

When an amount is due, the municipal council causes to be presented to the person liable for the payment, a bill for the sum claimed as due. If the sum is not paid within fifteen days from the presentation of the bill, the council may cause to be served upon the person liable for the payment, a notice of demand. If a person, on whom a notice of demand has been served, does not within thirty days from the service of notice, either pay the sum demanded or show cause to the satisfaction why he should not pay the same or prefer an appeal against the demand, he is deemed to be in default. Thereupon, a penalty not exceeding twenty per cent of the amount of the tax may be recovered from him in addition to the amount of tax. The tax and the penalty with all costs of recovery may be levied under a warrant issued by the council by distress and sale of movable property or attachment and sale of the immovable property of the defaulter. Every warrant is signed by the Municipal Commissioner or Chief Officer of the municipal council.

Improvement Board

The Government may, after consulting the municipal council, direct the establishment of an Improvement Board. The Board is established for the purpose of undertaking and executing improvement schemes in any municipality. It consists of seven members. The Chairman of the Board is appointed by the Government. The Municipal Commissioner or a Chief Officer, the Executive Engineer concerned and the nominee of the Director of Town Planning, two members appointed by the Government and two members to be elected by the municipal councillors from amongst themselves are the members. The Board is a body corporate and has perpetual succession and a common seal with power to acquire, hold and dispose of property and to contract, and may sue and be sued. The term of Chairman and other members, not being ex-officio, is three years from the date of publication of their names in the Official Gazette.

A person other than a person who is an ex-officio member, is disqualified for being chosen or for being a member of the Board, if he holds office of profit under the Board or the municipal council or the Government or is of unsound mind and stands so declared by a court or is an undischarged insolvent or has applied for being adjudged insolvent or has been convicted of an offence, which involves moral turpitude or has, directly or indirectly, by himself, by his wife or son or any other near relative dependent on him or by any partner, any share or interest in any contract or employment with, by or on behalf of the Board or is a secretary or manager or other salaried officer of any body corporate which has any share or interest in any contract or employment with the Board. The Government may, after inquiry, remove from office the Chairman or any other member, not being an ex-officio member, if he refuses to act or has become incapable of acting or has abused his position in the Board or fails to attend three consecutive meetings of the Board or ceases to reside within the limits of the municipality or has, since his appointment, incurred any of the disqualifications is otherwise unsuitable to continue on the Board. Such an order of removal can be made only after the member has been given an opportunity to submit his explanation to the Government.

The Board may enter into and perform all contracts necessary or expedient for carrying out the improvement schemes. All contracts are made on behalf of the Chairman. It is the duty of the Board to prepare improvement schemes and execute them and perform other functions for purposes of the improvement of the municipality. When the Government is satisfied that all the necessary improvement schemes have been executed by the Board and further measures may be undertaken conveniently by the municipal council, the Government may, by notification dissolve the Board.

Budget

The Chief Officer or the Municipal Commissioner on or before the 15th day of January each year prepares and submits to the municipal council a budget containing a detailed estimates of income and expenditure of the council for the ensuing year together with a complete account of the actual and expected receipts and expenditure for the year, ending on the 31st day of March next. The budget, as passed by the municipal council, is sent to the Government and a copy thereof is sent simultaneously to the Commissioner, and in the case of town municipalities, to the Deputy Commissioner of the district also for information. A balance of not less than the sum required to meet the establishment charges for a period of three months is also allowed. The municipal council may modify the budget in the course of the official year.

Accounts and Audit

The municipal council, at the general meeting in April or after audit of the past year's accounts, passes the accounts of the past year.

The municipal accounts, from time to time and once in every year at least, are audited by an auditor appointed by the Government. As soon as practicable after the completion of the audit, but not later than three months thereafter, the audit prepares a report and sends to the municipal council and to the Commissioner and Controller of State Accounts Department. On receipt of a report, the Municipal Commissioner or the Chief Officer has to remedy the defects or irregularities and, within two months places the report together with a statement of action taken before a meeting of the council. He has also, within three months, to send to the Controller of State Accounts Department intimation of his having remedied the defects or irregularities pointed out in the report. On receipt of such intimation, the Controller of State Accounts Department may accept the intimation and withdraw the objection or direct that the matter to be re-investigated at the next audit or at any earlier date or hold that the defects or irregularities pointed out in the report or any of them have not been removed or remedied. The Controller of State Accounts Department sends a report of his decision within one month to the Commissioner. The Commissioner may, after considering the recommendation of the Controller and after taking the explanation of the person concerned or making inquiry, disallow any item and surcharge the same on the person making or authorising the making of the illegal payment.

The municipal council, as soon as the accounts have been passed transmits to the Government a copy of account. The quarterly and annual accounts of receipts and expenditure are open to public inspection and are published.

Control

The Commissioner is the Chief Controlling Authority. The Commissioner, the Deputy Commissioner or any officer authorised by the Government, has the power to enter on and inspect any immovable property; to call for any extract from the proceedings of any council or of any committee or from any book or document and any return, statement, account or report to furnish, to require any information and to require a council to take into consideration any objection and to make a written reply within a reasonable time.

The Deputy Commissioner may, by order in writing under his signature, suspend the execution or prohibit the doing thereof, if in his opinion, the execution of any order or resolution of a council or doing of which is unlawful or is causing or is likely to cause injury or annoyance to the public or to lead to a breach of the peace. In such cases, the Deputy Commissioner has to forward to Government and to the Commissioner and to the council affected a copy of the order with a statement of the reason for making it. It is the discretion of the Government to rescind the order or to direct that it can continue in force with or without modification, permanently or for any period. In confirming, revising or modifying the order, the Government has to give the council a reasonable opportunity of showing cause against the order.

It is lawful for the Government to require the appointment of a Health Officer to be made by any council, to make an order vetoing the appointment or continuance of in office of any person selected or appointed by the council, and the tenure of such office ceases and determines on and from the date, on which such order is communicated to the council and to require that any person appointed to be a Chief Officer or a Municipal Commissioner is invested by any council with all or any of the powers, which can be delegated to him lawfully, in addition to powers conferred on him. The Government may order to perform certain duty within a fixed time. If that duty is not performed within a stipulated period of time, the Government may appoint some person to perform it and may direct the expenses incurred to be paid by the council. The Government may appoint administrators when any general election to a council has been stayed by a competent court or the election of all councillors or more than two-thirds of the councillors have been declared by a court to be void or all the councillors have resigned. The State Government may appoint an advisory council to advise and assist the administrator in the exercise of powers and the performance and discharge of the duties and functions conferred or imposed on him. The members of the advisory council hold office during the pleasure of the Government.

Dissolution

If, in the opinion of the Government, any council is not competent to perform or persistently makes default in the performance of its duties or exceeds or abuses its powers or refuses to carry out the directions or is functioning in a manner prejudicial to the council, the Government may, by an order publish together with a statement of reason therefor, in the Official Gazette, declare the council to be incompetent or in default and may dissolve it. Before making an order of dissolution, a reasonable opportunity is given to the council to show cause. Such an order of dissolution together with a statement of reason therefor is laid before both the Houses of the State Legislature as soon as may be.

The Commissioner may call for and examine the record of any proceedings including order of assessment of any subordinate officer and may pass appropriate orders. He may act as appellate authority.

Rules and Bye-Laws

The Government may, by notification and after previous publication, make rules for carrying out urban affairs.

Every municipal council may make, alter or rescind bye-laws. Before making any bye-law, the council publishes it together with a notice specifying a date on or after which the draft is taken into consideration. Such date is not less than thirty days. Objections and suggestions are received and considered. Every bye-law comes into effect once it is approved by the Government. The Government may make model bye-laws.

II. Municipal Corporation

The Governor may declare an area to be larger urban area if:

(a) it contains a population of not less than three lakhs;

(b) the density of population is not less than three thousand inhabitants to one square kilometre of area;

(c) the revenue generated from such area for the local administration in the year of the last preceding census is not less than rupees six crore per annum or an amount calculated at the rate of Rs. two hundred per capita per annum, whichever is higher; and

(d) the percentage of employment in non-agricultural activities is not less than fifty per cent of the total employment.

Any area specified as larger urban area is deemed to be a city and a corporation is established for the said city. The corporation is a body corporate. It has perpetual succession and common seal with power to acquire, hold and dispose of property and to contract. It may sue and be sued.

Municipal Authorities

The following are the municipal authorities:

(a) the Corporation,

(b) the Standing Committee, and

(c) the Commissioner.

Constitution

The corporation consists of:

(a) Elected Members : not being less than thirty and more than hundred.

(b) Nominated Members : not more than five persons nominated by the Government, who are

  (i) persons having special knowledge and experience in municipal administration or matters relating to health, town planning or education; or

  (ii) social workers.

(c) Ex-Officio Members :

  (a) the members of the House of People and the members of the State Legislative Assembly representing a part or whole of the city whose constituencies lie within the city and who are registered as electors within the city; and

  (b) the members of the Council of State and State Legislative Council, who are registered as electors within the city.

The nominated members have no right to vote in the meetings of the Corporation. Where two-thirds of the total number of councillors required to be elected have been elected, the corporation is deemed to have been duly justified.

Reservation

Seats are reserved in a corporation:

(a) for the Scheduled Castes and the Scheduled Tribes in the same proportion as the population of these classes in the city bears to the total population of the city;

(b) for persons belonging to the Other Backward Classes as nearly as may be one-third of the total number of seats to be filled by direct election, eighty per cent of seats are reserved for the persons falling under category 'A' and the remaining twenty per cent for the persons falling in category 'B'; and

(c) for women, not less than one-third of the seats reserved for each category belonging to Scheduled Castes, Scheduled Tribes and Other Backward Classes and those of the non-reserved seats to be filled by direct election.

Term of Office

The term of the Councillors commences on the date of the first meeting of the corporation. The term is five years. No election can be held if the vacancy occurs within four months before the expiry by efflux of time of the term of office of the councillors.

Election of Councillors

The elections are held wardwise. If there is equality of votes between two or more candidates, the Returning Officer decides by drawing lots. If a person is elected for more than one division, he has, within three days from the date of the last of such elections, by notice in writing delivered to the Commissioner, to intimate the division from which he chooses to serve and his that choice is final. If the candidate does not make a choice, the Commissioner determines by lot and notifies the division from which such candidate can serve. All elections of the Mayor and Deputy Mayor and that of councillors are notified by Government in the official gazette.

Election Petition

An election of a councillor can be questioned by an election petition presented for adjudication to the District Court within thirty days from the date of the publication of the result. The petition may be presented by any candidate or any voter of the division concerned.

An appeal can lie to the High Court from an order of the District Court within a period of thirty days from the date of the order of the court excluding the time required for obtaining a copy of the order.

Declaration of Assets

Every councillor is obliged within one month of the commencement of his term of office and in the same month of each succeeding year, to file with the Mayor a declaration of all assets owned by him and by any member of his family. Such declaration forms part of the Corporation records. If a councillor fails to file the declaration or files the same knowing it to be fake or incorrect, he ceases to be a councillor.

Disqualifications

A person is disqualified for being chosen as and for being a councillor:

(a) if he has been sentenced by a Criminal Court to imprisonment for an offence punishable with imprisonment for a term exceeding six months; or

(b) if he is convicted of an offence under the provisions of The Untouchability (Offences) Act, 1955 or The Prevention of Food Adulteration Act, 1954; or

(c) if he holds any office of profit under the Government of India or the Government of any state or of any local or other authority; or

(d) if he has been dismissed from service under a local authority or Government service; or

(e) if, having been a legal practitioner, he has been dismissed or suspended from practice by order of a competent authority; or

(f) if he has been deaf-mute; or

(g) if he is of unsound mind and stands so declared by a competent court; or

(h) if he is an undischarged insolvent; or

(i) if he is not a citizen of India, or has acquired voluntarily the citizenship of a foreign state or is under any acknowledgement of allegiance or adherence to a foreign state; or

(j) if he is disqualified by or under any law for the purpose of election to the State Legislature; or

(k) if he has, directly or indirectly, by himself or his partner, any share or interest in any work done by order of the Corporation, or in any contract or employment with or under or by or on behalf of the corporation; or

(l) if he is employed as a paid legal practitioner on behalf of the Corporation or accepts employment as legal practitioner against the Corporation; or

(m) if he is a licensed surveyor, or plumber or water supply contractor of the Corporation or he is a partner of a firm, of which any such licensed person is a partner; or

(n) if he fails to pay arrears of any kind due by him to the otherwise than as an agent, receiver, trustee or an executor to the Corporation within three months after a notice in this behalf has been served upon him; or

(o) if he has in proceedings questioning the validity or regularity of an election been found to have been guilty of any corrupt practice or any offence punishable under the Indian Penal Code, unless a period of six years has elapsed since the date of the finding or the disqualification has been removed by order by the Government.

A councillor becomes disqualified on following grounds in addition to the above, if he:

(a) votes or takes part as a councillor in the discussion of any matter in which he has, directly or indirectly, by himself or his partner, any share or interest; or

(b) in which he is professionally interested on behalf of a principal or other person; or

(c) in which he is engaged at the time in any proceeding against the Corporation; or

(d) absents himself from the meetings of the Corporation during three consecutive months except with the leave of the Corporation. No leave can be granted in case of absence from the meetings during a period exceeding six consecutive months.

Mayor and Deputy Mayor

The Corporation, at its first meeting after a general election of councillors and at its first meeting in the same month each year, elects one of its councillors to be the Mayor and one other councillor to be the Deputy Mayor. The seats are reserved on the pattern of the councillors. The Mayor or the Deputy Mayor holds office for one year from the date of his election. He can continue the office till his successor is elected. The retiring Mayor or Dy. Mayor is eligible for re-election. In case of casual vacancy in the office of the Mayor or Dy. Mayor, the Corporation chooses one of the councillors to fill the vacancy and every Mayor or Dy. Mayor so elected holds office for the remaining period.

The Mayor presides over every meeting of the Corporation. He has general powers of inspection and may give direction to the Commissioner with regard to the implementation of any resolution of the Corporation or a Standing Committee in the discharge of any obligatory and discretionary functions of the corporation. The Mayor may call any record of the Corporation from the Commissioner and the records made available to him are to be returned by him within fifteen days from the date they are made available. He may, by an order in writing, delegate any of his functions to the Dy. Mayor. The Mayor is not eligible to be elected as Chairman of any Standing Committee. If any vacancy occurs in the office of the Chairman of any Standing Committee, the Mayor has to convene a meeting for the election of another Chairman.

When the office of the Mayor is vacant, his functions are devolved on the Dy. Mayor until a new Mayor is elected. If the Mayor is absent from the city continuously for more than eight days, or is incapacitated for more than eight days, his functions are devolved on the Dy. Mayor. The Dy. Mayor has the power to direct the Commissioner to get the Administration and Audit Reports prepared in time. He discharges such functions of the Mayor as may be delegated to him by the Mayor.

Resignation

The Mayor resigns his office by notice in writing to the Dy. Mayor and delivered to the Commissioner and, in the absence of the Dy. Mayor, addressed to the Commissioner and delivered to him. The Dy. Mayor may resign his office by notice in writing addressed to the Mayor and delivered to the Commissioner and, in the absence of the Mayor, addressed to the Commissioner and delivered to him. A councillor may resign his office by notice in writing addressed to the Mayor and delivered to him. The resignation takes effect from the date on which it is delivered.

Allowances

Honoraria, fees or allowances as may be determined by the Government may be paid to the Mayor, the Dy. Mayor and the Councillors. The Corporation can place at the disposal of the Mayor annually by way of sumptuary allowance a sum not exceeding Rs. 25,000. Different limits may be prescribed for different Corporations.

Standing Committees

There are four Standing Committees of the Corporation:

(a) the Standing Committee for taxation, finance and appeals;

(b) the Standing Committee for public health, education and social justice;

(c) the Standing Committee for town planning and improvement; and

(d) the Standing Committee for accounts.

Each Standing Committee consists of seven Councillors. The members are elected at its first meeting after the general elections and at its first meeting in the same month in each succeeding year according to the principle of proportionate representation by means of single-transferable vote. The Standing Committee for public health, education and social justice consists of not less than two councillors belonging to the Scheduled Castes and the Scheduled Tribes. A councillor cannot be member of more than one Standing Committee at the same time. The Mayor and the Deputy Mayor are ex-officio members of all the Standing Committees but they have no right to vote.

The term of office of the members of the Standing Committee is one year from the date of their election. A person ceases to be a member of the Standing Committee if he ceases to be a councillor or if he absents himself without the permission of the standing committee for three consecutive meetings of the Standing Committee. A member of the Standing Committee may resign his office by notice in writing addressed to the Chairman of the Standing Committee, or where there is no Chairman, to the Mayor and deliver to the Chairman, or to the Mayor. Such resignation takes effect from the date on which it is delivered.

Each Standing Committee elects one of its members as Chairman. The Chairman holds office until his successor is elected but he is eligible for re-election. The Chairman vacates his office when he ceases to be a member of the Standing Committee. In case of casual vacancy, the Standing Committee elects one of its members as Chairman and every such person holds office during the remaining period of time.

The Standing Committee for taxation, finance and appeals deals with all matters relating to finance, taxation and appeals and all matters not specifically assigned to any other Standing Committee. Likewise, all Standing Committees deal with the matters relating to themselves. The

Standing Committee for accounts, in addition to the powers and duties assigned, supervise the utilisation of the budget grants, has access to the accounts of the Corporation and may require the Commissioner to furnish any clarification to the receipts and expenditure of the Corporation fund, may conduct a monthly audit of the Corporation accounts and is bound to check the monthly abstracts and receipts and disbursements for the preceding month as furnished by the Commissioner and may, subject to the approval of the Corporation, write off the amount of any loss, or depreciation caused to Corporation property which appears to the committee to be irrecoverable. The amount of any loss or depreciation exceeding rupees one thousand cannot be written off without the previous sanction of the Government.

The Standing Committee may, by resolution in writing, authorise the Commissioner to take action in anticipation of its approval, sanction, consent or concurrence.

Joint Committee

The Corporation may, and has to if required by the Government, join a local authority or a combination of local authorities in appointing a joint committee for purposes of joint interest. The committee may frame terms binding on each body as to the construction and future maintenance of any joint work. In case of any difference arisen between the constituents, the matter is referred to the Government whose decision is final and binding on all the parties.

Conduct of Business

The first meeting of the Corporation after the general election is convened by the Commissioner as early as possible after the publication of the results. It is presided over by the Divisional Commissioner. The meetings of the Corporation and the Standing Committees are held in the office of the Corporation. Notices of meetings are issued by the Council Secretary, who does so in consultation with the Mayor, in case of the Corporation and, with the Commissioner in case of the Standing Committee. Every notice has to specify the agenda for the meeting.

The Corporation meets in the Corporation office for the transaction of business at least once every month upon the day and hours arranged and convened by the Mayor. No meeting can be held unless at least six clear days before the day, of meeting, notice of the day and hour of the meeting and of the business to be transacted has been given to the members. In case of urgency, the Mayor may convene a meeting after giving shorter notice. In such cases, notice of the day and hour of the meeting is published in the manner as the Mayor may deem most expedient. The Mayor has to call a special meeting on receiving a request in writing, signed by not less than one-third of the members specifying the resolution proposed to move. No special meeting can be held unless at least four clear days notice has been given by a separate communication addressed to each member and by advertisement in the local newspapers. If the offices of Mayor and Deputy Mayor are vacant, the duties assigned for the purpose to the Mayor are performed by the Commissioner.

All the meetings are open to the public provided the presiding member may direct that the public generally or any particular person has to withdraw. All questions are decided by the majority of the votes of members present and voting at the meeting. In equality of votes, the presiding person can exercise a second vote. A business can be transacted if at least one-third of the total number of members is present. A resolution of the Corporation cannot be modified or cancelled within three months after its passing except at a meeting specially convened and by a resolution of the Corporation supported by not less than two-thirds of the total number of members.

Minutes of the proceedings are entered in Kannada and in English in a minute book specifying the names of the councillors who attended the meeting, the business transacted, the decision of the Corporation, the day of the meeting and the time of commencement and closing of the meeting and signed by the presiding member after each meeting. The minutes are recorded by the Council Secretary and are placed before the next meeting for confirmation. The minute book is open to the inspection of any councillor without payment and, to the inspection of any person, on payment of a fee of fifty paise.

The Commissioner has the right to attend the meeting of the Corporation and of any Standing Committee and to take part in the discussion but cannot vote or move any resolution. He is obliged to attend any meeting if required to do so by the Mayor.

The Mayor or Chairman may prohibit any councillor from voting or partaking in discussion on any matter in which the councillor is believed to have any interest, or he may require the councillor to absent himself during the discussion. If the Mayor or Chairman is alleged by any councillor present at the meeting to have any interest in the matter under discussion, he may on the motion of such councillor if carried, be required to absent himself from the meeting during the discussion.

Each Standing Committee meets at the Corporation office at least once a month. The Chairman of a Standing Committee may call a meeting at any time. He is obliged to call a meeting within forty-eight hours of the receipt of a requisition signed by the Commissioner or by the three members of the Committee and stating the business to be transacted. Every notice is issued by the Council Secretary. All questions are decided by the majority of votes of the members present and voting at the meeting. In case of equality of votes, the presiding member has a casting vote. All minutes of the proceedings are recorded by the Council Secretary in a book signed by the presiding member after each meeting. The minute book is placed before the Corporation at its next meeting. Any member, other than the Mayor or Dy. Mayor, who fails to attend three consecutive meetings ceases to be a member of such Standing Committee but may be re-elected by the Corporation. Every resolution of Standing Committee is made available to every member within fifteen days from the date of passing such resolution. The Corporation may, on a motion by any member of the Corporation, modify or amend or revoke any resolution.

Commissioner

The Commissioner is appointed by the Government after consultation with the Mayor. He is not the member of Corporation and holds office, subject to the pleasure of the Government, for a period of two years. The Commissioner can be removed from the office whenever the Corporation resolves by a majority of not less than two-thirds of its members. He is a whole-time officer of the Corporation. He is paid out of the Corporation fund such monthly salary and allowances as the Government may, by order, determine. During the absence of the Commissioner, the Government may appoint a person to act as the Commissioner. Every person so appointed exercises the powers and performs the duties conferred and imposed on the Commissioner.

The Commissioner performs all the duties and exercises all the powers imposed or conferred upon him. In emergency, he takes immediate action for the service or safety of the public or the protection of the property of the Corporation. He may, with the approval of the Standing

Committee concerned, by order in writing, empower any Corporation officer to exercise, perform or discharge any power, duty or function under his control.

All the correspondence is conducted by the Commissioner. He has to send copies of each correspondence to the Mayor. He may delegate to any officer subordinate to him any of his ordinary powers, duties and functions. The Commissioner may, on his own responsibility and by order in writing, authorise the Health Officer, the Engineer, the Revenue Officer or any other officer, who is the head of the Department working under him to exercise the extraordinary powers conferred on him.

The Commissioner is responsible for the custody of all records including all papers and documents connected with the proceedings of the Corporation, Standing Committees and other Committees. He has control over the Corporation establishment.

Corporation Officers and Servants

The Government appoints for every Corporation officers of the State Civil Services to be the Engineer, Health Officer, Revenue Officer, Chief Accounts Officer and Council Secretary for the efficient functioning of the Corporation. These officers are the heads of their respective departments and are subordinate to the Commissioner. The Government may also appoint one or more Dy. Commissioners and Asst. Commissioners. The Government appoints in consultation with the Mayor, an officer not below the rank of Assistant Commissioner to the Council Secretary. The officer is appointed on deputation ordinarily for a period of three years and if the corporation, by two-thirds of majority of its members so desire, he can be withdrawn earlier and another person is appointed.

The posts under every Corporation, which are included in the Karnataka Municipal Administrative Services are filled by the Government by appointment of officers belonging to Karnataka Municipal Administration Services.

The Corporation may appoint Special Health Officers for the purpose of making investigations and proposing preventive of remedial measures, Special engineers, architects or experts in town improvement or town planning for the purpose of preparing, executing or supervising any scheme of work undertaken by the Corporation and, Special Revenue Officer for the purpose of introducing a new tax or discharging any duty connected with the revenue administration of the Corporation. The special office can be created without the sanction of the Government. In the event of the occurrence of any unusual mortality or the prevalence or apprehended outbreak of any dangerous disease within the city, Government may, on its own motion, appoint a Special Health Officer for a period of not more than six months and the Corporation is not bound to pay more than five hundred rupees per month on this account.

The Commissioner lays before the Standing Committee for taxation, finance and appeals, a schedule setting forth the designations and grades of the officers and servants who should constitute Corporation establishment. The Standing Committee may either approve or amend the schedule and lays it before the Corporation with its remarks. The Corporation can sanction the schedule with or without any modifications and may amend it at the instance of the Commissioner and Standing Committee. A new office with maximum monthly salary exceeding nine hundred rupees cannot be created without the sanction of the Government. No officer or servant can be entertained on the Corporation establishment unless he is a member of the Karnataka Municipal Administrative Service or unless his office and emoluments are included in the schedule sanctioned.

The State Government may transfer any officer or servant of a corporation to a corresponding post in any other corporation or in any local authority.

General Powers

The municipal government of the city vests in the Corporation. It is the duty of the Corporation to exercise such powers, perform such functions and discharge such duties as are conferred on it and to consider all periodical statements relating to the receipts and disbursements and all progress reports and pass such resolutions thereon.

Obligatory Functions

It is incumbent on the Corporation to make reasonable and adequate provision by any means or measures, which it is lawfully competent to use or to take, for each of the following matters :

(a) erection of substantial boundary marks of the city;

(b) the watering and cleansing of all public streets and public places and the removal of all sweepings therefrom;

(c) the collection, removal, treatment and disposal of sweage, offensive matters and rubbish and the preparation of compost manure from such sewage, offensive matters and rubbish;

(d) the construction, maintenance and cleaning of drains and drainage works and of public privies, water closets, urinals and similar conveniences;

(e) the maintenance of a Corporation office and of all public monuments and open space and other property vesting in the Corporation and keeping a true and correct account of all Corporation property;

(f) the naming or numbering of streets and of public places vesting in the Corporation and the numbering or premises;

(g) the regulation and abatement of offensive and dangerous trades or practices;

(h) the maintenance, change and regulation of places for the disposal of the dead and the provision of new places for the purpose and disposing of unclaimed dead bodies;

(i) the construction or acquisition and maintenance of public markets and slaughter houses and the regulation of all markets and slaughter houses;

(j) the maintenance of an ambulance service and service for conveying dead bodies to crematoriums;

(k) the destruction of birds or animals causing nuisances or of vermin and confinement or destruction of stray or ownerless dogs;

(l) laying out new public streets;

(m) maintenance or aiding schools for pre-primary education;

(n) the construction or acquisition and maintenance of cattle ponds;

(o) establishing and maintaining a system of public vaccination;

(p) the reclamation of unhealthy localities, the removal of noxious vegetation and generally the abatement of all nuisances;

(q) the planting and maintenance of trees on road sides and elsewhere;

(r) the construction, maintenance, alteration and improvement of public streets, bridges, subways, culverts, causeways and the like,

(s) the removal of obstruction and projections upon streets, bridges and other public places;
(t) the management and maintenance of all municipal water works and the construction or acquisition of new works necessary for a sufficient supply of water for public and private purposes;
(u) preventing and checking the spread of dangerous diseases;
(v) the lighting of public streets, municipal markets and places of resort vested in the Corporation;
(w) the securing or removal of dangerous buildings and places;
(x) the construction and maintenance of residential quarters for the paura karmikas;
(y) the provision of public parks, gardens, playgrounds and recreation grounds;
(z) the regulation of lodging houses, camping grounds and rest houses in the city;
(aa) establishing and maintaining compost plants for disposal of sewage;
(ab) supplying, constructing and maintaining in accordance with the general system approved by the Corporation, receptacles, fittings, pipes and other appliances whatsoever on or for the use of premises for receiving and conducting the sewage thereof into drains under the control of the Corporation;
(ac) vital statistics including registration of births and deaths;
(ad) regulation of tanneries;
(ae) taking measures to meet any calamity affecting the public;
(af) fulfilment of any obligation imposed by the Government; and
(ag) subject to adequate provision being made for the matters, the provision of relief to destitute persons in the city in times of famine and scarcity and the establishment and maintenance of relief works in such times.

Discretionary Functions

The Corporation may, in its discretion, provide, either wholly or in part, for all or any of the following matters :

(a) the organisation, maintenance or management of institutions within or without the city for the care of persons who are infirm, sick or incurable, or for the care and training of the blind, deaf, mute or otherwise disabled mothers or infants or school children;

(b) the organisation, maintenance or management of maternity and infant welfare homes;

(c) the provision of milk to expectant nourishing mothers or infants or school children;

(d) the organisation, maintenance or management of chemical or bacteriological laboratories for the examination or analysis of water, food or drugs for the detection of diseases or for research connected with public health;

(e) the organisation, maintenance or management of swimming pools, public wash houses, bathing places and other institutions designed for the improvement of public health;

(f) the construction and maintenance in public streets or places of drinking fountains for human beings and water troughs for animals;

(g) survey of buildings or lands;

(h) the provision of music for the people;

(i) encouraging the development of planting and maintenance of trees and plants on private lands and within private compounds;

(j) maintenance of health museums;

(k) construction and maintenance of infirmaris or hospitals for animals;

(l) the organisation and maintenance in times of scarcity of shops or stalls for the sale of necessaries of life;

(m) the building or purchase and maintenance of residence for Corporation officers and servants;

(n) the grant of loans for building purposes to Corporation servants;

(o) the establishment and maintenance or the aiding of museums and art galleries or zoological collections and the purchase or construction of buildings therefore;

(p) constributing towards public funds raised for the relief of human suffering caused by natural calamities within the city or for the public welfare;

(q) the preparation or presentation of addresses to persons of distinction;

(r) granting rewards for information regarding the infringement of any provisions of the Act or of the rules etc.;

(s) the building or purchase and maintenance of suitable dwellings for the poors and working classes;

(t) the provisions of shelter for destitute or homeless persons and any form of poor relief;
(u) slum improvement and upgradation;
(v) urban forestry, protection of the environment and promotion of ecological aspects;
(w) urban poverty alleviation;
(x) promotion of cultural, educational and aestethic aspects;
(y) with the previous sanction of the Government, the making of a contribution towards any public ceremony or entertainment in the city; and
(z) any measures to promote public safety, health, convenience or instruction.

Enumeration of Tax

The Corporation can, with the sanction of the Government and at rates not exceeding to the prescribed limit, levy and one or more of the following taxes;

(a) a tax on buildings, or lands or both situated within city;
(b) a toll on vehicles, other than motor vehicles, entering the Corporation limits;
(c) a tax on advertisement;
(d) a duty on certain transfers of property in the shape of an additional stamp duty; and
(e) a water rate or water rates for water supply by the Corporation, which may be imposed in the form of a tax assessed on buildings and lands, including water charges.

In addition to tax on buildings or lands, the Corporation can levy a water supply cess at the rate of twenty per cent of such tax for the maintenance and improvement of water supply schemes in urban areas. The cess so collected is credited to the Government.

Imposition of Tax

Before imposing a tax, the Corporation has to select, by a resolution passed at a total general meeting for the purpose, one or other of the taxes and to specify the classes of persons or of property or of both and the amount or rate, at which the Corporation proposes to assess. After the resolution is passed, the Corporation is required to publish in the Official Gazette a notice of such resolution. Any inhabitant of the city may object within one month in writing to the Corporation. The Corporation takes all objections into consideration or can authorise the Standing Committee for taxation and finance to consider the same and report and submit the objections and modifications together with a copy of the notice to the Government. The Government may either refuse to sanction the resolution or may return it to the Corporation for further consideration or may sanction the resolution with or without modifications. All resolutions sanctioned with all modifications subject to which the sanction is given are published in the Official Gazette and in the offices of the Corporation in city together with a notice reciting the sanction and the date. The tax so published from a date specified in the notice, not less than one month from the date of publication of notice, is imposed accordingly.

The Corporation may, at any time for sufficient reasons, suspend, modify or abolish any existing tax. The Corporation can revise any tax imposed by it once every five years. The Government may, at any time, direct the Corporation to revise any tax imposed by it.

Property Tax

The property tax is levied on all buildings and lands within the city. It is levied on not less than twenty per cent and not more than twenty five per cent of the rateable value of the buildings and lands. The percentage may be different in different areas and for different classes of buildings and lands. Building includes a land appurtenant to building used as garden and grounds for the more beneficial enjoyment not exceeding thrice the area occupied by the building.

The rateable value of a building or land is deemed to be gross annual rent, at which the building or land may be expected to let, less a deduction, in the case of buildings, only of sixteen and two-third per cent of annual rent. In case of any Government or railway building or any building not ordinarily let, the rateable value is deemed to be six per cent of the total of the estimated market value of the land and the estimated cost of erecting the building after deducting for depreciation a reasonable amount, which in no case, be less than ten percent of such cost. Machinery and furniture are excluded for valuation.

The places set apart for public worship, choultries, places used for the charitable purpose, for sheltering the destitute or animals and orphanages, homes and schools for the deaf and dumb, asylum for the aged and fallen women, ancient monuments or parts, thereof as are used as residential quarters or public offices, charitable hospitals and dispensaries but not including residential quarters attached thereto, hospitals and dispensaries maintained by railway administration but not including residential quarters, burial and cremation grounds, Government lands set apart for free recreational purposes, buildings and lands exclusively used for student hostels, which are not established or conducted for profit, educational purposes by recognised educational institutions, the offices of labour associations, buildings and lands belonging to Central Government or any State Government used for purposes of Government and not used or intended to be used for residential or commercial purposes, buildings or lands belonging to the city of Mysore Improvement Trust Board, the Bangalore Development Authority, the Karanatka Housing Board or any local authority, the possession of which has not been delivered to any person and the agricultural lands are exempted from the property tax.

The property tax is paid by the person primarily liable within sixty days after the commencement of every half year. If default is made in making payment, the person liable to pay the tax has to pay a penalty at the rate of five per cent per annum of the amount of tax remaining unpaid.

If building, whether ordinarily let or occupied by the owner himself, has been vacant and unlet for thirty or more consecutive days in any half year, the Commissioner can remit, not exceeding one-half of the tax in that half year. The remission is allowed during that half year or in the following half year and not afterwards. The remission can be claimed only by delivering a notice to the Commissioner that the building is vacant or unlet or that the building will be vacant and unlet from a specified date.

In case of transfer of any property, the person whose title is transferred and the person to whom it is transferred, have to give notice of transfer within three months of such transfer. In the event of the death of the person liable, the person to whom the title of the deed is transferred has to give the notice of transfer to the Commissioner within one month from the death of the deceased. The Commissioner can review the transfer of title within a period of three years from the date of recording of transfer of title. The person likely to be affected is, however, given a reasonable opportunity of being heard.

If a building in the city is constructed or reconstructed, the owner has to give a notice thereof to the Commissioner within fifteen days from the date of completion. If the date falls within the last two months of the half year, a remission of the whole of the tax or enhanced tax is granted. If the date falls within the first four months, the owner is entitled to a remission not exceeding half of the tax or enhanced tax. In case of demolition or destruction of a building, if the notice is given during first two months, the remission is granted to whole of the tax for that half year and if the notice is given in last four months, the tax is remitted not more than half of that half year.

If any area is included in the city, no tax is liable if the date falls within the last two months. If date falls within the first four months, a remission not exceeding half of the tax is granted. In case of exclusion of any area from the city, whole of the tax is remitted, if the date falls within first four months. If date falls within last four months, a remission not exceeding half of the tax is allowed. A remission in such cases is allowed only if an application is made to the Commissioner within three months from the date of the exclusion of the area.

Assessment of Property Tax

An assessment book is maintained in which are recorded the particulars of each property. The assessment book is revised by the Commissioner once in every five years. The Commissioner may, after giving notice to the parties concerned and hearing their objections, amend the property tax assessment book at any time between two general revisions. In every case of assessing, any property for the first time or increase in assessment, the Commissioner has to intimate, by a special notice, to the owner or occupier that a petition for revising the assessment will be considered if reaches within thirty days from the date of service of notice. Immediately after the disposal of a revision petition, the Commissioner informs the petitioner and directs him to pay the amount fixed on revision within fifteen days and corrects the assessment book accordingly.

Revision of Assessment

An objector, who is dissatisfied with the assessment of any tax, other than the property tax, may make an application to the Commissioner for the revision of assessment stating the grounds of his objection. Such an application can be admitted if it has reached within seven days from the date of demand and the tax based on assessment prevailing was paid before making the application. The Commissioner hears the objections and passes the appropriate order, which is communicated to the objector by registered post. An objector dissatisfied with the order of the Commissioner may, within fifteen days from the date, on which order was sent by post, appeal against it to the Taxation Appeals Committee, consisting of three members of the Corporation elected by it.

The Divisional Commissioner may, suo motu or otherwise, call for and examine the record of any proceeding relating to assessment of any tax by the Commissioner or the Taxation Appeals Committee. He may, after giving the assessee an opportunity of being heard and after making necessary inquiry, pass necessary order. An appeal lies to the District Court against any decision of the Taxation Appeals Committee or any order of the Divisional Commissioner. But no such appeal can be heard by the court unless the petition is presented within thirty days from the date of decision or order and the tax has been paid.

Tax on Advertisement

Every person, who erects, exhibits, fixes or retains, upon or over any land, building, wall or structure any advertisement or who displays any advertisement to public view in any place, has to pay on every advertisement a tax calculated at the rates determined by the Corporation with the approval of the Government and subject to minimum and maximum fixed by the Government.

The Commissioner may farm out the collection of any tax on advertisement for any period not exceeding one year at a time.

Duty on Transfer of Immovable Properties

A duty on transfer of immovable property is levied in the form of an additional stamp duty on instrument of sale, gift, mortgage, exchange or lease in perpetuity at a rate not exceeding two per cent on the market value of the property or on the value of the rent for the first ten years in the case of a lease.

The Sub-Registrar, at the time of the registration of the instrument, maintains an amount of the duty of transfer levied in respect of each instrument and sends an amount thereof to the Corporation at the end of every month and also to the District Registrar of Stamps. Three per cent of the amount so collected is deducted towards expenses by the Government. The District Registrar sends intimation to the Commissioner of the Corporation once in every quarter about the amount payable to the Corporation. On the basis of the information, the Commissioner prepares a bill and draws the amount from the District Treasury concerned and credits the same to the Corporation fund.

Recovery or Dues

All costs, damages, penalties, compensation, charges, fees, rents, expenses, contributions and other sums are demanded by bill, containing particulars of the demand and notice of the liability incurred in default of payment and may be recovered within fifteen days from the date of service of the bill unless such person has applied to District Court. If the sum due is not paid by the party liable within fifteen days after demand, the sum may be recovered under a warrant of the District Court, by distress and sale of the movable property. No distraint can be made, no suit can be instituted and no prosecution can be commenced in respect of any sum due to the Corporation after the expiration of a period of six years from the date, on which distraint might first have been made.

Corporation Fund

All moneys received by or on behalf of the Corporation, all taxes, tolls and other imposts, fines, fees, penalties paid to or levied by it, all proceeds of land or other property sold by the Corporation and all rents accruing from its land or property and all interest, profits and other moneys accruing by gifts or transfers from the Government or private individuals or otherwise constitute the Corporation fund.

Accounts and Audit

All money received by the Corporation are lodged in a bank or treasury and are credited to an account entitled the Corporation Fund Account. All orders or cheques against the Corporation Fund are signed by the Commissioner or, in his absence, by the Revenue Officer. The Government appoints one of its officers as the Corporation Chief Auditor who conducts an audit of the Corporation accounts subject to the supervision and control of the Controller of State Accounts. He reports to the prescribed municipal authority any material impropriest or irregularity.

Sinking Fund

The Corporation maintains sinking funds for the repayment of money borrowed on debenture issued and pays by quarterly instalments into such sinking fund a sufficient sum for a repayment within a period fixed for the loan of all moneys borrowed or debentures issued. All money paid into the sinking fund are invested by the Commissioner.

Budget

The Commissioner prepares on or before the15th day of January each year and submits to the Standing Committee a budget containing a detailed estimate of income and expenditure for the ensuing year. The Standing Committee for taxation, finance and appeals, as soon as may be, considers the estimates and proposals of the Commissioner and after having obtained proposals of other Standing Committees, prepares a budget estimate of the income and expenditure of the Corporation for the next year. A balance of amount not less than one lakh of rupee under General Account Revenue is allowed in the estimate. The Commissioner gets the budget estimate as finally approved by the Standing Committee printed and not later than the 1st day of February forwards a printed copy thereof to each councillor. At a meeting of the Corporation called in the first week of February, the budget estimate prepared by the Standing Committee is laid before the Corporation. The Corporation may refer the budget estimate back to the Standing Committee for further consideration and resubmission within the specified period or adopt it. The Corporation has to pass finally the budget estimate atleast three weeks before the beginning of the year, to which it relates and forthwith submits a copy thereof to the Government. The Government may sanction the budget in its entirety or subject to certain modifications. However, if within two months from the date of receipt of the budget, the Government does not communicate any order thereon, the budget is deemed to have been sanctioned by the Government. The Corporation may, on the recommendation of the Standing Committee for taxation, finance and appeals, during the year, pass a supplemental budget estimate for the purpose of meeting any special or unforeseen requirement arising during the year.

The Standing Committee for taxation, finance and appeals may, at any time during the year, reduce the amount of the budget grant or transfer and add the amount or a portion of the amount of one budget grant to the amount of any other budget grant. Every such reduction or transfer has to be brought to the notice to the Corporation at its next meeting. If any reduction or transfer is of an amount exceeding Rs. 500, the Corporation may pass appropriate orders and it is incumbent on the Standing Committee and the Commissioner to give effect to it.

Corporation Property

All public parks, playgrounds, and open spaces reserved for ventilation, all public lamps, lamp-posts and apparatus connected therewith or appurtaining thereto, all gates, markets, slaughter houses, manure and refuse depots and public buildings of every description vest in the Corporation and be under its direction, management and control.

The Commissioner may acquire, on behalf of the Corporation, movable or immovable property within or without the city or any interest in such property. He is bound by the resolution of the Standing Committee in this regard. The sanction of the Standing Committee is required for the exchange of any immovable property, for the taking of any property on lease for a term exceeding twelve months or for the acceptance of any gifts or bequest of property burdened by an obligation. The sanction of Corporation and the Government is required for the acceptance or acquisition of any immovable property with value exceeding one thousand rupees or for the taking of any property on lease for a term exceeding three years or for the acceptance of any gift or bequest of property burdened by an obligation if the value of such property exceeds one thousand rupees.

The Commissioner may dispose of, by sale or exchange, any movable property, the value of which does not exceed two thousand rupees in each instance or grant for any term not exceeding twelve months a lease of any immovable property or a lease or concession of any right of fishing or grazing or of gathering and taking fruit and the like. Every such disposal is reported to the Standing Committee, within fifteen days. With the sanction of the Standing Committee the Commissioner may dispose of by sale or exchange any movable property, the value of which does not exceed five thousand rupees in each instance, or grant for any term not exceeding three years a lease of any immovable property, or a lease or concession of any such right. With the sanction of the Corporation, the Commissioner may lease, sale or otherwise dispose of any immovable property.

Every movable property exceeding a prescribed sum can not be sold otherwise than by public auction. No property can be transferred free of cost or for an upset price. A lease of any immovable property exceeding five years cannot be granted. No immovable property can be disposed of by sale or by other transfer except with the previous sanction of the Government.

Contracts

Every contract is made by or on behalf of the Corporation by the Commissioner. The common seal of the Corporation is affected to every contract, which is made between private persons. Every contract for the execution of any works or the supply of any materials or goods which will involve an expenditure exceeding one thousand rupees is made in writing and is sealed with the common seal. The seal is affixed in the presence of the Commissioner who signs the contract or instrument in token of his presence.

The Commissioner gives notice by advertisement inviting tenders at least seven days before entering into any contract or the execution of any work or the supply of any material or goods, which involves an expenditure exceeding ten thousand rupees. The Standing Committee may, at the instance of the Commissioner, authorise him to enter into a contract without inviting tenders.

The Commissioner may sanction an estimate amounting upto rupees ten lakh. When the amount of an estimate exceeds rupees ten lakh but is less than fifteen lakh rupees, the sanction of the Standing Committee is required. An estimate exceeding rupees fifteen lakhs but not exceeding rupees thirty lakh requires the sanction of the Corporation. Any estimate exceeding rupees thirty lakh requires the sanction of the Government. This power is applicable in the Corporation of the city of Bangalore. The respective powers of the several authorities of the Corporation of the Cities of Hubli-Dharwad and Mysore are different. The Commissioner may sanction an estimate not exceeding rupees two lakh, the sanction of the Standing Committee is required if the amount exceeds rupees two lakh but does not exceed rupees four lakh. The estimate excluding rupees four lakh but not exceeding rupees eight lakh can be sanctioned by the Corporation, while estimate exceeding rupees sight lakh requires sanction of the Government. The powers of several authorities of the Corporation in the cities of Belgaum, Mangalore and Gulbarga are also different. In these Corporations, the Commissioner may sanction an estimate, the amount of which does not exceed rupees one lakh. When the amount exceeds rupees one lakh but does not exceed rupees three lakh, sanction of the Standing Committee is required. Any estimate the amount of which exceed rupees three lakh but does not exceed rupees eight lakh, the sanction of the Corporation is necessary. Estimates exceeding rupees eight lakh require the sanction of the Government.

As regards restriction on the power to make contracts, the provisions differ. In the Corporation of the city of Bangalore, the Commissioner can make a contract involving the expenditure less than rupees ten lakh. The contract exceeding this amount needs the sanction of the Standing Committee. The Standing Committee cannot authorise making of contract involving an expenditure exceeding rupees fifteen lakh unless sanction of the Corporation is obtained. The Corporation cannot authorise contract exceeding rupees twenty lakh unless it has obtained sanction of the Government. In the cities of Hubli-Dharwad and Mysore, the Commissioner cannot make a contract involving an expenditure rupees three lakh unless he has obtained sanction of the Standing Committee. The Standing Committee cannot authorise a contract exceeding rupees five lakh without the sanction of the Corporation and the Corporation cannot authorise a contract involving expenditure exceeding rupees ten lakh unless a sanction of the Government is obtained. In case of Belgium, Mangalore and Gulbarga Corporations, the respective powers are rupees two lakh, rupees five lakh and rupees eight lakh.

Any variation in the contract involving an expenditure, which exceeds five per cent over the expenditure involved in the original contract requires the sanction of the authority superior to the original sanctioning one.

Regulation of Buildings

If any person intends to construct or reconstruct a building, he is required to send an application in writing for permission to execute the work together with a site plan of the land, ground plan, elevations and sanctions of the building, a specification of the work and other prescribed documents. The construction cannot be started unless and until the Commissioner grants the permission. The Commissioner has to either grant the permission or refuse it within thirty days after the receipt of application. If the Commissioner has not passed within thirty days any order, the applicant may address a letter to the Commissioner by name, requesting him to pass necessary orders on his application within thirty days. If the Commissioner again fails to either grant or refuse the permission, the Standing Committee is bound on the written request of the applicant, to determine by written order whether such approval should be given or not. If the Standing Committee does not, within one month from the receipt of such request, determine, approval is deemed to have been given and the applicant may proceed to execute the work. Whenever the Commissioner or the Standing Committee refuses to approve a site for a building or to grant permission to construct or reconstruct a building, the reasons for the refusal have to be stated specifically in the order.

If the construction of a building is not commenced within two years after the permission was granted, the work cannot be commenced until a fresh application is made and a fresh permission is granted.

Regulation of Huts

Every person, who intends to construct or reconstruct a hut, has to send to the Commissioner an application in writing for permission to execute the work and a site plan of the land. Within fourteen days after the receipt of application, the Commissioner either grants the permission or refuses. If Commissioner has neither granted nor refused the permission within the stipulated period of time, the Standing Committee is bound on the written request of the applicant to determine by written order whether permission should be granted or not. If the Standing Committee within thirty days does not determine, the applicant may proceed to execute the work. If the construction is not commenced within six months after the date of grant of the permission, the work can not be commenced until a fresh application is made and a fresh permission is granted.

Administrative Report

As soon as after the first day of April in every year, the Corporation is required to submit to the Government, a detailed report of the administration during the preceding year. The Commissioner prepares such report and the Corporation considers the report and forwards the same to the Government with its resolution thereon. Copies of the administration report are kept for sale at the Corporation office.

Licence

No place within the city can be used for any purpose inserted in Schedule 'X' in the Act without a licence obtained from the Commissioner. The Commissioner can, if required by the Corporation, publish a notification in the Official Gazette and in two or more local newspapers that any place at a distance within five kilometres of the limits of the city cannot be used for any purpose mentioned above without a licence obtained from the Commissioner.

Legal Cell

A Legal Cell is constituted in the Corporation. The Corporation consults the legal cell at all matters pertaining to the interpretation of the provisions of the Act and the rules, regulations and bye-laws and also in matters pertaining to the institution, defence or conduct of suits and other legal proceedings, to which the Corporation is a party. Head of the Legal Cell is a retired District and Sessions Judge or practising advocate having ten years of experience. The tenure does not exceed three years. The practising advocates having five years of experience are appointed as Legal Assistants for three years. There are other Deputy Law Officer, Assistant Officer and Junior Law Officer appointed on the Cell.

Sanction for Prosecution

When a Mayor or Deputy Mayor or any Councillor or the Commissioner or any officer of the Government working in the Corporation on deputation is accused of any offence alleged to have been committed by him while acting or purporting to act in the discharging of his official duty, no magistrate can take cognisance of such offence except with the previous sanction of the Government.

Security Force

There is constituted and maintained a force to be called the Corporation Security Force for the better protection and security of the property owned by the Corporation, for aiding the officers of the Corporation in the detection and investigation of any matter relating to leakage of revenue or any tax payable to the Corporation and for effective communication and obtaining of any information regarding any design to commit or the commission of any offence by any person.

The Supervisory Officers and other members come on deputation from the Karnataka State Public Service. There are one Sub-Inspector and a number of Head Constables, Constables and Arm Guards at the Force.

Rules, Regulations and Bye-Laws

The Government may, after previous publication by notification, make rules to carry out the urban affairs. Every rule is laid, as soon as may be after it is made, before each House of State Legislature while it is in session for a total period of thirty days, which may be comprised of one session or of two or more successive sessions.

The Corporation may, with the previous approval of the Government, by notification make regulations. The Corporation may make bye-laws for all matters expressly required or allowed by the Act. A bye-law gets validity only after it is sanctioned by the Government. If the sanction is not accorded within three months, the bye-laws are deemed to have been sanctioned.

The draft of a bye-law is published in the Official Gazette and in the local newspapers. Simultaneously, a printed copy of the draft is kept at the Corporation for at least thirty days for public inspection. Printed copies of draft are sold to any person requiring them on payment. All rules and bye-laws are published in the Official Gazette in English and in Kannada. A bye-law comes into operation three month after its publication. The regulations are published in such manner as the Corporation may determine.

Appeal

An appeal lies to the Standing Committee from any notice issued or other action taken or proposed to be taken by the Commissioner, any refusal by the Commissioner to grant permission to construct or reconstruct a building, any refusal by the Commissioner to grant permission or a licence or any other order of the Commissioner. If, on any such appeal, the Standing Committee reverses or modifies substantially any action taken or proposed to be taken by the Commissioner or any order passed by him, he may, within sixty days of the date of such decision, refer the matter to the Corporation, and pending the decision of the Corporation, the Commissioner is not bound to give effect to the decision of the Standing Committee. The decision of the Corporation is final. Where an appeal is against an order granting a licence or permission, it should be made within sixty days after the date of publication of the order on the notice board of the Corporation and, in other cases, within sixty days after the date of receipt of order or proceedings, against which the appeal is made.

Government Control

The Government may require the Corporation or the Commissioner to produce any record, proceedings, correspondence, plan or other document; furnish any return, plan, estimate, statement, account or statistics relating to the proceedings, duties or works of the Corporation or any of the municipal authorities; and to furnish or obtain and furnish any report. The Government may depute any officer to inspect or examine any Corporation department or office or any service or work undertaken by the Corporation or any of the municipal authorities, and all Corporation officers and employees are bound to afford the officer so deputed access to the premises or properties and to all records, accounts and other documents, the inspection of which he considers necessary to enable him to discharge his duties.

In case of matters pending before the Corporation for more than three months or pending before a Standing Committee for more than sixty days and urgent decision of which is necessary in the interest of administration of the Corporation, the Government may, before giving the Corporation notice of not less than fifteen days, pass such orders which are considered necessary or direct that the matter pending before the Standing Committee is deemed to be referred to the Corporation and be disposed of on that basis. In case of matter of public importance, no notice is necessary and the decision of the Government is final. Every such order passed by the Government is communicated to the Commissioner who gives effect to it expeditiously as if order is a resolution of the Corporation.

If on receipt of any report or information or otherwise the Government feels that any duty imposed on any Corporation authority has not been performed or has been performed in any imperfect, inefficient or unsuitable manner or that adequate financial provision has not been made for the performance of any such duty, the Government may, after giving the notice of not less than fifteen days, by order, direct the Corporation or the Commissioner to make arrangements for the performance of the duty or to make adequate financial provision. If no action has been taken, the Government may appoint an officer to take the action.

If the Government is of the opinion that the execution of any resolution or order or the doing of any act is in contravention of or in excess of the powers or is likely to lead to a breach of peace or to cause injury or annoyance to the public or to any class or body of persons or is prejudicial to the interest of the Corporation, it may suspend the execution of such resolution or order, or prohibit the doing of such act after using a notice to the Corporation to show cause within a period not less than fifteen days. Upon consideration of the reply, the Government may pass orders cancelling the resolution or order or repealing the bye-laws or regulation and communicate the same to the Corporation.

The Government may appoint an Administrator when the ordinary elections to the Corporation have been stayed by an order of a competent court or the election of all the Councillors or more than two-thirds of the Councillors have been declared by the competent court to be void or all the Councillors or more than two-thirds of the Councillors have resigned. An Administrator can be appointed for a period not exceeding six months.

If it appears to the Government on complaint made or otherwise that any tax or fee leviable by a Corporation is unfair in its incidence or that the levy is obnoxious to the interests of the general public, the Government may require the Corporation to take measures for removing any objection within a stipulated period, the requirements are not carried into effect to the satisfaction of the Government, it may, by notification, suspend the levy of such tax until such time as the objections thereto are removed. The Government may at any time, by a notification rescind any such suspension.

If it appears to the Government that the balance of the Corporation Fund of any Corporation is insufficient for meeting the expenditure or for the performance of any duties, the Government may, by notification, require the Corporation to impose any tax specified therein if no such tax is imposed thereon or to enhance any existing tax. The Government has to take into consideration any objection made by the Corporation or any inhabitant against the imposition or enhancement. The Corporation cannot abandon or modify or abolish such tax when imposed and the Government may cancel or modify any such requisition.

The Government may call for the records of any proceedings of a Corporation, Standing Committees, the Commissioner or any subordinate officer for satisfying itself as to the correctness, legality or propriety of any order or proceeding. After giving a reasonable opportunity of being heard, the Government may pass suitable order.

Dissolution

If, in the opinion of the Government, the Corporation is not competent to perform or makes default in the performance of any of the duties or exceeds or abuses its power or fails to carry out the directions or orders given by the Government to it or is acting in a manner prejudicial to the interests of the Corporation, the Government may, by order published together with a statement of all reasons therefor, in the Official Gazette, declare the Corporation to be incompetent or in default or to have exceeded or abused its power or to have failed to carry out the directions, and may dissolve it. Before making an order of dissolution, reasonable opportunity is given to the Corporation. The order of dissolution together with a statement of the reasons therefor has to be laid before the Houses of the State Legislature as soon as may be.

When the Corporation is dissolved, all powers and duties are exercised and performed by an Administrator appointed by the Government. An Advisory Committee consisting of not less than fifteen and not more than twenty-five persons, who are qualified to become Councillors, is formed to assist the Administrator.

A dissolved Corporation can be reconstituted before the end of six months from the date of dissolution. A reconstituted Corporation can continue only for the remainder of the period of the original Corporation.

Ward Committee III

In a city having population of three lakhs or more, Wards Committees are constituted. Each Wards Committee Consists of the Councillor of the Corporation representing the wards in the Corporation and not more than five persons having knowledge and experience in municipal administration are nominated by the Government and not more than two members are nominated by the Government from such non-governmental organisations and community based organisations working within the areas of the Wards Committee, as the Government may specify in this behalf.

The term of office of the members of the Wards Committee is co-extensive with the term of office of the Councillors of the Corporation. Where a Wards Committee consists of two or more wards, one of the members of the Wards Committee representing a ward is elected to be the Chairman of the Wards Committee.

Metropolitan Planning Committee

The Government is obliged to constitute a Metropolitan Planning Committee for the Bangalore Metropolitan Area to prepare a draft development plan for the area as a whole. The Committee consists of thirty persons, of which not less than two-thirds of the members are elected by and from amongst the elected members of the Corporation, the Municipal Councils and Town Panchayats and the Adhyakshas and Upadhyakshas of Zilla Panchayats, Taluk Panchayats and Grama Panchayats in the metropolitan area in proportion to the ratio between the urban and rural population and such number of representatives of the Government of India and State Government as may be determined by the State Government are nominated accordingly and such organisations and institutions as may be deemed necessary for carrying out the functions assigned to the Committee, are also nominated by the State Government. All the members of the House of People and State Legislative Assembly whose constituencies lie within the metropolitan area and the members of the Council of State and State Legislative Council who are registered as electors in the area are permanent invitees at the Committee. The Commissioner of the Bangalore Development Authority is the Secretary of the Committee. The Chairman of the Committee is chosen in the prescribed manner.

In preparing the draft development plan, the Committee has to have regard to the plans prepared by the local authorities in the area, matters of common interest between the local authorities, the overall objectives and priorities set by the Government of India and the State Government and the extent and the nature of investments likely to be made in the area by agencies of the Government and other available resources. The Committee has to consult such institutions and organisations as the Governor may, by order, specify. The Chairman has to forward the development plan, as recommended by the Committee, to the State Government.

District Planning Committee

The District Planning Committee in each district is constituted under Sec. 310 of the Karnataka Panchayat Raj Act, 1973. The Government has to constitute in every district a District Planning Committee to consolidate the plans prepared by the Municipal Corporations, Municipal Councils, Nagar Panchayats, Zilla Panchayats, Taluka Panchayats and Grama Panchayats. The Committee consists of :

(a) the numbers of the House of the People who represent the whole or part of the district;
(b) the members of the Council of States who are registered as electors in the district;
(c) Adhyaksha of the Zilla Panchayat;
(d) Mayor or the president of the Municipal Corporation or the Municipal Council respectively having jurisdiction over the headquarters of the district;
(e) such number of members, not less than four-fifths of total number of the members elected from amongst the members of the Zilla Panchayat, Nagar Panchayat and the councillors of the Municipal Corporation and the Municipal Council, in the district in proportion to the ratio between the population of the rural areas and the urban areas in the district;
(f) all the members of the State Legislative Assembly whose constituencies lie within the district, the number of the State Legislative Council who are registered as electors in the district and the Deputy Commissioner are permanent invitees of the Committee;
(g) the Chief Executive Officer is the Secretary of the Committee; and
(h) the Chairman of the Committee is chosen in the manner as prescribed.

The Chairpersons of every District Planning Committee forward the development plan as recommended to the Government.

Finance Commission

The Finance Commission is constituted under Sec. 267 of the Karnataka Panchayat Raj Act, 1973. The Commission has also to review the financial position of the urban local bodies. The Commission consists of a Chairman and two other members. The qualifications of the Chairman and other two members are prescribed by the Government.

State Election Commission

The State Election Commission is constituted under section 308 of the Karnataka Panchayat Raj Act, 1973.

4
Kerala

The ancient history of Kerala is shrouded, to a large extent, in the mists of tradition. The most popular legend is that Kerala was raised from the depth of the ocean. Legend apart, Kerala's culture has been an integral part of the mainstream of Indian culture. Its history is the story of synthesis, assimilation and fusion of old traditions and new values in every sphere of human thought and activity. In between the high Western Ghats on the east and the Arabian sea on the west, the width of the State varies from 35 to 120 km. According to the geographical features, the State can be divided into hills and valleys, midland plains and coastal belt. The total area of the State is 38,863 sq. km. covering 14 districts.

Agriculture is the main occupation of the people. About 50 per cent of the population depends upon agriculture for its livelihood. A unique feature of the State is the predominance of cash crops. Kerala is also rich in industrial potentialities and infrastructural facilities.

Urban Scene

The State accounts for about 3.54 per cent of country's urban population. The share in 1981 was 2.99. A little more than one-fourth (26.44 per cent) of the population of State lives in urban areas. The proportion in 1981 was 18.74 per cent. The State witnessed a tremendous decennial growth of 60.89 per cent in 1991 which was much more than that of 37.6 per cent recorded in 1981. The level of urbanisation is spread over whole of the State. Out of total 14, only one district of Kannur having 7.7 per cent of total population, witnessed highest urbanisation with 51.02 per cent in urban content. Ernakulam, which has 9.7 per cent of total population, has an urban content of 48.79 per cent. Three districts accounting for a little more than one-fourth poulation fall between 40–50 and five districts between 10–20 and three districts less than ten per cent, Kannur, Kozhikode, Alappuzha, Thiruvananthapuram and Ernakulam are districts with urban content of more than 30 per cent. Ernakulam having 17.9 per cent of urban population is the most urbanised district followed by Kannur (14.9), Kozhikude (13.1) and Thiruvananthapuram (13.0). All other districts could muster only single digit urban contents. Idukki (0.7) and Wayanad (0.3) are least urbanised, preceded by Pathanamthitta (2.0), Kasaragod (2.3), Malappuram (3.7), Kottayam (4.2), and Palakkad (4.9).

The number of towns has been increasing steadily over the decades. In 1991, there were 109 towns in the State. The number of towns in 1981 was 85 and in 1971, 78. The class one towns gained two digits in 1991. There were 14 class one towns with 66.34 per cent of urban population in 1991. The eight such towns in 1981 contained 53.4 per cent and six towns in 1971 accommodated 49.70 per cent of population.

Surprisingly, barring Iddukki (977) and Wayanad (967) all districts had, in 1991, sex ratio ranging between 1002 to 1088 as a whole. Likewise, these two districts had least sex ratio in urban as well as rural areas. The State has sex ratio of 1040 (total) and (1033) in urban areas. Kochi is the most populous town, followed by Thiruvananthapuram and Kozhikode. Vadakara is the least populous. Cherthala witnessed highest decadal growth of 228.14 per cent during 1981–91 followed by Kottayam (157.92) and Guruvayur (99.48). The growth rate during 1971–81 was highest in Kannur (206.83), Thrissure (134.46) and Kollam (108.16). Kannur experienced the least growth of 11.21 in 1991 while Alappuzha (6.10) and Kottayam (7.90) were in the category in 1981. The sex ratio in all the class one towns was found ranging between 1003 and 1061.

Kerala is the most literate state in the country. The literacy rate in 1981 was 81.1 per cent. Kannur (81.4), Kozhikode (80.3), Thrissur (82.1), Ernakulam (83.4), Iddukki (80.6), Alappuzha (83) and Thiruvananthapuram (80.8) districts had more than 80 per cent literacy, while Kottayam (85.6) is at the top followed by Pathanamthitta (85.4). Wayanad (72.61) was the least literate preceded by Malappuram (74.4) and Palakkad (75.8) and Kollam (79.3). The literacy in female population also ranged between Malappuram (72.2) and Kottayam (84.3); Kannur (78.9), Thrissur (80.2), Ernakulam (81.2), Alappuzha (80.6) and Pathanamthitta (83.9) were the districts having female literacy more than that of the whole State (78.7). The demographic profile of the State is detailed out in Table 1.

Thiruvananthapuram, Ernakulam and Kozhikode are Municipal Corporations. There are in all 58 municipal institutions including three Corporations. The combined share of Corporations is 36 per cent of Nagarpalika population and the Municipalities cater to the 64 per cent of the population spread over the State.

Prior to the Constitution (seventy-fourth Amendment) Act, 1992, the urban affairs in the State were being managed by the Kerala Municipalities Act, 1960; the Kerala Municipal Corporations Act, 1961; and the Guruvayur Township Act, 1961. All these Acts have now been repealed and there is only the Kerala Municipality Act, 1994 to regulate the municipal affairs in the State. Further, the State Government setup a Committee on Decentralisation of Powers to local government units. The major recommendations of the Committee are also incorporated and discussed.

Demographic Profile

	1971	*1981*	*1991*
Total population (lakh)	–	254.54	290.99
Decadal growth (percentage)	–	–	14.06
Urban population (lakh)	–	47.71	76.80
Decadal growth (percentage)	–	37.64	60.89
Proportion of urban to the total population	–	18.74	26.44
Area (km^2)	–	38863 (1788)	38863 (3364.80)
Number of towns	78	85	109
Proportion of population in class I towns	49.70	53.14	66.34
Number of class I towns	6	8	14
Sex ratio	–	1032 (1021)	1040 (1033)
Literacy	–	70.42 (76.11)	81.10 (81.10)
No. of households (lakh)	–	44.23 (7.92)	55.13 (14.11)
No. of occupied residential houses (lakh)	–	42.97 (7.48)	54.59 (13.83)
Total main workers (lakh)	–	67.91 (11.86)	83.01 (21.24)
Marginal workers (lakh)	–	9.80 (1.22)	8.45 (1.50)
Non-workers (lakh)	–	176.82 (34.63)	199.52 (54.06)

Figures in parentheses denote urban.

I. Municipality

The Government has to constitute a Town Panchayat for a transitional area, a Municipal Council for a smaller urban area and a Municipal Corporation for a larger urban area.

Every Municipality is a body corporate and has perpetual succession and a common seal. It may sue and be sued. It has the power of acquiring, holding and transferring property, of entering into contracts and of doing all things necessary, proper or expedient for the purposes for which it is constituted. A Municipality has such powers, authority and responsibilities of the Government as may be necessary to enable it to function as an institution of self-government in respect of the matters entrusted to it.

Composition

A Municipality consists of the following types of the members.

1. ***Elected Councillors***

   As notified by the Government in accordance with the following:

Population	*Number of councillors*
Not exceeding 20,000	16
Exceeding 20,000 but not exceeding 30,000	20
Exceeding 30,000 but not exceeding 40,000	24
Exceeding 40,000 but not exceeding 50,000	28
Exceeding 50,000 but not exceeding one lakh	32
Exceeding one lakh	36

A Muncipal Corporation consists of councillors not less than 40 nor more than fifty.

The Committee on Decentralisation of Powers suggests that in a Town Panchayat or Municipal Council, the number of councillors should be 20 for a population upto 20,000 and be increased at the rate of one for every 2,500, subject to maximum of 50 seats. In a Municipal Corporation, the number should be 50 for a population upto 4 lakh and be increased at the rate of one for every 10,000, subject to maximum of 100 seats.

2. ***Special Councillors***

Not more than two persons having special knowledge or experience in municipal administration.

The Special Councillors have all the rights of a Councillor, except the right to vote. If for any reason, a Councillor could not be elected from any ward at an election, the State Election Commission has to hold an election within three months to elect a councillor. The term of office of such a councillor is coterminus with the term of the Municipality.

Reservation

Seats are reserved in every Municipality:

(i) for the Scheduled Castes and the Scheduled Tribes. The number of seats to be reserved is determined by the Government. The number, however, bears as nearly as may be the same proportion to the total number of seats to be filled by direct election as their population bears to the total population of that area.

In case of population of these classes being insufficient to make them eligible for the reservation of any seat, one seat is reserved in that municipality for the Scheduled Castes or the Scheduled Tribes having higher population.

(ii) for the women to the tune of not less than one-third, including the one-third seats reserved for women belonging to the Scheduled Castes and the Scheduled Tribes.

Disqualifications of Candidates

A person is disqualified in the circumstances for being chosen as and for being a Councillor of a Municipality if he is so disqualified under the Constitution or under any law; OR has been sentenced by a criminal court to imprisonment for a period of more than one year for any offence not involving moral delinquency while he is undergoing the sentence and for six years from the date of expiration thereof; OR has been adjudged to be of unsound mind; OR has voluntarily acquired the citizenship of a foreign State, OR has been sentenced by a criminal court for any electoral offence or has been disqualified from exercising any electoral right on account of corrupt practices in connection with an election, and six years have not elapsed from the date of such sentence or disqualification, OR is an applicant for being adjudicated as an insolvent, or is undischarged insolvent, OR is interested in a subsisting contract made with or any work being done for, the Government of the

Municipality as a shareholder in a company, OR is employed as a paid legal practitioner on behalf of the Municipality or as a legal practitioner against a Municipality, OR is already a Councillor whose term of office as such will not expire before his fresh election can take effect or has already been elected as Councillor whose term of office has not yet commenced, OR is in arrears of any kind of due by him to the Municipality upto and inclusive of the previous year in respect of which, a bill or notice has been duly served upon him and the time specified therein for payment has expired, OR is dismissed or removed from any of the services of a State or Central Government or a local authority or a Corporation owned or controlled by a State or the Central Government or of a Company in which the State or Central Government or local authority has not less than 51 per cent share or of Boards or any University and five years have not elapsed from the date of such dismissal or removal, OR is debarred from practising as an Advocate or Vakil, OR is a deaf-mute, OR is disqualified under any other provision of the Act, OR is blacklisted consequent on defaulted performance under any contract or auction with the Government.

If any question arises as to whether a candidate has become subject to any of the disqualification, the question is referred to for the decision of the State Election Commission and the decision of the Commission is final.

Disqualifications of Councillors

A Councillor ceases to hold office, if he is sentenced by a criminal court, OR has been adjudged to be of unsound mind, OR has voluntarily acquired the citizenship of a foreign State, OR has been sentenced by a criminal court for any electoral offence or has been disqualified from exercising in connection with an election, and six years have not elapsed from the date of such sentence or disqualification, OR has applied for being adjudicated, or is adjudicated as an insolvent, OR acquires any interest in any subsisting contract made with, or work being done for the Government or the Municipality except as a shareholder in a company or except as permitted by rules, OR is employed as a paid legal practitioner on behalf of the Municipality or accepts employment as a legal practitioner against the Municipality, OR ceases to reside in the Municipality, OR is debarred from practising as an Advocate or Vakil, OR is in arrears of any kind of due by him to the Municipality upto and inclusive of the previous year in respect of which, a bill or notice has been duly served upon him and the time specified therein has expired, OR absents himself without the permission of the Municipality from the meetings of the Council or any Commitee thereof for a period of six consecutive months reckoned from the date of commencement of his term of office, or of the last meeting which he attended, or of the restoration of office or if within the said period, not less than three meetings have been held, absents himself from three consecutive meetings held after the said date, OR is disqualified under the Constitution or by or under any law relating to election to the State Legislative Assembly, OR is disqualified under the Act, OR a councillor belonging to a political party recognised by the National Election Commission as a National or State Party and was elected under the election symbol of such political party is disqualified if he votes or abstains from voting in an election to the office of Chairperson or Deputy Chairperson or in respect of a no-confidence motion, contrary to any written direction issued by such political party, OR has been elected or nominated as a member of the House of People or a member of the Council of States or a member of State Legislative Assembly and assumed that office, OR has been subjected to realisation of any amount on account of any loss, wastage or misuse or other property of the Municipality, OR has failed twice consecutively, to convene the meetings of the Ward Sabha or Ward Committee due once in three months and of which he is the convenor Or has failed to file declaration of assets within three months of his election.

Whenever a question arises as to whether a Councillor has become disqualified after having been elected as such, any Councillor or a Municipality or any other person entitled to vote at the election, in which the Councillor was elected or the Government or any officer authorised by them or the Chairperson may file a petition before the State Election Commission for decision. The question of disqualification can be referred by the Secretary to the Election Commission for decision, as and when such question comes to his notice. The Commission, after making necessary enquiry, decides the matter and that decision is final. However, the Commission may pass interim order as to whether the Councillor can continue to hold office or not during the pendency of the decision. Where a person ceases to be a Councillor as a result of absence, the Secretary has, at once, to intimate the fact in writing to such person and report the same to the Council, at its next meeting. If such person applies for restoration to the Council on or before the date of its next meeting or within fifteen days of the receipt by him of such intimation, the Council may at the meeting next after the receipt of such application, restore him to his office of Councillor. A Councillor cannot be restored more than once during his term of office.

Election Petition

An election cannot be called in question except by an election petition. An election petition may be presented to the Munsiff's Court by any candidate at such election or any elector within thirty days from, but nor earlier than the date of election of the returned candidate. Every election petition should be accompanied by as many copies thereof as there are respondents mentioned in the petition and every such copy has to be attested by the petitioner under his own signature to be the true copy of the petition. The court, as soon as may be after the conclusion of the trial of an election petition, intimates the substance of the order to the State Election Commission and the Chairperson of the Municipality and, as soon as may be, sends to the State Election Commission an authenticated copy of the order. After receipt of the order, the Commission forwards copies of the order to the Chairperson of the Municipality and causes the order to be published. The order takes effect as soon as it is pronounced by the Court.

Any person aggrieved by an order made by the Court, may prefer an appeal to the District Court within thirty days from the date of the order of the court. As soon as the appeal is decided, the District Court intimates the substance of the decision to the State Election Commission and the Chairperson of the Municipality and, thereafter, sends to the Commission an authenticated copy of the decision. The State Election Commission, thereafter, forwards a copy to the Chairperson and causes the decision to be published.

Chairman or Mayor

There is a Chairman for every Town Panchayat and Municipal Council and a Mayor in every Municipal Corporation. They are elected by the elected Councillors from amongst themselves.

The meeting to elect the Chairperson or Mayor is convened within three weeks from the date of publication of the names of the elected Councillors by the State Election Commission. The Commission designates or nominates an officer of the Government as the returning officer for the election. If the Chairperson is not elected at such an election, a fresh election is conducted within six months for the election of the Chairman.

When any dispute arises as to the validity of the election of the Chairperson, any Councillor may file a petition before the District Court having jurisdiction over the area of the headquarters of that Municipality for decision and such a decision is final.

Where the office of a Chairperson is vacant, the Deputy Chairperson exercises the powers and discharges the duties of the Chairperson until a newly elected Chairperson assumes the office.

Where a Chairperson has been absent from jurisdiction continuously for more than fifteen days or is incapacitated and there is vacancy in the office of the Deputy Chairperson or the Deputy Chairperson has been absent from jurisdiction continuously for more than fifteen days or is incapacitated and the Chairperson has not delegated his functions to any Councillor, the Chairperson of the Standing Committee can exercise the power and perform the functions of the Chairperson until the Deputy Chairperson returns to jurisdiction or recovers from his incapacity.

Where there is no Chairman of Standing Committee to hold the office of the Chairperson, an elected Councillor nominated by the Government can exercise the powers and perform the duties of the Chairperson of the Municipality.

The Chairman of the Municipality can convene the meeting of the Council, exercise the powers and discharge the duties conferred or imposed specifically on him under the Act and exercise overall supervision over the working of the Municipality and can coordinate the functions of the Municipality, the Secretary and the Committees thereof.

The Chairperson has the power of inspection and may give instructions and orders with regard to the implementation of any resolution of the Council or Committees in the discharge of any function of a Municipality and the Secretary is bound to comply with such instructions. The administrative powers to implement the provisions and the resolutions passed by a Council vest in the Chairperson. He is directly responsible for the proper discharge of the functions imposed by or under the Act. The Chairperson has to preside over and control the proceedings of the meetings of the Council of the Municipality, of which he is the Chairperson. He has to supervise and control the acts done and steps taken by the officers and employees of the Municipality, prepare the confidential reports of the Secretary and also to review the confidential reports prepared by the Secretary in respect of other employees. The Chairperson can meet the contingent expenditure to the extent fixed by the Government and can authorise the payment and repayment of money relating to the Municipality. He can cause the required statements and reports to be prepared and can exercise such other powers and performs such other functions, which may be conferred or entrusted under the Act or rules made thereunder.

The Chairperson may, in emergent circumstances, direct the execution of any work or performance of any act, in respect of which the sanction of the Council is necessary, and in his opinion, the immediate execution or performance of which is necessary for the safety of the public. He may also direct that the expenses incurred for execution of such work or performance of such act be paid from the fund of the Municipality.

The Chairperson has power to inspect all records of the Municipality and can direct the Secretary to submit such records for inspection. All official correspondence from the Secretary to the Government and to other authorities, not below the rank of Collector has to be made through the Chairperson. The Chairperson be an is ex-officio member of every Committee of a Municipality and has all powers of a member of such committee except the right to vote.

The Chairperson may, by order in writing, delegate any of his functions to the Deputy Chairperson. He, however, cannot delegate any of his functions, which the Council expressly prohibits him from delegating. Where the Chairperson is absent from jurisdiction continuously for more than fifteen days or is incapacitated, his functions during his absence or incapacity devolve on the Deputy Chairperson. However, where the Chairperson is within the State during such absence and is on business connected with the affairs of the Municipality, his functions are not devolved on the Deputy Chairperson. Where the Deputy Chairperson is also continuously absent from jurisdiction for more than fifteen days or is incapacitated or the office of the Deputy Chairperson is vacant, the Chairperson can by an order in writing, delegate his functions to the Chairman of the Standing Committee. Every such order is communicated to the Council. The Chairperson may, by an order in writing, delegate to the Secretary the powers and functions vested in him to meet the expenses relating to administration.

Deputy Chairperson

There is a Vice-Chairman in every Town Panchayat and Municipal Council and a Deputy Mayor in every Municipal Corporation, who is elected by the elected Councillors from amongst themselves.

No-Confidence Motion

A motion expressing want of confidence in the Chairperson or Deputy Chairperson or the Chairman of a Standing Committee may be moved by a written notice signed by elected Councillors not less than one-third of the sanctioned strength of the Council together with a copy of the motion proposed to be made and delivered by any one of the Councillors signing the notice, in person to the officer authorised by the Government in this behalf. The officer, thereupon, convenes a meeting of the elected Councillors for consideration of the motion not later than 15 days from the date, on which the notice was delivered to him. He has to give to the elected Councillors notice of not less than ten clear days of such meeting. A notice is also exhibited in the Municipal office. Such a meeting is presided over by the Chairperson, if the motion is against a Deputy Chairperson or Chairman of a Standing Committee, by the Deputy Chairperson, if the motion is against the Chairperson and by the Chairman of the Standing Committee, if the Chairperson or the Deputy Chairperson is unable to preside over the meeting due to absence from station or otherwise. If no one is able to preside over the meeting, the elected Councillors present at the meeting elect a Councillor from amongst themselves to preside over. Such a meeting cannot, except reasons beyond control, be adjourned. As soon as the meeting commences, the person presiding reads the motion and declares it to be open for debate. The person presiding over cannot speak on the merit of the motion but is entitled to vote without the right to exercise a casting vote. The debate terminates automatically on the expiry of four hours, if it is not concluded earlier. After the expiry of the debate, the motion is put to vote, by means of secret ballot. On the conclusion of the meeting, a copy of the minutes of the meeting together with a copy of the motion and the result of the voting thereon is forthwith forwarded by the person presiding over the Government. If the motion is carried with the support of more than one-half of the sanctioned strength of the Councillors, the Chairperson or the Deputy Chairperson or the Chairman of the Standing Committee ceases to function and the Government notified the fact of his removal from office. If the motion is not carried out or if the meeting could not be held for want of quorum, no notice of any subsequent motion expressing want of confidence in the same person can be entertained until after the expiry of six months from the date of meeting. No notice of a motion can also be entertained within six months of the assumption of office by a Chairperson or Deputy Chairperson or the Chairman of the Standing Committee.

Removal

The Government may, on the recommendation of the prescribed authority, remove from office any Councillor, the Chairperson or the Deputy Chairperson after giving him an opportunity of being heard, if such Councillor, Chairperson or the Deputy Chairperson has been found guilty of misconduct in the discharge of his duties or abuses his powers or makes persistent default in the performance of his duties and functions. The Chairperson or the Deputy Chairperson so removed may, at the discretion of the Government, also be removed from the Councillorship of the Municipality.

The Government may disqualify for a period not exceeding five years any person who has resigned his office as a Councillor, Chairperson or Deputy Chairperson or, otherwise, ceased to hold any such office and has been guilty of misconduct. Such an action, however, can be taken within six months from the date on which the person resigns or ceases to hold any such office. The Decentralisation Committee finds it against the spirit of decentralisation. It thinks proper not to remove elected members or elected office holders particularly in the context of Ombudsman.

Resignation

The Chairperson of a Municipality may resign his office in writing under his own hand by tendering resignation to the Deputy Chairperson of the Municipality and in his absence, to the Secretary. The resignation takes effect from the date of receipt of it by the Deputy Chairperson or the Secretary. The Deputy Chairperson or the Secretary has to report the fact to the Council.

A Deputy Chairperson or any Councillor of a Municipality may resign his office in writing under his own hand by tendering resignation to the Chairperson of the Municipality. The resignation takes effect from the date of receipt by the Chairperson.

A person who resigns his office may, either tender the resignation to the person concerned or send it by registered post with acknowledgement due. Where any dispute arises with regard to any resignation, it is referred to the State Election Commission for decision and the decision of the Commission is final. A dispute cannot be taken for consideration by the State Election Commission after the expiry of 30 days from the date of effect of resignation.

Rights and Powers of Councillors

Every Councillor of Municipality has the right to call the attention of the Chairperson or Secretary of the Municipality to any neglect in the execution of municipal work, to any waste of municipal property, or to the needs of any locality in the municipal area and may suggest improvements, which may appear to him desirable and to move resolutions and to interpellate the Chairperson on matters connected with the administration of a municipality. He has the right of access to the records of the Municipality during office hours after due notice to the Secretary.

Allowances

The Chairperson, Deputy Chairperson and other Councillors are paid allowances on such rates as are prescribed. The Chairperson and Deputy Chairperson are eligible for travelling allowances and daily allowance while travelling in public purpose.

Councillors to Declare Assets

The Committee on Decentralisation recommends that every Councillor is bound to file a declaration of assets and interests in property of himself and of his family, within three months from the date of assuming his office. Where a Councillor, after filing a declaration acquires or disposes any assets or interest in property, he has to file further declaration to that effect before the competent authority, within three months from the date of acquisition or disposal. A Councillor, who makes a false declaration, is liable to be proceeded against in accordance with law. Failure to file a declaration attracts the provisions for disqualification of the Councillor.

Council's Power

The Council may, at the time, require the Secretary to produce any record or document in his custody relating to the Municipality. It may call for any extract from the proceedings of the Standing Committees or of any other committee or any return, statement, account or report relating to any matter, which such committee is empowered to deal with and every such requisition is compiled with by the Secretary.

The Council may constitute committees for the purpose of exercising such powers, discharging such duties or performing such functions as may be delegated to them. It may appoint any Councillor or Committee to enquire into and report or advise on any matter referred to him or it. The Council may especially invite as members of any Committee, persons who are not Councillors but who may posseses special knowledge/ qualifications for serving in such Committee.

Standing Committees

In every municipality, Standing Committees are constituted as under:-

(a) in a Town Panchayat — One Standing Committee;

(b) in a Municipal Council —
 (i) Standing Committee for Taxation, Finance and Accounts,
 (ii) Standing Committee for the Public Works, and
 (iii) Standing Committee for matters relating to Health and matters relating to Environment; and

(c) in a Municipal Corporation —
 (i) Standing Committee for Taxation, Finance and Accounts,
 (ii) Standing Committee for Public Works,
 (iii) Standing Committee for Health,
 (iv) Standing Committee for Town Planning Tradition and Heritage, and
 (v) Standing Committee for Appeals relating to Tax.

The Government may constitute a Standing Committee for Appeals relating to Tax and Town Planning, in a Municipal Council or in a Town Panchayat also.

The Committee on Decentralisation of Powers recommends three Standing Committees in Town Panchayats, five in Municipal Councils and seven in Municipal Corporation, as under:

Standing Committee		*Town Panchyat*	*Municipal Council*	*Municipal Corporation*
1.	Finance and General Administration	Yes	Yes	Yes
2.	Planning and Development	Yes	Yes	Yes
3.	Infrastructure	Yes	Yes	Yes
4.	Welfare	–	Yes	Yes
5.	Health and Education	–	Yes	Yes
6.	Town Planning and Heritage	–	–	Yes
7.	Tax Appeals	–	–	Yes

Every Standing Committee consists of five members, including the Chairman. The Standing Committee for Taxation, Finance and Accounts consists of four elected members. The members are elected by the elected Councillors from amongst themselves under the proportional representation system by single transferable vote. A Councillor cannot be a member of more than one Standing Committee at the same time. A Councillor elected as a member of a Standing Committee holds office for a period of 30 months from the date of first meeting of the Committee. A member elected to fill a casual vacancy can hold office only for the remaining term of office of the person in whose place he is elected.

The Committee on Decentralisation of Powers suggests that the number of members of the Standing Committee be fixed by the Council. The numbers should, as far as possible, be equal. The term of a member be co-terminus with his term as a Councillor.

Functions of the Standing Committee

The powers and functions of the Standing Committee are given below.

(a) In a Town Panchayat the Standing Committee:

(i) supervises the utilisation of the budget grants, and watches the timely assessment and collection of taxes, fees, rent or other sums due to the Town Panchayat;

(ii) has the freedom to inspect the accounts of the Town Panchayat;

(iii) conducts monthly audit of the accounts and checks the monthly demand, collection and balance and abstract of receipts and disbursements of the preceding months as furnished by the Secretary;

(iv) may, write off such sums due to the Council as appear to the Committee to be irrecoverable;

(v) Scrutinises the annual accounts and demands, collection and balance; and

(vi) monitors the annual execution of public works and watches the issue of licences under the Building Rules;

(b) In a Municipal Council, the Standing Committee for Taxation, Finance and Accounts:

(i) supervises the utilisation of the budget grants and keeps watch on the timely assessment and collection of taxes, fees, rents or other sums due to the Municipal Council;

(ii) has the right to inspect the accounts of the Municipal Council;

(iii) conducts monthly audit of accounts and checks the monthly demands, collection and balance and monthly abstract of receipts and disbursements of the preceding month as furnished by the Secretary;

(iv) writes off such sum due to the Council as appears to the Committee to be irrecoverable; and

(v) scrutinises the annual accounts and demands, collection and balance.

The Standing Committee for Health deals with all matters relating to public health and sanitation. It watches the issue of licences under dangerous and offensive trades and other allied matters.

The Standing Committee for Public Works deals with all matters relating to public works and town planning. It keeps watch on the issue of licences under the Building Rules.

(c) In a Municipal Corporation, the Standing Committee for Taxation, Finance and Accounts:

(i) supervises the utilisation of budget grants and watches the timely assessment and collection of taxes, fees, rents and other sums due to the Municipal Corporation;

(ii) has the right to inspect the accounts of the Municipal Corporation. It may require the Secretary to furnish any explanation which it considers necessary as to the receipts and expenditure of the Municipal funds;

(iii) conducts monthly audit of accounts and checks the monthly demands, collection and balance of the preceding month. It scrutinises the annual account and demand, collection and balance as furnished by the Secretary;

(iv) brings to the specific notice of the Council, any laxity or irregularity in maintaining the accounts of the Municipal Corporation; and

(v) writes off such sums due to the Municipal Corporation which the Committee is satisfied to be irrecoverable.

The Standing Committee for Public Works deals with all matters relating to public works.

The Standing Committee for Health deals with all matters relating to public health, and sanitation. It watches the issue of licences under dangerous and offensive trades and other allied matters.

The Standing Committee for Town Planning, Tradition and Heritage deals with all matters connected with town planning, urban beautification, development plans, street lighting, promotions of art, culture, sports, language, preservation of monuments and watches the issue of licences under the Building Rules.

The Standing Committees for Tax Appeals deals with tax appeals in respect of any assessment of tax by Secretary which is appealable.

The Committee on Decentralisation of Powers provides for a bunch of functions to each of the Standing Committees linked to its nature.

A Standing Committee may require the Secretary or any other employee of the Municipality to produce any record, report, return, document and other particulars. It may require him to be present at meeting of the Committee for seeking further information and the person concerned is bound to comply with such requisition.

Each Standing Committee elects one of its members to be its Chairman. The Deputy Mayor in a Municipal Corporation and the Deputy Chairperson in a Municipal Council is an ex-officio member and Chairman of the Standing Committee for Taxation, Finance and Accounts. The Chairman presides the meeting and in his absence, a member chosen by the members present from amongst themselves presides over the meeting. A member presiding over a meeting has all the powers and be subject to all obligations of the Chairman.

The Chairman of a Standing Committee holds office as long as he continues to be a member of that committee. A member elected to fill the casual vacancy can hold office for the remaining term of office of the person in whose place he was elected. Where a vacancy occurs in the office of the Chairman of Standing Committee for Taxation, Finance and Accounts, a member chosen by the members from amongst themselves can act as Chairman until a person to fill the vacancy is elected.

The Chairman of a Standing Committee may resign his office by giving notice to the Chairperson of the Municipality. A member of a

Standing Committee may resign from the Committee by giving notice to the Chairman of that Standing Committee. Such a resignation takes effect from the date on which it is received by the Chairman of the Standing Committee or the Chairperson of the Municipality.

Steering Committee

In every Municipal Corporation, a Steering Committee is constituted. It consists of the Mayor, Deputy Mayor and Chairman of the Standing Committee. The Mayor is the Chairman of the Committee.

The Decentralisation Committee provides for constituting Steering Committee in every Municipality. It consists of the Chairperson and the Chairman of the Standing Committees. The Chairperson is the Chairman of the Steering Committee.

The Steering Committee has to coordinate and monitor the functioning of the Wards Committees, examine the functioning of the Wards Committees, and give them guidelines and discharge the powers and functions entrusted to it by the Council.

A Municipal Council may constitute a Joint Committee of the Standing Committees for any purpose of joint interest. The Chairperson may nominate the Chairman of any Standing Committee as the Chairman of such a Joint Committee.

Joint Committee

The Council of a Municipality may, if so required by the Government, join a Council of any other Municipality to constitute a Joint Committee for any purpose of joint interest or for any matter, for which they are jointly responsible. A Joint Committee may include as member, persons who are not Councillors but who possess special qualifications for serving in such committee. The number of such persons cannot exceed one-third of the total number of the members of that Committee. The members so appointed have no right to vote in the Committee.

Conduct of Business

Every meeting of the Council of a Municipality is presided over by the Chairperson or in his absence, by the Deputy Chairperson or the Chairman of the Standing Committees and in his absence, by a Councillor chosen by the Councillors present from amongst themselves. Where two or more Councillors are proposed and seconded, the Secretary or in his absence, the officer authorised to perform the function of the Secretary, conducts the election.

Every matter coming before the Council for decision is decided by the majority of votes of the elected Councillors present. In case of equality of votes, the person presiding over the meeting has a casting vote.

A copy of the minutes of every meeting of a Municipality and a copy of the notes of dissent regarding such proceedings received within 48 hours of the conclusion of the meeting are, with the approval of the Chairperson, forwarded by the Secretary, within seven days after the date of the meeting, to the officer authorised by the Government in this behalf.

The Chairperson or the person presiding has to control the meeting and to decide all points of order arising at or in connection with a meeting. The decision of the Chairperson or the person presiding is final. Where any member behaves in a disorderly manner and causes obstruction to the conduct of a meeting, the Chairperson or the person presiding can direct such member to withdraw forthwith and if disobeyed, he can be suspended from the meeting for such period as the Chairperson or the person presiding may decide. The member so suspended has to withdraw from the meeting immediately thereafter, failing which he can be removed by using reasonable force. The Chairperson or the person presiding may, at any time at his discretion, and has to at the instance of the Council supported by a resolution passed to that effect, cancel the order of suspension.

No Councillor can take part in or vote on a discussion on any question, in which he has any interest. The Chairperson may prohibit any Councillor from voting on, or taking part in the discussion of any matter in which he believes such Councillor to have interest or he may require such Councillor to absent himself from the meeting during such discussion. Such Councillor may challenge the decision of the Chairperson, who puts the question to the meeting for a decision which becomes final. Where a Chairperson is believed by a Councillor present at a meeting to have any pecuniary interest in any matter under discussion, he may, if a motion to that effect is carried, be required to absent himself from the meeting during such discussion.

Secretary

For every Municipality, there is a Secretary appointed by the Government in consultation with that Municipality. He is an officer of the Government and the Executive Officer of the Municipality. Other Officers and employees of the Municipality are subordinate to him. The Secretary cannot, without the sanction of the Municipality or the Government, undertake any work unconnected with his office. The pay and allowances of the Secretary are paid from the State funds and whole of the sum is credited monthly to the State funds by the Municipality. The Government may grant leave to the Secretary and appoint a substitute or nominate an officer to hold charge of his office during his absence. The Secretary is the custodian of all Municipal properties and records including all papers and documents connected with the proceedings of the Council and the Standing Committees and other Committees.

The Government may transfer the Secretary from a Municipality and if the Council, on the strength of a resolution passed at a special meeting convened for this purpose, by a simple majority vote of the approved strength of the Council, recommends transfer and the Government is obliged to do so.

The Secretary may, with the approval of the Chairperson, require the village officer any village in the Municipal area to furnish him with any information or any matter falling within the categories as may be prescribed in respect of that village or any person or property therein and every such order has to be complied with by the village officer. Where village officer fails to comply with any such order, the Secretary may report the matter to the District Collector, who can initiate disciplinary action against the Village Officer and make arrangements for furnishing the information required by the Secretary.

The Council is competent to impose minor penalties on its Secretary. An appeal may be filed against the order of the Council imposing any minor penalty, before the authority authorised by the Government in this behalf. On receipt of an appeal, the authority, after giving the person filing the appeal an opportunity of being heard, may either confirm, cancel or revise the order, against which the appeal is preferred or pass appropriate order. The Government may, either suo motu or on application, call for the records of any order in that regard. No application, for review can be entertained if it is preferred after 30 days from the date of receipt by the applicant of the order sought to be reviewed. The Government cannot pass any order affecting any party without giving an opportunity for submitting a representation. The Government can not suo motu review an order if more than one year has elapsed since the date of the order sought to be reviewed.

Functions of the Secretary

The Secretary is obliged to:

(a) carry into effect the resolutions of the council;

(b) furnish to the Council such periodical reports regarding the progress made in carrying into effect the resolutions of the Council relating to the collections of taxes as the Council may direct;

(c) implement all the directions of the Chairperson;

(d) exercise the powers and discharge the duties specially conferred or imposed on the Secretary;

(e) incur expenditure authorised by the Chairperson;

(f) make payments for all kinds of expenditure authenticated by the Municipality either by cheque or by cash;

(g) maintain and keep the accounts of receipts and expenditure by the Municipality;

(h) be responsible for the safe custody of the Municipal fund;

(i) maintain the records in respect of the meetings and proceedings of the Council; and

(j) have the right to take disciplinary action against municipal employees with the knowledge of the Chairperson.

Rights and Duties

The Secretary has to attend the meetings of the Council and the Standing Committees or any other Committee of a Municipality and may take part in the discussion as an advisor, but does not have the right to move any resolution or to vote. He may, by order in writing, delegate any of his functions to any officer or employee of the Municipality who is bound to carry out such functions. The officer or employee to whom the power is delegated has all rights, privileges and authority of the Secretary with respect to such functions. The Secretary has the power after informing the Chairperson to incur expenditure not exceeding Rs. 25,000 out of the Municipal Fund.

Establishment

The Government may constitute a common Municipal Service for the employees under the service of the Municipality in the State and regulate the recruitment and conditions of service of the employees of the Municipalities.

The power to sanction the leave to the officers and employees of the Municipality vests in the Secretary. The Municipal Council has the power to impose minor penalties on any officer or employee of the Municipality. An appeal may be preferred against an order of the Council imposing a minor penalty to the authority empowered in this behalf. The Authority has to give the applicant an opportunity of being heard and may either confirm, cancel and modify the order appealed against or may pass suitable orders. The Government may, either suo motu or on application, call for the records and may pass appropriate order. A review application cannot be entertained after expiry of thirty days from the date of the order.

No post in the service of the Municipality can be created except with the previous sanction of the Government.

The Council is the appointing authority in respect of the contingent posts in the Municipal Service and appointment orders in respect of them are issued by the Secretary, with the approval of the Council. The Government or the officer authorised is the appointing authority in respect of other posts, whether they are included in the Municipal Council Service or not.

The Government may, after consulting the Municipality, sanction a post of Health Officer and a post of Municipal Engineer for that Municipality. The Government may, after consulting a Municipality which has undertaken the generation, transmission or supply of electrical energy, sanction a post of Municipal Electrical Engineer. The Government may sanction the posts of Deputy Secretary, Finance Manager, Accounts Officer, Revenue Officer and such other posts in a Municipal Corporation and giving regard to the necessity and financial soundness of a Municipality may also sanction similar posts in a Town Panchayat and a Municipal Council. The Finance Manager in addition to his duty as such, functions as the Advisor and Secretary to the Standing Committee for Taxation, Finance and Accounts of the Municipality.

In Municipalities where there are no Health Officers, the Health Supervisors and in absence of both, the first grade Health Inspectors can exercise the functions of the Health Officer. The power to control the Health Officer vests in the Secretary. But the Secretary cannot dismiss or remove the Health Officer from service.

The Government may, on the application of any Municipality, place the service of any Government servant at the disposal of the Municipality to be employed by it. The Municipality has to pay the salary and other allowances as may be payable to him. Such a Government servant, except in cases of emergency, can be withdrawn from the service of the Municipality without its consent, or unless and until the Government has given three months notice in writing to that effect to the Municipality, or unless some other Government servant has been deputed to replace the one withdrawn. The Chairperson of the Municipality has right to conduct enquiry against such officer and to submit report to Government. The council has the power to impose minor penalties on any such Government servant.

The Secretary can specify the duties of the Municipal establishment and can exercise supervision and control over all officers and staff under Municipality. The Chairperson can exercise supervisory control over the work of all officers and staff under the Municipality and may require the Secretary to produce or make available all necessary reports and information relating to their work and has authority to issue all directions necessary for the speedy implementation of the decisions of the Council or any Committee thereof.

Relationship between Elected Functionaries and Officers

The Decentralisation Committee suggests that the Government should prescribe a code of conduct governing the relationship between the elected functionaries and the officers and employees of municipality. It is required for the purpose of protection of the right of officers and employees to tender advice on the matters dealt with by them, and their professional freedom or statutory rights. The minutes of discussion should reflect the points of view expressed by the officials. There should be mutual respect in behaviour, avoiding rude language, gesture or action totally. Complaints on the infringement of the code of conduct by the elected functionaries be considered by the Ombudsman and the report furnished to the Government for appropriate action. Oral instructions by the elected functionaries to the officials be confirmed in writing before they are acted upon.

Municipal Property

All public roads, streets, lanes and paths, bridges, ditches, dykes and fences on or beside the same, and all adjacent land not being private property appertaining thereto in any Municipal area other than roads classified as National Highways and State Highways vest absolutely in the Municipality together with all pavements, stones and other materials and other things provided therein, all sewers, drains, drainage works, tunnels and culverts, whether made at the cost of the Municipal funds or otherwise, in, alongside or under such roads and all works, materials and things appertaining thereto. All rubbish and filth and other matter collected by a Municipality belong to the Municipality and it can dispose of the same by auction or otherwise.

The management, control and administration of every public institution maintained exclusively out of the municipal fund vest in the Municipality.

The Secretary maintains an inventory of all immovable property owned by the Municipality or to which the Municipality has a reversionary right. A copy of the inventory is deposited with the Government and all changes are communicated to them.

A Municipality may, with the previous sanction of the Government, acquire any property whether land or building within or without its area for any public purpose. A Municipality may construct commercial or other buildings and let them out to the public on licence and may charge fees. In all cases except renewal of licence or rehabilitation of a licensee, licence is granted only by public auction or tender.

Contracts

Every Municipality may enter into contracts with any person or agency for the performance of its works. Subject to the availability of resources, the authority competent to accord administrative sanction to any estimate for works or to sanction any expenditure and the limit upto which such sanction may be accorded are as under:

		Town Panchayat	*Municipal Council*	*Municipal Corporation*
(i)	The Chairman/ Mayor	upto Rs. 5000	upto Rs. 10,000	upto Rs. 25,000
(ii)	The Standing Committee	Rs. 5000 to 25,000	Rs. 10,000 to 50,000	Rs. 25,000 to 3 lakh
(iii)	The Council	Rs. 25,000 to 10 lakh	Rs. 50,000 to 25 lakh	Rs. 3 to 50 lakh
(iv)	The Government	Rs. 10 lakh and above	Rs. 25 lakh and above	Rs. 50 lakh and above

The Decentralisation Committee has recommended the exercise of according administrative sanction to any estimate for work as under:

		Town Panchayat	*Municipal Council*	*Municipal Corporation*
(i)	The Standing Committee	upto Rs. 25,000	upto Rs. 50,000	upto Rs. 1 lakh
(ii)	The Council	Rs. 25,000 and above	Rs. 50,000 and above	Rs. 1 lakh and above

Every contract is made on behalf of the Municipality by the Secretary. The Secretary may not carryout contract without the sanction of one or the other municipal authorities. Where tender is necessary, a contract cannot be made by the Secretary unless the tender is accepted by the competent authority. In case of every contract for works, supplies or services made by the Secretary, the estimate for which he is competent to sanction, is reported to the Standing Committee within 15 days. The common seal of the Municipality is affixed to every contract. In case of contracts for the execution of any work or the supply of any materials or services, the cost of which exceeds Rs. 1000, and in the case of all other contracts whatever be their value, the contract is made in writing and is sealed with the common seal. The common seal remains in the custody of the Secretary and cannot be affixed to any contract or other instrument except in his presence.

Municipal Fund

All moneys received by a Municipality except those collected as fees for licences and permissions constitute a fund, which is called the Municipal Fund.

The Secretary has to publish, not later than the first week of June, an annual financial statement of the preceding year, approved by the Council embodying a classified abstract of receipts and payments of the Municipality under Revenue, Capital and Debt heads, a demand, collection and balance statement and a statement of the general financial position of the Municipality. As soon as after the publication, the Secretary forwards a copy thereof to the auditors.

Poverty Alleviation Fund

Every Municipality has to provide in its Annual Budget 2 per cent of the revenue receipt for constituting a separate Poverty Alleviation Fund for implementing poverty alleviation programmes in the municipal area.

Sinking Funds

The Municipality has to maintain Sinking Funds for the repayment of money borrowed on debentures issued. It has to pay by quarterly instalments such sum as is sufficient for the repayment within the period fixed for the loan of all moneys borrowed on debentures issued.

Budget

The Secretary has to prepare and submit to the Standing Committee, on or before the 15th day of January each year, a budget containing a detailed estimate of receipt and expenditure for the ensuing year. The Standing Committee considers the estimates and proposals of the Secretary and frames therefrom a budget estimate of the receipt and expenditure of the Municipality for the next year. The budget has to provide for the payment of all instalments of principal and interest of loan and allow for a cash balance at the end of the year not less than 5 per cent of the revenue of the Municipality. The budget estimates prepared by the Standing Committee are laid before the Council not later than the first week of March. The Council may refer the budget estimates back to the Standing Committee for further consideration and resubmission within a specified time, or adopt the budget estimates or any revised budget estimates submitted to it. The Council has to, finally, pass the budget estimates before the beginning of the year to which it relates. The Council has to forthwith submit copies of the budget to the Government and the officer authorized by the Government in this behalf and to the auditors. If the Standing Committee fails or omits or delays the preparation of the budget estimates within the specified period, the Chairman gets the proposals prepared by the Secretary to be laid before the Council and the Council has to pass the budget estimate as proposed by the Secretary with or without modification before the beginning of the ensuing year.

The Council may pass a supplementary budget on the recommendation of the Standing Committee concerned during the year for the purpose of meeting any special or unforeseen requirement arising during the year.

The Standing Committee may, at any time during the year, reduce the amount of the budget grant or transfer and add the amount or a portion of the amount of one budget grant to the amount of any other budget grant. Every such reduction or transfer has to be brought to the notice of the Council at its next meeting. Where any reduction or transfer is of an amount exceeding Rs. 20.000, the Council may pass appropriate orders and it is incumbent on the Standing Committee concerned and the Secretary to give effect to it.

Accounts and Audit

The responsibility to maintain or cause to maintain the accounts and the connected books of the Municipality and to submit or cause to submit accounts to the Local Fund Examiner for conducting audit in time vests with the Secretary.

The Examiner of the Local Fund Accounts and his nominees are the auditors of the Municipality. The auditors maintain a continuous audit of the accounts of the Municipality and, after completing the audit, are required to send a report to the Municipality concerned and a copy thereof to the Government. The Municipality has to remedy any defect or irregularity pointed out by the auditors and to report the action taken to the Government within three months.

Functions of the Municipality

The administration of a municipal area in respect of the following matters vests in the Municipality:

(i) Preparation of annual long-term schemes for urban planning and town development and their implementation;

(ii) Regulation of building construction and land assignment;

(iii) Preparation and implementation of socio-economic development schemes;

(iv) Road and Bridges—Maintenance of roads, culverts and drains and construction and maintenance of new roads;

(v) Water Supply—implementation of water supply schemes required for domestic, industrial, commercial purposes, digging of wells and the tube wells for obtaining drinking water and their maintenance, protection of public ponds;

(vi) Public Health—Control and management of Taluk hospitals, Government dispensaries and health centres; preservation and improvement of public health; control and management of maternity and child welfare centres; implementation of health education programmes and preventive measures including vaccination against epidemic diseases; cleaning of roads; drains; markets and other public places and removal of solid wastes; destruction of stray dogs; mosquito control; regulation of sale of meat; fish and other perishable food items; licensing of eating establishments; disposal of unclaimed corpuses and carcasses of animals; establishment of bathing ghats in rivers and ponds and establishment of special cleaning places for cattle; popularisation of water tight closets; licensing of dangerous and offensive trades;

(vii) Providing assistance to fire extinguishing and protection steps and machineries;

(viii) Social Forestry and Environmental Protection—improvement of urban forestry scheme; organising campaigns for free planting; planting and maintenance of avenue trees and social forestry strips; raising and distribution of fuel wood; cultivation of fodder and soft wood trees; setting up nurseries for raising seedlings; directly and by assisting educational institutions and voluntary agencies; and creation of awareness about ecological factors;

(ix) Social Welfare and Welfare of Scheduled Castes and Scheduled Tribes—Implementation of feeding programmes for preschool students; implementation of child welfare schemes; control and supervision of anganwadies functioning under ICDS scheme; construction and handing over buildings to anganwady centres; management of care homes for disabled children; children's homes; a balamandirs, homes for physically handicapped and aged; custodian care homes, day care centres for children of weaker section; destitute homes and beggar homes; distribution of pension to destitutes, widows and the aged, and financial assistance for the marriage of daughters of poor widows and to inter-caste couples, distribution of agricultural labourers pension and unemployment dole; payment of scholarship to physically handicapped students; providing financial assistance to educational institutions for such students; payment of grants to orphanages; payment of grants to the inmates of homes for the physically handicapped; campaigning against superstitions; casteism and untouchability; campaigning against smuggling; black marketing; hoarding; tax evasion and other social evils; implementation of preventive awareness creation of programmes on legal protection to women; implementation of adult education programme for the Scheduled Castes and Scheduled Tribes; providing financial assistance to Scheduled Castes and Scheduled Tribes for thatching of houses and for house construction; providing public facilities in SC and ST colonies; providing financial assistance to SC/ST for marriage, medical treatment, higher studies etc.; introduction of welfare programmes for the children belonging to SC and ST; construction of legal aid committees for the weaker sections, implementation of other welfare programmes for the SC and ST;

(x) Implementation of slums development schemes, rehabilitation of paramboke dwellers;

(xi) Eradication of Poverty—implementation of Nehru Rozgar Yojana, urban basic services scheme; and promotion of urban community, societies;

(xii) Construction or maintenance of parks, gardens, playgrounds, traffic islands etc. in the urban areas;

(xiii) Cultural-Educational activities—control and supervision of Government lower primary, upper primary and high schools; construction and maintenance of Government school buildings, noon-feeding of school children; management of educational institutions established by the Municipalities including pre-primary schools and industrial training centres; distribution of scholarships and grants to students; implementation of non-formal education, adult education and other literacy programmes; management of municipal libraries and payment of financial aid to other libraries; payment of grants to Nilathezhithu Assano; promotion of awareness of physical labour in schools; management and control of Government technical schools, constitution of Municipal Education Committee; promotion of social and cultural activities, construction of community halls and open air theatres; providing assistance to school youth festivals, art-cultural-sports and games, festivals and other local festivals and controlling melas and festivals; establishment of memorials for celebrities and historical personages and protection of other historical monuments;

(xiv) Opening and maintenance of public burial and burning grounds and electric crematoria;

(xv) Opening cattle pounds and taking steps for prevention of cruelty to animals;

(xvi) Registration of births, deaths and marriages;

(xvii) Introducing public facilities—installation of street lights and their maintenance; specifying bus stops and constructing waiting sheds thereat; providing parking places for vehicles including taxies and autorikshaws; providing parking places on canals for boats and canoes;

(xviii) Management and control of slaughter houses, and regulation of tanneries;

(xix) Agriculture—improvement of agriculture and establishment of model agricultural farms; establishment of granaries; bringing under cultivation waste and fellow lands belonging to or invested in the Municipalities and promotion of optimum utilisation of land; ensuring conservation of manurial resources; cultivation of green manure; preparing compost and selling manure; promotion of organic manure, establishment and maintenance of nurseries of improved varieties of seeds, seedlings and planting materials; provision of implements, stores, pesticides etc.; promotion of cooperative and group farming; conducting crop experiments and launching crop protection schemes; encouraging crop experiments and group farming; assisting Government in the implementation of land reform schemes; execution of social conservation schemes; promotion of horticulture; development and maintenance of grazing lands; plant-protection measures against pests and serious diseases and eradication of weeds; conducting the agricultural exhibitions; crop-development programmes for optimum utilisation of land and increase in production, activities for the promotion of the use of fertilisers; introduction of partial mechanisation; promotion of seed production; conduct of melas; seminars, farmer's day, input fortnight etc.; promotion of processing agricultural produce at farmers level;

(xx) Animal Husbandry and Dairy Development—improvement of cattle and cattle breeding and general care of livestock, promotion of dairy farming, promotion of poultry farming, bee keeping and piggery, grassland development, conduct of cattle and poultry shows, providing artificial insemination facilities, veterinary public health, veterinary care including treatment of animals, assisting the authorities concerned in the prevention and eradication of animal diseases, management of veterinary dispensaries and hospitals, veterinary polytechnics, and clinical laboratories transferred by Government, management of dairy extension service units, establishment of cattle feed units, promotion of milk cooperative societies management of breeding farms and distribution of improved varieties of animals and poultry;

(xxi) Minor Irrigation—maintenance of community pump sets, tube wells, and public tanks, digging of wells for irrigation, execution of works assigned by the Command Area, Development Authority, management and proper use of water for irrigation, construction of field channels and fields boothes with the cooperation of the farmers, construction and maintenance of minor irrigation and lift irrigation schemes benefiting upto 15 hectares if the entire command area is within the Municipality;

(xxii) Fisheries—development of inland fisheries through leasing of public waters; promotion of entrepreneurs; distribution of fish etc.; management and upkeep of traditional landing centres, and upkeep of fishery roads, dispensaries and schools; extension of educational facilities to the fisherman by giving scholarship, stipend, grants, or subsidised books for students; organising nursery schools and literacy programmes in coastal areas; implementation of welfare schemes for the uplift and development of fishermen; establishment of housing colonies for fishermen; promotion of fish marketing cooperative societies; and

(xxiii) Small Scale Industries—identification of traditional skills in the locality and developing cottage industries; licensing of smail scale industries and workshops; arranging training programmes for artisans and craftsmen; promotion of sericulture, establishment and management of small scale industrial estates; assisting the development of raw materials locally; creation of community; interest in village industries and their products; promotion of household, cooperative and private small scale industries through the provision of an integrated counselling and clearance service; promotion of the marketing of the products of small scale and cottage industries, entrepreneurship development; organising training programmes of khadi, handloom weavers and artisans and craftsmen; distribution of financial assistance to self-employment schemes; registration and control of small scale industrial units; and management and control of khadi-village industry, handloom, coir, handicrafts and other traditional industries;

(xxiv) Housing—identification of houseless families, and poramboke dwellers; acquisition of house sites and their distribution to the houseless; popularising of low cost housing and building materials; implementation of shelter upgradation programmes, provision of public amenities in housing colonies; construction of housing colonies, flats and those under Rajiv One Million Housing Scheme, and the development of house sites and their distribution; and promotion of housing cooperative societies;

(xxv) Electricity and Non-Conventional Energy—identification of electrification works to be attended by Electricity Board; popularisation of non-conventional energy including biogas plants; promotion and popularisation of energy saving devices; and setting up micro power projects and the distribution of electricity thus generated;

(xxvi) Public Distribution System—examination of complaints against the public distribution system and taking of remedial measures; campaigning against weights and measures offences; general supervision and guidance of ration shops and Maveli Stores, inspection of ration shops; detection of irregularities and action against hoarding of essential commodities, activities for price control; and creating consumer protection awareness;

(xxvii) Employment—supervision of Industrial Technical Institutes and Industrial Technical Colleges;

(xxviii) Cooperation—providing incentives, deposit mobilisation campaigns; distribution of subsidy for the salary of employees of cooperative societies; distribution of subsidy to marketing cooperative societies, SC/ST Cooperative societies; and

(xxix) General—organising relief measures during natural calamities and drought; distribution of financial assistance from the Revenue Department and the Chief Minister's Relief Fund; preparation of annual budget; organising voluntary labour for community development programmes; providing first aid training, awareness against motor accidents, awareness of traffic rules; providing legal aid; promotion of civic responsibility etc.; participation in National Saving Programme encouraging saving habits and thrift; maintenance of ambulance service; providing ferries and their licensing; maintenance of waterways and public canals; and management of public markets, shopping complexes, bus stands, rest houses etc.

The Committee on Decentralisation of Powers suggests a separate list of mandatory functions, general functions and sectorwise distribution of responsibility as under:

Mandatory Functions

1. Regulation of building construction;

2. Protection of public land from encroachment;
3. Protection of traditional drinking water sources;
4. Preservation of ponds and other water bodies;
5. Maintenance of water-ways and canals under their charge;
6. Collection and disposal of solid waste and control of liquid waste;
7. Storm water drainage;
8. Maintenance of environment hygiene;
9. Management of markets;
10. Vector control;
11. Regulation of slaughtering of animals and sale of meat, fish and other perishable food items;
12. Regulation of eating establishments;
13. Prevention of food adulteration;
14. Maintenance of roads and other public streets;
15. Street lighting and their maintenance;
16. Immunisation;
17. Carrying into effect National and State level strategies and programmes for disease prevention and control;
18. Opening and maintenance of burial and burning grounds;
19. Licensing the dangerous and offensive trades and industries;
20. Registration of births and deaths;
21. Providing bathing and washing ghats;
22. Provisions of ferries;
23. Provide parking space for vehicles;
24. Provide waiting sheds for travellers;
25. Provide toilet facilities in public places;
26. Regulate conduct of fairs and festivals;
27. Licensing the pet dogs and destroying stray dogs;
28. Provision of basic minimum service in slums;
29. Amenities for pedestrians including footpath and road crossing facilities;
30. Preparation of detailed town plans and action plan for phased implementation.

General Functions

1. Collection and updating of essential statistics;
2. Organising voluntary labour and contribution for community works;

3. Carrying and campaigns for thrift;
4. Awareness building on control of social evils like drinking, consumption of narcotics, dowry and abuse of women and children;
5. Ensuring maximum people's participation in all stages of development;
6. Organising relief during natural calamities;
7. Inculcating environmental awareness and motivating local action for environmental upgradation;
8. Promoting cooperatives;
9. Enhancing communal harmony;
10. Mobilising local resources in cash and in kind, including free surrenders of land for development purpose;
11. Spreading legal awareness among the weaker sections;
12. Campaigning against economic crimes;
13. Organising neighbourhood groups and self help groups with focus on poor;
14. Awareness building on civic duties.

Taxation

Every Municipality may levy:

(a) a property tax,

(b) a profession tax,

(c) a tax on animals and vessels,

(d) a show tax,

(e) a tax on advertisement,

(f) a tax on timber brought into the municipal area, and

(g) a duty on certain transfer of immovable property in the shape of an additional stamp duty.

The Municipality may for the purpose of providing any specific service on amenity levy a surcharge on any tax other than profession tax levied by the Municipality. The surcharge cannot exceed 10 per cent of the amount of the tax. The Municipality may levy a land conversion cost not exceeding Rs. 75 per acre from the landholder in respect of paddy field, marshy land, pond or watershed held by him which is converted in to garden land or building site.

Imposition of Tax

The Council has to resolve the decision to levy a tax specifying the rate at which, and the date from which the tax can be levied. Before passing a resolution imposing a tax for the first time or increasing the rate of an existing tax, the Municipality has to publish a notice in the Gazette, at least in one newspaper published in the language of the locality having wide circulation in the Municipality, on the notice board of the Municipality and in other places in the municipal area of its intention. A reasonable period of not less than one month is fixed for submission of objections. The Council considers the objections and finalises the impositions. When a Council determines to levy any tax for the first time or at a new rate, the Secretary has to forthwith publish in the prescribed manner the rate at which, and the date from which, and the period of levy, for which the tax is levied.

Abolition of Tax

A resolution abolishing an existing tax or reducing the existing rate has to immediately be reported to the Government. In the case of a Municipality which has an outstanding loan either from the Government or from the public or any other local body, abolition or reduction cannot have effect without the sanction of the Government.

Property Tax

The property tax may comprise of a tax for general purpose and a service tax. The service tax may comprise of:

(a) a water and drainage tax to provide for expenses in connection with the construction, maintenance, repair, extension or improvement of water or drainage work;

(b) a lighting tax to provide for expenses connected with the lighting of the municipal area by gas, electricity or any other means; and

(c) a sanitary tax to provide for expenses connected with the general sanitation of the municipal area and the removal of rubbish, filth or carcasses of animals from private premises.

The property tax cannot be less than 8 per cent and more than 20 per cent in Town Panchayat, 10 and 25 per cent in a Municipal Council and 15 and 25 per cent in a Municipal Corporation of the annual value of all buildings or lands or both. The different components at the minimum rates are:—

Minimum Rates (%)

	Town Panchayat	*Municipal Council*	*Municipal Corporation*
(i) Tax for general purposes	5	5	7
(ii) Lighting tax	2	2	2
(iii) Drainage tax	–	–	2
(iv) Water tax	–	–	1
(v) Sanitary tax	1	3	3

The Municipal Council can levy these taxes on land used exclusively for agricultural purposes and which is more than one hectare in extent on its annual value excluding one hectare therefrom at the percentage fixed by it but not exceeding the maximum.

Assessment

Every building is assessed together with its site and other adjacent premises occupied as an appurtenance thereto. The annual value of buildings and lands is deemed to be the gross annual rent, at which they may reasonably be expected to be let less a deduction, in case of buildings, of 20 per cent of that portion of such annual rent which is attributable to the buildings alone apart from their sites and adjacent lands occupied as an appurtenance thereto.

In the case of any Government building or any building of a class not ordinarily let, the gross annual rent of which cannot be estimated, the annual value of the premises is deemed to be 6 per cent of the total of the estimated value of the land and the estimated present cost of erecting the building after deducting for depreciation a reasonable amount in no case be less than 20 per cent of such cost. Machinery and furnitures are excluded from valuations. In the alternative, the annual value of a building may be determined based on the letting value calculated on plinth area basis, less a deduction of 20 per cent for depreciation of buildings.

In the case of owner occupied residential buildings, the annual value arrived at is reduced by a rebate of 25 per cent in value.

Places set apart for public worship, and either actually so used for no other purpose, buildings used exclusively for public worship, choultries for the occupation of which no rent is charged and choultries where the rent is charged for the occupation is used exclusively for charitable purposes, buildings recognised by the Government or registered with the Municipality and owned and occupied by educational institutions and used only for teaching and libraries open to public, ancient monuments as are not used as residential quarters or as public offices, burial and burning grounds included in the register kept at the office of the Municipality, buildings or lands belonging to the Municipality, such property of Government not being buildings, as may be notified by the Government and public buildings and places used for charitable purposes of sheltering the destitutes, or animals are exempted from the property tax. These exemptions are not extended to buildings and lands, for which rent realised by the owners thereof and to residential quarters attached to the schools and colleges not being hostels or residential quarters attached to hospitals, dispensaries and libraries. The council may by a general resolution exempt any building, or land from property tax if the annual value does not exceed three hundred rupees and the proprietor does not own any other building or land assessed to the property tax and is not liable to profession tax or income tax or agricultural income tax. In the case of properties exempted from the property tax, the Municipality can claim the cost of services covered by the service taxes.

When any building whether ordinarily let or occupied by the owner himself has been vacant and unlet for a half year, the owner is entitled to a remission of tax for that half year. A remission is admissible only when the owner or his agent has previously delivered notice to the Secretary that the building is vacant and unlet or the building will be vacant and unlet from a specified date either in that half year or in the succeeding half year.

Whenever the title of the person liable to payment of property tax is transferred, the person whose title is transferred and the person to whom it is transferred are required to give notice to the Secretary within three months after the execution of the instrument of transfer or after its registration. In the event of death of the person liable, the person to whom the title of the deceased is devolved as heir or otherwise has to give notice of such transfer to the Secretary within one year from the date of death of the deceased.

If any building is constructed or reconstructed in a municipal area, the owner has to give notice to the Secretary within 15 days from the date of completion or occupation of the building whichever is earlier. If such date falls within the last two months of a half year, the owner is entitled to a remission of the whole of the tax or enhanced tax for that half year. If such date falls within the first four months of a half year, the owner is entitled to a remission of not exceeding a half of the tax or enhanced tax payable for that half year, as is proportionate to the number of days in that half year.

If any building is demolished or destroyed, the owner has to give notice to the Secretary. If the notice is given within the first two months of a half year, the owner is entitled to a remission of the whole of the tax payable for that half year. If the notice is given in the last four months, the owner is entitled to a remission not exceeding a half of the tax for that half year, as is proportionate to the number of days in the half year succeeding the demolition or destruction.

Where a person has constructed any building unlawfully, such building is liable to tax from the date of completion or occupation whichever is earlier till the date of demolition of that building.

Where any area is included within the municipal area, the owner of every building or area is essential for remission. If the date of inclusion falls within the last two months of a half year, the owner is not liable to pay property tax for that half year. If such date falls within the first four months, the owner is entitled to a remission of tax not exceeding half of the property tax payable for that year.

When any area is excluded from the municipal area, the owner of every building or land is entitled for remission. If the date of exclusion falls within the first two months of a half year, every owner is entitled for that half year. If such date falls within the last four months every owner is entitled for remission of tax not exceeding half of the property tax payable for that half year. A remission in case of exclusion cannot be granted unless an application in writing for such remission is made to the Secretary within three months from the date of exclusion of the area.

Profession Tax

A profession tax is levied on every company which transacts business in the Municipal area for not less than 60 days in aggregate in any half year or transacts business outside the limit of the municipal area but has its head office or place from which its business is controlled within the area for not less than sixty days in the aggregate in any half year. The tax is imposed on every person who exercises a profession, art or calling or transacts business or holds any appointment, public or private, within the municipal area for not less than 60 days in the aggregate or outside to municipal area, but who resides within the area for not less than 60 days in the aggregate or transacts business outside the area but has his head office or place from which his business is controlled within the municipal area for not less than 60 days in the aggregate or resides in the municipal area for not less than 60 days in the aggregate or resides in the municipal area for not less than 60 days in the aggregate and is in receipt of any income from investments. They have to pay half yearly tax assessed in accordance with the rules.

The Secretary during the month of May and November in every half year sends a notice requiring every employer or head of office to assess every employee in his institution liable to profession tax and every self-drawing officer to remit the profession tax due in accordance with the notice. Before the end of February of every year, head of office or employer has to assess every employee liable to tax and recover the amount from him and pay over to the Municipality. The Secretary maintains a Ward-wise Demand Register by providing independent pages for every institution.

Tax over Animals and Vessels

The Council may levy a tax on animals and vessels kept or used within the municipal area. Every person having possession, custody or control of any taxable animal or vessel is liable for half yearly tax if the animal or vessel has been kept or used within the municipal area for an aggregate period of not less than 60 days in a half year. If such aggregate period does not exceed 15 days, no tax is liable for that half year.

A tax is not levied on animals and vessels belonging to the Government or the Municipality and animals and vessels kept solely for sale by dealers, animals kept for the reception of infirm or disabled animals and vessels kept for the repairs.

Show Tax

A show tax is levied on all shows within the municipal area, calculated as under:

(a) Regular cinematographic exhibitions at licensed theatres @ Rs. two per show.

(b) Other cinematographic exhibition @ Rs. 10 per show.

(c) Regular shows other than cinematographic exhibitions connected at the same place daily @ Rs. 5 per show.

(d) Other shows @ Rs.30 per show.

A show tax is not levied in respect of any show on which no entertainment tax is levied and for which no rent is paid to the owner of the premises for the show.

Tax on Timber

A tax is levied on timber brought into the municipal area at the rate not exceeding Rs. 24 per tonne.

The Secretary may, with the sanction of the Council farm out of the collection of tax on timber for a period not exceeding one year.

Levy of Tax on Direction

The Government may, by order published in the Gazette direct a Municipality to levy either retrospectively or prospectively the property tax or any other tax and authorise a Municipality to levy, collect and appropriate such taxes, duties, and tolls and fees as may be specified in the order.

Assignment of Tax

The Government may, by order published in the Gazette, assign to a Municipality such taxes, duties, tolls and fees levied by the Government for such purposes and subject to such conditions and limits as may be specified in the order.

Recovery of Dues

All the dues are demanded by bill. If amount exceeds Rs. 50,000, it is recovered together with penalty at the rate of 2 per cent per annum from the date which it becomes due. No distraint can be made, no suit can be instituted and no prosecution can be commenced in respect of any sum due to a Municipality after the expiration of a period of three years.

Where an amount due to the Municipality has been barred by limitation due to the default of not taking steps at the appropriate time, and it is found in a lawful enquiry that it was lost due to the default of any officer, the amount so lost to the Municipality is realised with 12 per cent interest from such officer.

Registration of Hospitals

No private hospital or paramedical institution can be estimated within the territorial area of a Municipality without prior registration in that Municipality. Any person maintaining or running an unregistered private hospital or private paramedical institution is punished with fine which may extend to give 1000 rupees.

Registration of Tutorial Institutions

A tutorial institution cannot be established within the Municipal area without prior registration obtained from Municipality. Any person who establishes or maintains a tutorial institution without registration can on conviction be punished with fine, which may extend to one thousand rupees.

Appeals

An appeal can lie to the Council from any notice issued or other action taken or proposed to be taken by the Secretary, or any order of the Secretary granting or refusing to grant a licence or permission or any order of the Secretary suspending or revoking a licence or any other order of the Secretary that may be appealable. Pending decision on an appeal, the Chairman may on application, by order stay the operation of the notice, order or other action appealed against. Every case has to be reported by the Chairperson to the Council at its next ordinary meeting with the reasons in full for making such order and the Council can either confirm such order with or without modification or revoke it. An appeal has to be disposed of by the Council within three months of receipt of such appeal.

An appeal from an order passed by the Secretary regarding approval of site or alteration in work or demolition of building can lie to the Government. The Government may, either suo motu or on application call for and examine the records of any order passes or proceedings taken for the purpose of satisfying themselves as to the legality or propriety of such order or as to the regularity of such proceedings and pass such order as they think fit.

An appeal can be presented within 30 days after the date of publication of the order granting a licence or permission and in other cases, within 30 days after the date of the receipt of the order or proceedings against which the appeal is made.

Rules, Bye-Laws and Regulations

The Government may by notification in the Gazette make rules either prospectively or retrospectively to carry out the Municipal administration. Every rule has to be laid before the Legislative Assembly while it is in session for a total period of 14 days.

The Council may make bye-laws. The Council with the previous sanction of the Government make bye-laws with respective effect. The Council may make regulations. After making or altering any bye-law or regulation, the Council has to publish a draft of the proposed bye-law or regulation together with a notice specifying a date on or after which the draft will be taken into consideration, receive objections/suggestions and consider them. A bye-law or regulation or any cancellation or alteration thereof cannot have effect until the same is approved and confirmed by the Government. A bye-law or regulation or cancellation or alteration, approved and confirmed has to be published in the Gazette and comes into operation on the date of publication unless a different date is provided therein. The Government may cancel any bye-law, or regulation. Before cancellation, the Council has to be given an opportunity to express its views regarding cancellation.

Control

The Government or other officer authorised in this behalf may inspect any office under the control of the Municipality or any movable property kept therein or any immovable property or any work which is in progress. He may call for any document in the custody of the Municipality, require the Chairman to furnish any return, plan, estimate, statement, account or statics, require the Chairperson to furnish any information or report on any matter relating to the Municipality and record in writing any observation for the consideration of the Council, Chairperson or Secretary in regard to the proceedings or functions of the Council, Chairperson or Secretary.

The Government may by order, for reasons to be recorded in writing, amend, cancel or suspend for a period not more than three months any resolution passed, order issued, licence or permission granted, or prohibit the doing of any act by the Municipality if it may cause or likely to cause any pecuniary loss or damage to the Municipality or affect the financial interest of the Municipality or the execution of such resolution or order, the continuance in force of such licence, or permission or the doing of such act is likely to cause danger to human life, health or safety, is likely to lead to a riot or affray. The Government may issue appropriate order or direction if any action taken or order issued or licence or permission granted by any Municipal Authority is erroneous, improper or against the financial or other interests of the Municipality or is likely to cause financial loss or causes or is likely to cause injustice to or denies the legal right of any person, or causes or is likely to cause undue hardship, damage or injury to any person, or wilfully or otherwise omits to discharge a legal duty or fails to fulfil an obligation cast upon it by any law, or is against public interest and better administration of a Municipality.

If it appears to the Government that a Municipal Authority has made default in performing any duty imposed on it, it may, by order, in writing, direct such authority to perform the duty with a specified period of time, and such authority is bound to comply with such direction. The Government may, with the consent of a Municipality, undertake on its behalf the construction of water supply, drainage or any other work, appoint any officer or person to carry out the construction of such works and direct that the expenses including pay and allowances of such officers be paid from the Municipal fund in priority to any other charges except charges for the service of authorised loans.

Where the duration of a Municipality has expired and a new Municipality has not been constituted or where the councillors of a Municipality have resigned in block or where there are vacancies in the Council of a Municipality either by resignation or otherwise of the Councillors and the number of remaining Councillors cannot constitute the quorum for the meeting of the Council, the Government may by notification in Gazette, appoint an Administrative Committee and a Chairman thereof, or a Special Officer for a specified period of time not exceeding six months. The Administrative Committee or the Special

Officer have all the powers and functions of the Council, the Chairperson, the Deputy Chairperson and the Committees of the Municipality and take all such actions as may be required in the interest of the Municipality.

Dissolution

If the Government is of opinion that a Municipality persistently makes default in performing its duties or in carrying out the orders or directions lawfully issued by the Government or abuses its powers, the Government may by notification in the Gazette, dissolve the Municipality and forward a copy thereof to the State Election Commission. A dissolved Municipality has to be reconstituted within six months from the date of its dissolution. Before publishing a notification of dissolution, however, the Government has to communicate to the Municipality the grounds on which it proposes to do so, give the Municipality a reasonable period to show cause against the proposal and consider its explanation or objection.

Upon the dissolution, all the Councillors including the Chairperson or the Deputy Chairperson deemed to have vacated their offices. During the interim period between the dissolution and the reconstitution of a Municipality, all powers, functions and duties of a Municipality including those of the Chairperson, the Deputy Chairperson, the Standing Committees and other Committees thereof are exercised, performed or discharged by the Secretary or such officer as may be authorised by the Government in that behalf.

A Municipality which is constituted upon dissolution before the expiration of its due can continue only for the remainder of the period for which the dissolved Municipality would have continued had it not been dissolved.

Every notification of dissolution is laid before the Legislative Assembly and the approval of the Assembly is obtained.

People's Participation

The corner stone of decentralised democratic governance is people's participation. Genuine participation consists of dialogue and partnership leading to full involvement in decision making in the allocation and utilisation of resources meant for collective good that constitutes genuine participation. Thus it is a people centred view of local self-government that the Committee has taken. In order to ensure people's participation, there has to be an enabling environment. Thus the right of information is incorporated as a prominent feature in the Acts and rules governing local self-government institutions. The Committee believes that accountability to the people is best ensured through transparency. Transparent administration enable people to achieve an on-line monitoring of the administrative process.

The State Government set up a Committee on Decentralisation of Powers to local self-government institutions in pursuance of the 73rd and 74th Amendments to the Constitution. The Committee submitted its interim report in August 1996 and final report in December 1997. The Committee adopted a rigorous methodology in identifying various issues concerning decentralisation and suggesting measures to tone up the local self-government institutions in the State. The Committee attempted to bring about a restructuring of Kerala Panchayat Raj Act, the Kerala Municipality Act, and the allied Acts besides making appropriate recommendations to strengthen the local self-government institutions with adequate staff support. In making its recommendations, the Committee had been guided by vision of an effective local self-government capable of providing good governance at the local level with full participation of the people. In order to realise this vision, the Committee has focused on certain critical issues. Some of them are broadly outlined below.

Institutionalising Local Self-Government

The Constitution envisages the functioning of municipal bodies as ''institutions of local self-government''. Therefore, the Committee has recommended that the powers, functions and responsibilities be redefined more clearly so that sphere of activity of each local body is fairly clear. For the local self-government to function, it has to be relatively free from interference and executive control from above. The Committee has reduced the scope of government interference in its day to day affairs. The resolution can be cancelled only in extraordinary circumstances.

Local self-government implies control over its staff and power to utilise staff transferred to it according to the division of responsibility to be decided by the local bodies. The division of work should be more functional rather than departmental.

To protect the autonomy of the local self-government institutions, the Committee recommends the delayering by removing superfluous committees and bodies, which run parallel to them. Thus the Development Authorities, Metropolitan Planning Committee and other Committees are recommended to be abolished.

New Checks and Balances

The Committee feels that the reduced role of Government, a new system of checks and balances has to emerge with account on control from below. In order to ensure fairness in decisions, propriety in expenditure, legality in actions and legitimacy in policy, these new checks and balances will have to be in place. Of course, social audit both formal, through Gram Sabhas/Ward Sabhas/Wards Committees, community structures and people's committees is expected to be the main deterrent against possible waywardness in performance of duties of municipalities. The rights of people's groups coupled with the duties of municipalities in maintaining transparency and providing information would provide a powerful check on the municipalities. At the same time, the audit system needs to be strengthened.

New Institutions

As decentralised governance becomes a reality, some of the existing institutions need to be strengthened and new institutions of people's participation like Ward Committees need to get strengthened considerably. Also, the State Election Commission would have to be given more powers particularly in delimitation of constituencies, reservation of constituencies and office of President and in disqualification of members. Among the new institutions which become inevitable, are the Appellate Tribunal and the Ombudsman.

Public Accounts and Vigilance Committee

In every Municipal Corporation, a Public Accounts and Vigilance Committee is constituted. It consists, including its Chairman, of not less than five but not more than seven members elected by the Councillors from amongst themselves. The Leader of Opposition in the Council is the Chairman and ex-officio member of the Committee. The Committee can scrutinise the accounts, inspect the works and enquire into the observations in the audit and inspection reports and present periodical reports to the Council for timely action. The Committee has to keep surveillance on administrative and financial transactions of the Municipal Corporation and make observations thereon in the periodical reports.

Right to Information

Every bonafide person has right to information from a Municipality in accordance with the prescribed procedure. The Government may, in the interest of public and local administration, classify any documents containing categories of information, to which no person shall have right to information and any request for such information is liable to be rejected by the Municipality. The Government may direct the Municipalities to publish the categories of information for general information of the inhabitants of the area of that Municipality.

A person requiring any information from the Municipality has to make an application to the Secretary and pay the fee prescribed therefor. The Secretary or any officer authorised by the Council furnishes the information to the applicant within the period prescribed, unless the application is rejected or, otherwise, disposed of within that period. In case of rejection of any application, the reasons for rejection have to be given in writing. The Secretary or the officer made responsible for furnishing the information is liable personally for furnishing the same within the period prescribed, unless such information is in respect of a notified document. When such information is not furnished within the period prescribed, the officer responsible for non-supply is punishable with a fine of fifty rupees for every day of delay after the due date and such fine is credited to the fund of municipality. If the Secretary or any officer made responsible fails to furnish the information or furnishes a false information, he is punishable with fine of not less than 1000 rupees. If the Secretary or the officer responsible for supply of information, after making thorough search finds that the document is not available or traceable, by reason of expiry of period for preservation of document or for any other reason and the information cannot be made available, he has to inform the applicant accordingly and dispose of application.

Citizens Charter

Every Municipality has to formulate and publish a Citizen's Charter which specifies the categories of service guaranteed by the Municipality to the citizen, the standard of such service and also the time limit or periodicity within which such service is tendered. The Charter is renewed and updated periodically at least once in a year.

Ombudsman

The State Government has, by notification in the Official Gazette, to constitute an authority for local self-government institutions known as Ombudsman at the State level for the purpose of conducting investigations and inquiries on any complaint with regard to any action involving corruption, maladministration or irregularities in the administration by the local self-government institutions. The Ombudsman consists of a High Court Judge, appointed by the Government with the approval of the Chief Justice of the High Court, who acts as Chairman, two judicial officers of the rank of District Judge appointed by the Government with the approval of the Chief Justice of High Court, two officers of the Government, not below the rank of Secretary and two public men of repute having known integrity appointed by the Government with the approval of the Leader of Opposition of the Legislative Assembly of the State. In the absence of the Chairman, the senior in service among the judicial officers exercises the powers and performs the functions of the Chairman.

A member holds office for a term of five years or till attains 62 years of age. A member may, by writing under his hand and addressed to the Government, resign his office. A member may be removed from office by an order of the Governor, passed after an address by the State Legislative Assembly supported by a majority of the total membership of the House and by a majority of not less than two-thirds of the members of the Legislative Assembly present and voting, has been presented to the Governor in the same session for such removal on the ground of proved misbehaviour or incapacity.

The Ombudsman has a secretary and other officers and employees determined by the Government in consultation with the Ombudsman to assist Ombudsman in the exercise of its powers and discharge of its functions. The Ombudsman may request the assistance of any officer in any Department of Government in order to ascertain the veracity of any complaint in an investigation and such officer is duty-bound to render the assistance in addition and without deteriment to his official duties. The Ombudsman may engage the services of any person having experience and expertise in any particular subject for arriving at a decision on matters before it.

The Ombudsman can perform all or any of the following functions:

(a) causing investigation into any allegation, contained in a complaint or on a reference from Government, or that has come to the notice of the Ombudsman;

(b) inquiring into any allegation against a public servant alleging corruption or maladministration;

(c) pass an order on the allegations in the following manner:

  (i) where the irregularity involves commission of a criminal offence by a public servant, refer the matter to the appropriate authority to cause further investigation and intimation of prosecution;

  (ii) where the irregularity leads to loss or inconvenience to a citizen, award compensation to the victim by the local self-government institution concerned and cause to recover such amount from the persons responsible for the irregularity;

  (iii) where the irregularity involves any loss, waste, mis-application of funds of local self-government institution, cause to recover such loss from the person responsible for the irregularity; and

  (iv) where the irregularity is by reason of omission or inaction, cause to supply the omission or to cause rectification.

In addition, the Ombudsman may pass interim order restraining the local self-government institution from doing any thing detrimental to the interest of the complainant, if the Ombudsman is convinced that the complainant may suffer imminent loss or injury by the act of the institution complained of. It may, in its order, impose fine in addition to the award of compensation if it is of the opinion that the irregularity involves some corrupt practice for personal gain.

For the purpose of any investigation or inquiry, the Ombudsman has the power of a civil court in respect of summoning and enforcing the attendance of any witness and examining him, requiring the discovery and production of any document, receiving evidence on affidavits, requisitioning any public records or copy thereof from any public court or office and issuing commissions for the examination of witness.

Where the Ombudsman finds that the allegations contained in a complaint are without substance or trivial in nature, it may order the complainant to pay amount of cost to the opposition party. Where the allegation is about the loss, waste or misapplication of fund of the local self-government institution or the loss or inconvenience to the citizen, the Ombudsman may during the enquiry collect evidence, quantify such loss and specify in its order the amount to be realised from the person responsible. The amount due as per order of the Ombudsman, if not paid within the specified time, is recoverable under revenue recovery proceedings as if it were the arrears of tax due on land.

Appellate Tribunals

The Government can constitute in every district an Appellate Tribunal for local self-government institutions to consider and dispose of the appeal or revision against the decisions of the local self-government institutions. It consists of one Judicial Officer only, not below the rank of a District Judge having not less than three years of service as a District Judge or Additional District Judge. He is appointed by the Government in consultation with the Chief Justice of the High Court.

The Tribunal has the powers of a civil court in respect of summoning and enforcing the attendance of any person and examining him on oath, requiring the discovery and production of any document or other material object productive as evidence, receiving evidence on affidavits, requisitioning any public record or a copy thereof from any court of office and issuing commissions for the examination of witness or documents.

Any proceedings before the Tribunal are deemed to be a judicial proceedings within the Indian Penal Code.

The Tribunal is assisted by officers and staff as decided by the Government.

The Tribunals can, on a reference from the Government, with regard to the legality or sustainability of any decision of the local self-government institutions, tender its opinion to the Government thereon if necessary, after giving opportunity of being heard to the President of the local self-government institution concerned.

Ward Committees

In every municipality where population exceeds one lakh, a Ward Committee is constituted for every ward within three months of the constitution of the municipality. The Ward Committee is a body nominated by the Chairperson in consultation with the ward members. A Ward Committee consists of the elected Councillor of the Ward and not more than 50 persons nominated by the Chairperson in consultation with the Councillor of the Ward from the following:

(i) heads of enducational institutions in the Ward;
(ii) presidents of the residents' associations of housing colonies in that Ward, registered with the Municipality;
(iii) presidents of the area development societies formed by the urban poor in that Ward, registered with the Municipality;
(iv) representatives of important industrial or commercial establishments in that ward;
(v) representatives of organisations of traders in that ward;
(vi) representatives of recognised trade unions;
(vii) union chairmen of educational institutions in that Ward;
(viii) representatives of arts, sports and games, cultural organisations in that Ward, registered with the Municipality; and
(ix) doctors of Government and private hospitals functioning in that ward.

In addition, three prominent citizens are nominated by the Chairperson. The elected Councillor is the Chairman of the Committee.

The Committee has to meet at least once in three months for discharging the duties and performing its functions. The meeting is convened by its Chairman. The Chairman, or in his absence, a member chosen by the members present from amongst themselves has to preside over the meeting. The Secretary and the Heads of Department in the services under the Municipality have to attend the meetings and produce any document or furnish any information or report required by the Committee.

Ward Sabhas

In every municipality, where the population does not exceed one lakh, a Ward Sabha is constituted in every ward. It consists of all persons registered in the electoral roll of that ward. The councillor representing the ward is the convenor of the Ward Sabha. In case of his inability to perform his functions, the Chairperson may appoint a councillor representing any adjacent ward as the convenor.

The Ward Sabha meets once in three months. Every meeting is presided over by the Chairperson or, in his absence, by the Deputy Chairperson or Standing-Committee Chairman authorised by the Chairperson. The convenor of the Ward Sabha can convene extraordinary meetings of the Sabha as and when a request is made by not less than 10 percent of the electors in the ward, with the items of agenda specified in the request.

The quorum at the meeting is 10 per cent of its members. The council can take every measure required to achieve maximum participation of all the sections of its members.

The convenor places before the Ward Sabha a report relating to the developmental programmes relating to the ward during the previous year and those that are proposed to be undertaken during the current year and the expenditure thereof, the annual statement of accounts, and the administration report of the preceding year.

An officer is nominated specifically by the council as the Coordinator of the Ward Sabha to assist the convenor of the Sabha in convening its meetings, in recording its decisions in a minutes book and also in taking follow up action thereon. The officers of the municipality can attend the meetings of the Sabha as may be required by the Chairperson.

Ward Sabha may appoint, elect or constitute sub-committees of not less than five members for general or specific purposes for effective implementation of schemes, policies or decisions of the Sabha and in furtherance of the rights and responsibilities of the Ward Sabha.

Functions of the Ward Committee/Ward Sabha

A Ward Committee or Ward Sabha is obliged to exercise power and perform functions such as :

(a) rendering assistance in the collection and compilation of details required for formulation of development plans of the municipality;

(b) generating proposals and fixing priority of the development programmes to be implemented in the area of the ward and getting information on the action plans for the next three months;

(c) preparing a list of eligible beneficiaries, in the order of priority, in respect of the beneficiaries oriented schemes from the area of the ward, on the basis of the criteria fixed by the municipality or Government, by identification of most eligible applicants;

(d) rendering assistance in effective implementation of development schemes by providing facilities required locally;

(e) selecting and obtaining detailed information on the development programmes being carried out in the ward and monitoring their implementation vis-a-vis their specifications;

(f) providing and mobilising voluntary labour and contributions in cash and kind for community welfare programmes;
(g) preparing priority list as to the location of street lights, street- or community-water taps, public sanitation units, irrigation facilities and such other public amenity schemes;
(h) discussing and formulating literacy programmes required for the area of the ward, formulating schemes of imparting matters of public interests like cleanliness, preservation of environment and prevention of pollution, and guarding against social evils like corruption, illicit and clandestine transactions;
(i) promoting harmony and unity among various groups of people in the area of the ward and arranging art festivals and sport meets to give expression to the goodwill of the people of the locality;
(j) nominating members to the beneficiary committees proposed by the council;
(k) verifying the eligibility of persons getting various kinds of welfare assistance from Government such as pensions and subsidies;
(l) creating awareness among the people about prompt payment of taxes, fees, rents and other sums due to the municipality;
(m) cooperating with the employees of the municipality in the sanitation arrangements in the area and rendering voluntary service in the removal of garbage;
(n) encouraging the residents to start kitchen gardens and horticulture activities;
(o) identifying the deficiencies in the water supply and street-lightening arrangements in the area and suggesting remedial steps;
(p) identifying the lacunae and lapses in the observance of the rules governing building construction and in the implementation of special planning;
(q) assisting the activities of the parent–teacher associations in the schools in the area; and
(r) assisting the activities of public health centres in the area; and such other functions as may be presented.

Duties of Ward Committees and Ward Sabhas

Ward Committee or Ward Sabha has the following duties and responsibilities:

(a) dissemination of information on development and welfare programmes;

(b) conversing participation in health, literacy and similar development campaigns;

(c) collecting essential socio-economic data;

(d) providing feedback on the performance of development programmes;

(e) resorting to moral persuasion to pay taxes, repay loans, promote environmental cleanliness, maintain social harmony, etc.

(f) mobilising local resources to augment the resources of the municipality;

(g) supervising developmental works as volunteer teams; and

(h) creating arrangements to report quickly the incidence of epidemics, natural calamities, etc.

Rights of Ward Committee or Ward Sabha

The Ward Committee or Ward Sabha has following rights:

(a) to get information from the officials concerned as to the services they will render and the works they proposed to do in the succeeding three months;

(b) to get information on the detailed estimates of the works proposed to be taken;

(c) to know the rationale of every decision of the Council concerning the area of the Ward;

(d) to know the follow up action taken on the decision of the Ward Sabha and Ward Committee and to know the detailed reasons for not implementing any of the decisions; and

(e) to obtain information about detailed town planning schedules, building permits, etc. in the ward.

District Planning Committee

The Government has to constitute in every district a District Planning Committee at district level to consolidate the plans prepared by the Panchayats and the Municipalities in the district and to prepare a draft development plan for the district as a whole. The Committee consists of fifteen members of whom (a), twelve members are elected by and from amongst the elected members of the Panchayats at the district level and of the municipalities in the district in the proportion to the ratio between the population of the rural areas and of the urban areas in the district; (b), the President of the District Panchayat in that district; (c), one person having considerable experience in administration and planning, nominated by the Government; and (d), the District Collector as, ex-officio member. The members are elected under the guidance, supervision and control of the State Election Commission. The President of the District Panchayat is the Chairman and the District Collector is the Secretary to the Committee. The district level officers of the departments of the Government in the district are the Joint Secretaries to the Committee. The members of the House of the People and the Members of the State Legislative Assembly are permanent invitees to the Committee. A member of the Council of States representing the state is also a permanent invitee to the Committee of the district in which he is registered as elector in the electoral roll of any municipality or Panchayat. A member nominated to the State Legislative Assembly is a permanent invitee to the Committee of the district in which he ordinarily resides. Where a member of Parliament or a member of State Legislative Assembly is appointed as Minister or elected as Speaker or Deputy Speaker or appointed as the Government Chief Whip or recognised as leader of the Opposition, he may nominate a person from the area he represents as member to represent him in the committee.

The Committee on Decentralisation of powers recommends that the District Planning Office has to work as the Secretariat of the District Planning Committee. The Town Planning wing in the district and the Development Authorities can form its spatial planning wing while the District Planning Office can serve its socio-economic planning unit. The District Statistical Office along with the offices below it, can work under the DPC to provide it with necessary data base. The National Informatics Centre can serve the DPC with its computer facilities. Thus, the DPC would be made a professionally well-supported organisation.

The functions of the Committee could be listed out as follows:

(a) to chalk out the strategies and prepare action plan in accordance with National and State policies and in keeping with the resource endowments of the district, to bring about balanced development within the district.

(b) to ensure that plans prepared at the Block Panchayat, District Panchayat and Municipality levels are appropriate to that level and the totality of all the places do not have contradictions, duplications or gaps. The DPC will take every effort to bring about an organic integration;

(c) to prepare spatial plans for the district;

(d) to plan for infrastructure development indicating the priorities and the criteria followed for fixing the priorities;

(e) to suggest the criteria for allocation of resources among different sectors for particular groups of local self-government institutions;

(f) to assist the local self-government institutions in preparation of integrated local plans. Model projects which could be adopted by various institutions can be got prepared by experts;

(g) to suggest the measures for the optimum use of natural resources available in the district, upgradation of the environment, employment generation, poverty alleviation with special reference to Scheduled Castes and Scheduled Tribes and women and children;

(h) to prepare a phased plan for provision of basic needs;

(i) to identify the backward and forward linkages required for getting the optimal returns from plan investments;

(j) to coordinate input supplies, marketing arrangements, training and skill upgradation etc. in connection with plan implementation;

(k) to assess the credit requirements of the district and prepare a potential-linked credit plan;

(l) to prepare and update a detailed data base required for socio-economic and spatial planning;

(m) to conduct regular monitoring of plan progress and hold monthly plan review meetings; and

(n) to carry out evaluation studies.

The DPC should have an Advisory Group of top professionals drawn from the Government and non-government sector. It should have the power to ask for expertise in areas required by it and it will be the duty of the Government to assign such experts to it. In order to perform its functions well, the DPC must be authorised to constitute sub-committees, particularly for the development of Scheduled Castes and Scheduled Tribes, development of women and children, spatial planning and infrastructure development, etc. The Committee should render professional assistance to the panchayats and municipalities in the preparation of draft development plans for the respective areas and should have power to direct them to revise the plans. The State Government, while finalising the state plans, should give due regard for the suggestions and priorities given by the District Planning Committee in the draft development plans for the respective districts. The Committee should monitor the plan progress, both qualitatively and quantitatively with special reference to the physical and financial targets attained by the implementation of the approved District Plan and also the State Plan so far as it relates to the district, and should evaluate the programmes implemented.

Metropolitan Planning Committee

The Government has, by notification in the Gazette, to constitute a Metropolitan Planning Committee in a metropolitan area to prepare a draft development plan for such area as a whole. The Committee has to consist of (a), ten members elected by and from amongst themselves the elected members of the municipalities and the Presidents of the village panchayats in the metropolitan area in proportion to the ratio between the population of the municipalities and village panchayats in that area; (b), five members are nominated by the Government of whom one should be an officer of the rank of Secretary to Government or an eminent person having experience in local administration or public administration; one should be an officer not below the rank of Senior Town Planner of the Town Planning Department; one should be an officer not below the rank of Superintending Engineer of Public Works Department; one should be an officer of any Government Department not below the rank of a Deputy Secretary to Government, one should be the Collector of the district in which the metropolitan area is comprised. The officer of the Government not below the rank of Deputy Secretary as nominated by the Government is appointed as the Member Secretary of the Committee. Where the Government feels that representation of the Central or State Government and of any organisation or institution is necessary for carrying out the functions assigned to the Committee, they may provide for the inclusions as invitees of the representatives.

The Committee has to prepare a draft development plan for the metropolitan area as a whole and perform such other functions relating to planning and coordination for the metropolitan area as may be assigned to it by the Government.

The Committee on Decentralisation of Powers has suggested to scrap the Metropolitan Planning Committee. The Committee feels that unless a metropolitan area spans across the jurisdiction of more than one district, there is no need of a Metropolitan Planning Committee. Such a Committee for a single district would only create confusion *vis-a-vis* the functions of the District Planning Committee. However, urbanisation needs to be well anticipated and planned to limit the ills associated with it. Thus, there would be need for spatial planning particularly for zonning infrastructure planning and detailed town planning in areas covering more than one local authority. In such cases, the State Government can be empowered to notify such urban agglomerations and creation create Urban Area Planning Committee consisting of the heads of local authorities within that area and making this body responsible for spatial planning and empowered to prepare the spatial plans under the Town Planning Act. These Committees can be serviced by Town Planners from the District Planning Committee.

High Level Committee

A high level committee is constituted for each metropolitan area. The Committee covering the state capital may be known as the High Level Committee for the capital region. The Committee consists of the Chief Minister, the Ministers in charge of Transport, Water Supply, Finance, Electricity and Public Works, the Chief Secretary to the Government, the Secretaries in charge of Transport, Local Administration, Transport, Public Works, Water Supply and Electricity, the Chairman of the Metropolitan Planning Committee, the Chairman of the District Planning Committee, the members of the House of the People and the State Legislative Assembly, the constituencies represented by whom lie in part or in whole within the metropolitan area, the nominated member of the State Legislative Assembly who is registered as an elector in the electoral roll of any local authority within the metropolitan area, the President of the District Panchayat of the district which the metropolitan area is comprised of, the Mayor of the Municipal Corporation within the metropolitan area and the Chairman of Development Authority in the metropolitan area.

The Committee is provided with the avowed purpose of coordinating and monitoring the urban development activities of the Government and other agencies.

The Committee on Decentralisation of Powers feels that this function can be more effectively done by a DPC sub-committee. The Committee therefore recommends that the High Level Committee may be dissolved and a new Committee be created.

State Development Council

The Committee recommends to constitute a State Development Council on the lines of the National Development Council. The Council consists of the Chief Minister, the Leader of Opposition, the members of the Council of Ministers in the state, the Chairman of the District Planning Committees in the state, the Mayors of the Municipal Corporations, one Municipal Chairman nominated by the Government, the Vice-Chairman of the State Planning Board and the Chief Secretary to the Government. The Chief Minister is the Chairman, the Leader of Opposition is the Vice-Chairman and the Chief Secretary is the Member-Secretary.

The Council has to formulate the development policy concerning local-level and regional development; to harmonise the District Plans and the State Plans; to formulate policy matters necessary for strengthening; and to tackle inter-district issues concerning development.

The Council meets periodically, at least once in six months.

Finance Commission

A Finance Commission has to be constituted in the state in accordance with the provisions of the Constitution. The Commission consists of members not exceeding three including Chairman. The members may be appointed on part time basis. The Chairman and the members are elected from amongst the persons who had experience in public administration or have special knowledge of the finances and accounts of Government and local authorities or have special knowledge and experience in financial matters or have special knowledge of economics.

State Election Commission

The State Election Commission is appointed under the Article 243 of the Constitution under the superintendence, direction and control of the State Election Commission, the District Election Officers can coordinate and supervise all works in connection with the conduct of elections to the municipalities. For every municipality and for every election in a municipality, the State Election Commission, in consultation with the Government, designates or nominates a Returning Officer, who may be an officer of the Government or of a local authority. The Commission may appoint one or more Assistant Returning Officers to assist any Returning Officer in the performance of his functions.

5
Tamil Nadu

The history of Tamil Nadu is very old. It is traced in the olden literature and archaeological findings. The edicts of Ashoka Pillars also refer the Cher, Chola and Pandya emperors. In olden days the area was known as Kumari Kandam or Lemuria. It was later on submerged into the Indian Ocean. The geological and anthropological findings corroborate the fact.

Tamil Nadu has a hoary antiquity. Though early Sangam classics throw vague historical references, only from the Pallavas a recorded history is available. At the end of 11th century, Tamil Nadu was ruled by several dynasties, like the Chalukyas, Cholas and Pandyas. In the two centuries that followed, the imperial Cholas gained paramountcy over South India. Muslims gradually strengthened their position which led to the establishment of the Bahamani sultanate by the middle of the 14th century. At the same time the Vijayanagar kingdom quickly consolidated itself and extended its sway over the whole of South India and at the close of the century, Vijayanagar became the supreme power in South. The Portuguese, the Dutch, the French and the English came in quick succession and established trading centres. Tamil Nadu was one of the first British settlements in India. The State is the successor to the old Madras Presidency which in 1901 covered the bulk of the southern Peninsula. The composite Madras State was later recognised and the present Tamil Nadu was formed.

Tamil Nadu is bounded on north by Andhra Pradesh and Karnataksa, on west by Kerala, on east by the Bay of Bengal and on south by the Indian Ocean. The total area of the state is 130,058 km. consisting of 23 districts.

The economy of the State depends largely on agricultural sector as more than 70 per cent of the population are engaged in agriculture. Tamil Nadu occupies a premier position in the production and executive application of bio-fertiliser. Major industries are cotton textiles, chemical fertilisers, paper and its products, printing and allied industries. Tamil Nadu accounts for nearly one-fourth of the spinning capacity in India. One-fifth of cement and one-tenth of the nation's production of sugar are produced here.

Urban Scenario

Tamil Nadu accounted for about 8.76 per cent of the country's total urban population. The proportion of urban population to total population of the state was more than one-third (34.20 per cent) in 1991. The State is divided into 23 districts. Madras is the district with the highest urban population and with hundred per cent urban, followed by Coimbatore (53.20 per cent) and Nilgiri (49.81 per cent). Dharmapuri (9.41 per cent) is the least urbanised district, preceded by Tiruvannamalai Sambuvarayar (12.10 per cent). Madras (100), Nilgiri (49.81), North Arcot Ambedkar (31.76), Coimbatore (53.20), Madurai (44.99), Kamarajar (37.55), Chindambaranar (41.39), Tirunelveli-Kattabomman (31.72) and Chengai Anna (44.83) are the districts with more than 30 per cent urban content. The level of urbanisation is dispersed. One district falls between 50-60 percent and four show 40-50 per cent and three between 30-40. Seven districts witness urbanisation between 20-30 and four between 10-20 while one is below 10 per cent.

The number of towns has been found increasing over the years. There were 240 towns in 1971 which increased to 245 in 1981 and further to 260 in 1991. The corresponding number of class one towns was 16, 20 and 25 respectively. Majority of the urban population is found in these towns increased from 62.22 (1981) to 65.96 in 1991. The figure in 1971 was 57.74.

The sex ratio in the state was 972 (total) and 951 in urban areas. Chidambarbar (1047) recorded highest sex ratio followed by Tirunelveli (1036), Pasumpon Thevar (1029), Ramanathapuram (1026) and Pudukhottai (1006). In class one cities, Tiruppur (41.55) experienced highest decadal growth, followed by Erode (29.51), Neyveli (27.94) and Chennai (24.99). Chennai is the most populous city. Arcot has the highest sex ratio of 1006, followed by Tirunelveli (1005) and Nagercoil city (1000). Barring Chennai (927), Coimbatore (808), Tiruppur (924), Erode (939) and Neyveli (903) all other class one towns have sex ratio more than the urban state (951).

As regards literacy, the state has 68.1 per cent in total and 60.9 percent in female population. The district of Kanniya Kumari tops in literacy with 78.4 per cent, followed by Madras (72.5), Tirucherappali (71.4), Pudukhotai (70.8), Chidambarnagar (70.7), and Coimbatore (70.6), Madurai (58.9) is least literate preceded by Salem (60.9), Dharma Puri (62.1) and North Arcot (62.8) districts. In towns Nagercoil tops with 80.68, followed by Neyveli (76.22), Thaiyavur (74.79), Coimbatore (74.05), Tirucherappali (73.19), Kumabakonam (73.18), Tuticorin (73.10) and Chennai (72.17).

The state had a host of Municipal Acts for urban governance. Each corporation had a separate Act of its own. The municipalities were governed by the Tamil Nadu District Municipalities Act, 1920. Recently, the State Government has enacted a unified legislation and all other Acts have been repealed.

Demographic Profile

	1971	*1981*	*1991*
Total population (lakh)	–	484.08	558.59
Decadal growth (percentage)	–	–	–
Urban population (lakh)	–	159.52	190.78
Decadal growth (percentage)	–	27.98	19.28
Proportion of urban to total population	–	32.95	34.20
Area (km²)	–	130058.00 (5860.70)	130058.00 (6175.59)
Number of towns	240	245.00	260.00
No. of class I towns	16	20.00	25.00
Urban content (percentage)	57.74	62.22	65.96
Literacy	–	46.76 (63.45)	54.61 (68.11)
Sex ratio		977.00 (956.00)	972.00 (951.00)
Total main workers (lakh)		190.26 (50.04)	227.99 (62.21)
Marginal workers (lakh)		11.72 (1.08)	13.95 (1.39)
Non-workers (lakh)		282.09 (108.39)	316.65 (127.1)
No. of total households (lakh)		102.81 (70.24)	125.43 (41.09)
No. of Occupied Residential Houses (lakh)		99.83 (31.04)	124.13 (40.43)

Figures in parentheses denote urban.

I. Constitution

The Governor may constitute any local area as Town Panchayat, where the population is estimated at not less than 20,000 and the annual income of such area is not less than 30 lakhs of rupees; a Municipality, where the population is not less than 30,000 and the annual income is not less than 50 lakhs of rupees an a Municipal Corporation, where the population is estimated at not less than 5 lakhs and the annual income of the area is not less than 30 crores of rupees.

Every municipality is a body corporate and has perpetual succession and a common seal. It can acquire, hold and transfer property or enter into contracts.

Municipal Authorities

For the efficient performance of the functions of the municipality, there are following authorities in a municipality:

(a) a Council,
(b) a Chairperson,
(c) Standing Committee,
(d) Wards Committee, and
(e) a Commissioner.

Composition

The municipal administration vests in the council. The council consists of:

1. Elected councillors including Chairperson; and
2. Ex-officio Members:
   (a) members of the House of the People and members of the State Legislative Assembly representing the constituency comprising the whole or any part of the municipality; and
   (b) the members of the Council of States, who are registered as elector within the area of the municipality.

The ex-officio members are entitled to take part in the proceedings of the council but can not take part in voting.

Reservation

In every municipal council seats are reserved for :

(a) the persons belonging to the Scheduled Castes and the

Scheduled Tribes in such proportion as their population shares in the total population;

(b) the women belonging to the Scheduled Castes and the Scheduled Tribes from among the seats reserved for these classes to the tune of not less than one-third of the total number of their seats; and

(c) women to the tune of not less than one-third of the total number of seats in a municipality.

The office of Mayor of the corporations is reserved for the persons belonging to the Scheduled Castes or Scheduled Tribes. The number of offices so reserved bear the same proportion to the total number of offices as their population in all the corporations bears to the total population of all the corporations in the state. Where no office of Mayor can be reserved for these classes based on the total percentage of population, one office of the Mayor of a corporation having the highest percentage of population of these castes is reserved for women belonging to these classes out of the total number of offices reserved for women.

At least one-third of the total number of office of the Mayors are reserved for women.

The offices of the Chairperson of the municipalities are reserved for the persons belonging to the Scheduled Castes and the Scheduled Tribes and the number so reserved bears the same proportion to the total number of offices as the population of these classes in all the municipalities bears to the total population of all the municipalities. One-third of offices reserved for these castes is reserved for the women belonging to these classes.

The one-third offices are reserved for the women. The offices of the Chairperson of the Town Panchayats are reserved for the persons belonging to the Scheduled Castes and the Scheduled Tribes in the proportion of their population in all the Panchayats in the total population of all the panchayats in the state. One-third of such offices reserved are reserved for the women of these classes. one-third of the offices are reserved for women.

Election of Councillors

For the purpose of election of councillors, the Commissioner of the municipality in consultation with the council prepares a draft proposal for delimitation of the wards and publishes in prescribed manner for objections. After disposing off the objections, the Commissioner forwards the proposal to the Director, whc can either confirms the same or modifies the proposal and directs the Commissioner for publishing the same. Any modification or revision to delimitation of wards is made in five years before the general election to the municipality. Only one member is elected for each ward. If any person has been elected for two or more wards, he has to initimate the Commissioner within seven days, the ward for which he chooses to serve. In default of such intimation, the Commissioner can determine by lot and notify the ward for which such person can serve.

Disqualification of Candidates

A person is not qualified for election as a Chairman of a council if:

(a) his name is not included in the electoral roll of the municipality;

(b) he has not completed his twenty-one years of age;

(c) he is an officer or employee of the Central or State Government or any local authority, remunerated by either salary or fees or honoraria;

(d) he has any share or interest in any contract or engagement with, by or on behalf of the municipality;

(e) he has been sentenced by a Criminal Court to transportation or to imprisonment for a period of more than six months and disqualifies for five years from the date of the expiration of the sentence;

(f) he is convicted of an offence punishable under the Protection of Civil Rights Act, 1955, and disqualified for five years from the date of such conviction;

(g) he is of unsound mind and he is declared so by the competent court;

(h) he is an undischarged insolvent or an applicant to be adjudicated as an insolvent;

(i) he is directly or indirectly in a subsisting contract made with or any work being done for, the municipal council except as a shareholder in a company;

(j) he is a person convicted of an offence punishable under the Act or under the Indian Penal Code;

(k) he is a representative or office bearer of any association or union representing any section of municipal establishment or any class of municipal employees;

(l) he is already a councillor whose term of office does not expire before his fresh election can take effect, or has already been elected as a councillor whose term of office has not yet commenced;

(m) he is disqualified to stand for being elected as a member of the Legislative Assembly or a Member of the Parliament;

(n) he is a person having held an office under the Central or State Government or a local body has been dismissed from office for corruption or for disloyalty to the state; and

(o) he is in arrears of any kind due by him to the municipality upto and inclusive of the previous year.

Disqualifications of the Chairman or Councillors

The Chairman or a Councillor ceases to hold his office, if he:

(a) is sentenced by a Criminal Court to transportation or to imprisonment for a period more than six months. He is disqualified for the five years from the date of expiration of the sentence;

(b) is convicted of an offence punishable under the Protection of Civil Rights Act, 1955;

(c) becomes of unsound mind;

(d) applies to be adjudicated as an insolvent or is an insolvent;

(e) acquires any interest in any subsisting contract made with, or work being done, for the council except as a shareholder in a company;

(f) is employed as paid legal practitioner on behalf of the council or accepts employment as legal practitioner against the council;

(g) becomes a representative or office bearer of any association or union representing the employees of the municipality;

(h) loses any of the qualification for having been elected as a councillor or Chairman;

(i) ceases to reside in the municipality;

(j) fails to pay arrears of any kind due by him to the municipality within three months after a bill or notice has been served upon him or where the service of any bill or notice is not required within three months after a notice requiring payment of the arrear;

(k) ceases to be a voter in the municipality in which he was elected; and

(l) absents himself from the meetings of the council for a period of three consecutive months reckoned from the date of commencement of his term of office, or of the last meeting which he attended.

Whenever the allegedly disqualified person does not admit the allegation or he himself is in doubt whether or not he has been disqualified, such Chairman or councillor or any other councillor may, and the Commissioner at the request of the council or Chairperson or a direction from the Government has to apply to the Principal District Judge in which the municipality is situated. The Judge after making necessary inquiry determines whether or not such person is disqualified. Pending such decision, the Chairperson or the Councillor is entitled to act as he was not disqualified. Any councillor or Chairperson may and the Commissioner, at the request of the council, or on direction from the Government, can appeal to the High Court against the decision. No such appeal can be entertained after the expiry of thirty days from the date of decision unless the High Court is satisfied otherwise.

Restoration

The Chairman or a councillor when becomes disqualified on account of his absence in meetings, the matter is reported by the Commissioner at the ordinary meeting and the Council may at that meeting restore such person on application to office. The council however, may consider the restoration on application made by him and such restoration cannot be made for more than twice during his tenure of office.

When a person ceases to be councillor or Chairman under clause (a) and (b) he can be restored to office for such portion of his period for which he was elected as may remain unexpired at the date of restoration if and when the conviction, sentence or order is annulled on appeal or revision or disqualification caused by the conviction or sentence is removed by an order of the State Election Commissioner. Any person elected to fill the vacancy in the interim period has to vacate office on such restoration.

Resignation

The Chairman may resign his office by giving notice in person and in writing to the Commissioner. The Commissioner after verifying the bonafides of notice, convene a special meeting of the council within seven days from the date of receipt of such notice and places it before the council. The meeting is presided over by the Deputy Chairperson or in his absence by any one of the councillors elected by the councillors from amongst themselves. The resignation takes effect from the date on which it is placed before the special meeting of the council.

The Deputy Chairperson or any councillor may resign his office by giving notice in person and in writing to the Chairperson. The Chairperson after verifying the bonafides of notice, within a period of five days accepts the resignation. The resignation takes effect from the date on which it is accepted by the Chairperson.

Election Petition

An election can be questioned only by an election petition presented to the Principal District Judge, within 45 days from the date of the publication of the result of the elections. The petition may be presented by any candidate at such election, or by an elector of the ward concerned, or by any returned candidate. The petition should contain a concise statement of the material facts on which petitioner relies. If the Principal District Judge is of opinion that on the date of his election a returned candidate was not qualified or was disqualified to be chosen as councillor or that any corrupt practice has been committed by a returned candidate or his agent or by any other person with the consent of returned candidate or his agent or any nomination paper has been improperly rejected or that result of the election has been materially effected by improper acceptance of any nomination or by any corrupt practice or by any improper acceptance or refusal of any vote or reception of any vote or by the non-compliance with the provisions of the Act.

Duties and Powers of Councillor

Any Councillor may call the attention of the Commissioner or the Chairperson to any neglect in the execution of any municipal work. Every councillor has the right to interpellate the Chairperson in any council meeting as matters connected with the municipal administration. Every councillor has access during the office hours to the records of the municipality after giving notice to the Commissioner. The Commissioner may for the reasons given in writing forbid such access. The councillor may appeal against such an order of the Commissioner to the Chairperson and any person aggrieved by the order of the Chairperson may refer an appeal to the Director whose decision thereon is final.

Chairperson/Mayor

Every municipality has a Chairperson directly elected by the persons. The term of office of the Chairperson is five years from the date notified by the State Election Commissioner. A casual vacancy in the office of the Chairperson is filled by a fresh election and a person so elected holds the office for remainder of the term. The Chairperson is an ex-officio member of the council. The Chairperson is an ex-officio member of every Standing Committee, Wards Committee and of other Committees except Taxation Appeals Committee/Tribunal but is not eligible to be elected as the Chairman of any Standing Committee or Wards Committee. He has no right to vote at any meeting of the Standing Committee or any Wards Committee.

The Chairperson convenes and presides over all the meetings of the council. He exercises all the powers and performs all the duties conferred or imposed on him. He coordinates with the Commissioner and the Committees constituted under the Act. He has the power to inspect any municipal work, project or other schedules. The Chairperson can carry out such work and perform such duties as entrusted to him by the Government.

Deputy Chairperson/Deputy Mayor

Every municipality has a Deputy Chairperson who is elected by and from amongst the councillors. The term of the office of the Deputy Chairperson is five years from the date notified by the State Election Commission for assumption of office. The Deputy Chairperson is deemed to have vacated his office on cessation as a councillor.

The Chairperson may in writing delegate any of his powers and functions with the approval of the council to the Deputy Chairperson. In the event of any vacancy in the office of the Chairperson by reason of his death, resignation or removal or otherwise, the Deputy Chairperson can act as Chairperson until the date on which a new Chairperson is elected to fill the vacancy and enters upon the office. When the Chairperson is unable to discharge his functions owing to absence or illness or for any other cause, the Chairperson may in writing, authorise the Deputy Chairperson to discharge his functions until the date on which the Chairperson resumes his duties.

In case if the Chairperson fails to authorise the Deputy Chairperson and if the Chairperson continuously absents for more than 15 days owing to illness or for any other reason, the powers and functions of the Chairperson are devolved on the Deputy Chairperson till such time the Chairperson resumes his duties.

During the first meeting of the council or from time to time, the council may nominate from among the councillors, a panel of three councillors and one of whom can exercise the powers and performs the duties of the Chairperson until the Chairperson or Deputy Chairperson resumes his duties.

Honoraria, Fees or Allowances

From out of the municipal funds, such honoraria, fees or allowances as may be determined by the Government may be paid to Chairperson, Deputy Chairperson and the councillors. The municipality places at the disposal of the Chairperson annually by way of sumptuary allowance a sum not more than fifty thousand rupees. The limit may differ for different types of municipalities.

Removal of Councillor or Chairperson

The councillors consisting of more than one half of the total strength of elected councillors as on date may present a written representation, signed by them, through any two of them to the Director for the removal of Chairperson or any councillor on the ground that the Chairperson or councillor wilfully omits or refuses to carry out or disobey or act in contradiction of the Act or abuses his office or any power vested in him. The Director may in writing, get the views of the Chairperson or councillor on the representation. On receiving the replies, if the Director finds the representation baseless, he may inform his decision to the councillors who have signed the representation. If the Director is satisfied that the representation has some base, he nominates an officer to convene the meeting for consideration of the matter at a time appointed by him within one month from the date of his appointment. A clear seven days notice of meeting is given to all elected councillors including Chairperson. If three-fourths of the total strength of the elected councillors on date are present, the officer reads the motion and puts the motion to vote. If the motion is carried out by three-fourths, of the total strength of the elected councillors by giving their approval, the officer forwards a report to the Director with a copy of the motion passed by the council, who in turn, forwards the same to the Government. The Government within fifteen days from the receipt of the report, give the Chairperson or the councillor a reasonable opportunity to make his representation within the period specified by the Government in the notice. The Government after considering the representation may notify the removal of the Chairperson or councillor or allow him to continue.

If the meeting could not be held for want of quorum, or if the motion is not carried out, the motion is deemed to have been lapsed and no notice of any subsequent motion can be entertained until the expiry of six months from the date of meeting. No motion expressing removal against any Chairperson or councillor can be entertained till the expiry of six months from the date of assumption of office or where the term of office is less than six months.

No-Confidence Against Deputy Chairperson

A motion expressing no-confidence against the Deputy Chairperson can be in writing signed by not less than one-third of total elected councillors on date and delivered by any two of them to the Director. The Director nominates an officer to convene a special meeting of the council. The officer has to convene the meeting at any time appointed by him within 15 days of his appointment. A clear seven days notice of such meeting is given to all the elected councillors including Chairperson. If more than two-third of the elected councillors on date are present, the officer reads the motion and puts to vote. If the motion is carried out by more than two-third of the total strength of elected councillors on date by giving their approval, the officer forwards a report to the Director with a copy of the motion passed by the council, who in turn, forwards the same to the Government. The Government within 15 days notifies the removal of the Deputy Chairperson, who ceases to hold office but continues to be a member of the council.

If the meeting could not be held for want of quorum or if the motion is not carried out, the motion is deemed to have been elapsed and no notice of any subsequent motion expressing no-confidence in the same Deputy Chairperson can be entertained until the expiry of six months from the date of meeting. No motion of want of confidence against a Deputy Chairperson can be entertained till the expiry of six months from the date of assumption of office or where the term of office is less than six months.

Functions

The council has both obligatory and discretionary functions.

Obligatory Functions

(a) Construction and maintenance of roads, culverts and drains;

(b) Execution and maintenance of water supply schemes required for domestic, industrial or commercial purposes, except in the municipality where there is a separate authority to which such functions are assigned;

(c) Protection of public ponds and fountains;

(d) Maintenance of sewerage and drainage schemes except in the municipality where there is a separate authority for the purpose;

(e) Destruction of stray dogs;

(f) Mosquito control;

(g) Regulation of sale of meat, fish and other perishable food items and sale of other consumer items;

(h) Regulation of dangerous trades or trade practices;

(i) Licencing of eating establishments;

(j) Disposal of unclaimed corpses or carcasses of animals;

(k) Estabalishment of public comfort stations, latrine and bathing places;

(l) Construction and maintenance of parks, gardens, play grounds, traffic islands in the urban areas;

(m) Opening and maintenance of public burial and burning grounds and electric crematoria;

(n) Registration of briths and deaths;

(o) Installation of street lights and their maintenance;

(p) Providing parking places for vehicles;

(q) Public health matters including vaccination and innoculation;

(r) Maintenance of public markets, shopping complexes, bus stands, rest houses;

(s) Solid waste management;

(t) Prevention or removal of obstructions and projections in or upon streets, bridges and other public places;

(u) Numbering and naming of streets;

(v) Regulation of hoardings and advertisements, put up for public view on public or private land;

(w) Civic reception to persons of distinction; and
(x) Organisation of fairs and exhibitions.

Discretionary Functions

The council may carry out any work or perform any of the functions or implement the schemes delegated to the council by the Government in relation to following matters:

(a) Urban planning including town planning;
(b) Regulation of land use and construction of buildings;
(c) Regulation of slaughter house and tanneries;
(d) Planning for economic and social development;
(e) Fire services;
(f) Urban forestry, protection of the environment and promotion of ecological aspects;
(g) Safeguarding the interests of weaker sections of society, including the handicapped and mentally retarded;
(h) Slum improvement and upgradation;
(i) Urban poverty alleviation;
(j) Promotion of cultural, educational and aesthetic aspects; and
(k) Cattle pounds, prevention of cruelty to animals.

Taxation

It is mandatory for the council to levy following taxes :

(a) property Tax,
(b) water Tax,
(c) sewerage Tax,
(d) education Tax,
(e) advertisement Tax, and
(f) a duty on transfer of property.

Imposition of Taxes

For the purpose of imposing a tax, the council has to pass a resolution determining the levy of tax specifying the rate and the date from which the tax is to be levied. A proposal to levy or increase the rate of any tax or to effect any change in the mode of levy or the manner of collection has to be placed before the council and the council after due consideration passes necessary resolution approving or modifying the proposal. The resolution passed by the council is published calling for objections and suggestions in regard to proposed levy, increase or change in the mode or manner of collection within a prescribed period. After disposing of the objections, the council passes necessary resolution approving the proposal with or without modification.

Property Tax

The property tax is levied on all buildings and lands within the municipality. In the case of reassessment or general revision of any property tax, the owner or the occupier of any building or land has to furnish to the Commissioner within the prescribed period a return containing details for the purpose. If any one fails to furnish a return or furnishes an incomplete or incorrect return, the Commissioner can cause an inspection to be made and also to make local inquiries and prepares a return and a copy of the same is furnished to the owner or occupier. On receipt of a return or on the basis of a prepared one and after considering the objections, the Commissioner determines the tax payable and sends an intimation to that effect to the person concerned. In the case of failure to furnish a return, the Commissioner, in addition to the tax determined directs the owner or occupier to pay by way of penalty a sum of rupees two hundred and fifty or five per cent of the property tax determined, whichever is higher.

The Government prescribes the minimum and maximum rates of basic property tax for the building or land having regard to the existing property tax, the value of the building and land and the use of the building and in regard to additional basic property tax for every building with reference to its location and type of construction. The Government can prescribe the concession with regard to age of the building.

The basic property tax for every building relates to the carpet area of the building and its usage. In carpet area open verandah, open courtyard or any other open space is not included. The additional property tax relates to location and type of construction of the building. The location of the building is classified as : arterial roads, bus-route roads, leading to arterial roads and main roads, bus-route roads other than earlier ones and roads and streets in primarily residential colonies. The type of construction is classified into : thatched or tiled roof, reinforced concrete cement roof, reinforced concrete cement roof with mosaic or ceramic tiled flooring and granite and marble flooring and walls.

For the purpose of levy of property tax, every building is assessed together with its site and other adjacent premises occupied as an appurtenance thereto. The basic property tax is calculated at the rate fixed by the council. The additional basic property tax is calculated at the rate fixed by the council and added to the basic property tax. On the quantum of amount arrived at by adding the above two, concession in respect of the building at the rate fixed by the council is deducted and the amount thus arrived at is the property tax payable for every half year.

Where there is any land without any building situated within the municipal limit, the Commissioner determines the property tax payable for such land at the rate fixed by the council. In case of any land with building and if the extent of the land left vacant is twice the plinth area of the building, the Commissioner determines the tax on vacant land which exceeds twice the plinth area of the building at the rate fixed by the council. No property tax however, can be levied if the extent of such land with or without any building thereon does not exceed two thousand and four hundred square feet.

The Commissioner issues a property tax book containing all details of the building or land and the property tax payable.

The general revision of the assessment of property tax is made once in five years.

The council may exempt any building having a carpet area not exceeding one hundred square feet, constructed with mud walls and thatched roof, from the levy of property tax. The places set apart for public worship and either actually so used or used for no other purpose, choultries for which no rent is charged and choultries the rent charged for which is used exclusively for charitable purpose, buildings used for educational purpose including hostels and places used for sheltering the destitute or animals and orphanages, homes and schools for deaf and dumb, asylum for the aged and fallen women and other institutions run purely on philanthropic lines, ancient monuments, charitable hospitals and dispensaries, hospitals and dispensaries maintained by railway administration, burial and burning grounds and the bed of any river or canal and which do not provide any income are exempt from the property tax. However, it is open to the council to collect any service charges for providing the civic amenities and for any other general or special services rendered.

Water Tax

The council may levy water tax at a rate not exceeding 35 per cent of the property tax as the council may determine.

Sewerage Tax

The council may levy sewerage tax at a rate not exceeding 15 per cent of the property tax.

Education Tax

The council may levy education tax at the rate not exceeding five per cent of the property tax.

Advertisement Tax

Every person who erects, exhibits, fixes or retains upon or over any land, building or wall, hoardings or structure any advertisement or who displays any advertisement to public view has to pay on every advertisement a tax at the rate determined by the council.

Duty on Transfer of Property

The duty on transfer of property is charged in the form of a surcharge on the duty imposed on every instrument which relates to immovable property. The rate should not exceed five per cent on the amount specified below against such instrument.

(a)	Sale of immovable property	— The market value of the property;
(b)	Exchange of immovable property	— The market value of the property of the greater value as set forth in the instrument;
(c)	Gift of immovable property	— The market value of the property;
(d)	Mortgage with transfer of possession of immovable property	— The amount secured by the mortgage as set forth in the instrument; and
(e)	Lease in perpetuity of immovable property	— An amount equal to one-sixth of the whole amount or value of the rents which would be paid or delivered in respect of the first fifty years of the lease, as set forth in the instrument.

Taxation Appeals Committee

There is a Taxation Appeals Committee for hearing and disposing of an appeal preferred by any person who is not satisfied with the assessment order made by the Commissioner. For every Town Panchayat, the Committee consists of the Chairperson of the council who acts as the Chairman, and other members as notified by the Government from among the members of the Town Panchayat. For every municipality, the Committee consists of the Chairperson of the council, who acts as Chairman and four elected councillors elected by the council.

An appeal against the decision of the Taxation Appeals Committee may be filed within thirty days from the date of the order to the Principal District Judge. The appeal can be entertained by the Principal District Judge only if the appellant has deposited with the Town Panchayat or the municipality the entire amount of tax as decided by the Taxation Appeals Committee and continues to deposit till the disposal of the appeal by the Principal District Judge.

Taxation Appeals Tribunal

There is one or more Taxation Appeals Tribunals for the corporation for hearing and disposing of any appeal preferred by any person who is not satisfied with the assessment order made by the Commissioner. The Tribunal consists of a Judicial Officer who is or has been a Civil Judge. The salary and other allowances payable to Tribunal are borne from the funds of the corporation. The Tribunal has to dispose off the appeal within five months from the date of filing of the appeals. Any person preferring an appeal may either appear in person or through an authorised agent before the Tribunal. An appeal against the decision of the Tribunal may be filed within 30 days from the date of the order to the Principal District Judge.

Tolls, Licence, Fees etc.

The council may levy tolls in respect of any road or bridge made or repaired by it. No person can carry on any trade or business without the licence granted by the Commissioner. The council may determine the licence fees within the prescribed minimum and maximum rates and can review once in three years. Any person desiring to keep a bird or animal has to obtain a licence from the Commissioner. All markets whether public or private can be run on a licence issued by the council.

No enclosed place or building can be used for public resort or entertainment within the municipal limit other than in a corporation limit without a licence by the Commissioner.

The council may levy charges on every motor vehicle entering into any pilgrim or tourist resorts in any municipal area.

The Commissioner may for reasons to be recorded restore or suspend the licence granted. Anybody aggrieved by the order of the Commissioner in refusing to grant or renew a licence or cancelling or suspending a licence may appeal to the Director within 30 days from the receipt of the order appealled against.

Building Regulations

Any person intend to construct or reconstruct a building has to sent to the Commissioner an application in writing for approval of the site together with a site plan of the land and an application for permission to execute the work together with a ground plan, elevations and sections of the building and a specification of the work. The Commissioner cannot grant permission to construct or reconstruct a building unless and until he has approved the site in accordance with the Tamil Nadu Town and Country Planning Act, 1971. The construction or reconstruction of a building can not began unless and until the Commissioner has granted permission for the execution of the work. In receipt of an application, the Commissioner has to grant the permission within 30 days. Any person objecting to an order passed by the Commissioner may within a period of 45 days prefer an appeal to the Government.

Where the construction or reconstruction or modification is commenced or completed in contravention, the owner is liable to a penalty of an amount not exceeding rupees ten thousand and in case of a continuing contravention, a further sum not exceeding 50 rupees per square feet every day during the period of contravention.

In hill areas, no person other than the Central or State or local authority can construct or reconstruct a building on any land or put to use any agricultural land to any non-agricultural purpose or carry out any engineering or mining or other allied operations on any land within the area of the hill station without a licence granted by the Government. Every application for a licence can be submitted to the Commissioner. The Commissioner after examining the application forwards the application to the Committee for Architectural and Aesthetic Aspect. The Government may set up such a committee for all the hill stations in a district with officials and non-officials as its members. The committee examines the application and forwards to the Government, which may grant or refuse a licence.

The Commissioner can grant licence for construction and reconstruction of residential buildings on any land within the hill areas having plinth area not exceeding two hundred and fifty square metres in the ground floor and in the first floor in the aggregate or in the case of improvement or enlargement of an existing residential building the construction of which does not exceed two hundred and fifty square metre.

Any person aggrieved by an order of the Commissioner may within sixty days prefer an appeal to the Government. The Government after hearing the appellant may pass an order. The order of the Government is final.

Commissioner or Executive Officer

There is a Commissioner for each municipal corporation and for each municipality who is appointed by the Government. For each Town Panchayat, there is an Executive Officer who is appointed by the Director.

All the executive powers for the purpose of carrying out the provisions of the Act vest in the Commissioner. The Commissioner is responsible for the custody of all the records of the municipality. He may delegate any of the powers, duties or functions conferred or imposed upon or vested in him to the holder of any municipal office. The Commissioner may in cases of emergency direct the execution of any work or the doing of any act and the immediate execution or doing of which is necessary for the service or safety of the public and may direct that the expenses of executing such work are paid from the municipal fund.

The Commissioner is the appointing authority for all Class IV posts and to the posts of Class II and Class III as delegated to him by the Government.

The Commissioner may without the sanction of the council incur petty contingent expenditure incidental to the municipal administration, not exceeding the amount notified by the Government. The Commissioner has to report any such expenditure and the reasons therefor to the council at its next meeting.

The Commissioner is entitled to take part in the proceedings of the council or standing committee or any other committee but can not vote.

Municipal Establishment

The municipal establishment consists of the following classes of officers:

(a) Class I — All Heads of Departments in the municipality;

(b) Class II — All Officers who are next in rank immediately to Class I Officers;

(c) Class III— All others appointed to serve under the municipality; and

(d) Class IV— All persons holding posts in the service classified by the Government as basic service.

All appointments to the posts included in Class I are made by the Government. Appointments to the posts in Class IV and to the posts in Class II and Class III as delegated by the Government are made by the Commissioner. A Selection Committee comprising of the Chairperson, Commissioner and other members notified by the council, selects persons for appointment to the posts included in Class III and Class IV. Town Panchayats have only Class III and IV employees.

Every appointment to any post included in Class I and Class II are made from the list of candidates selected by the State Public Service Commission.

The Director can fix the cadre strength for all municipalities taking into consideration the financial position of the municipalities and municipal services to be rendered and other local conditions. The total expenditure on the establishment however, should not exceed 45 per cent of the total income of municipality. The cadre strength is reviewed once in every five years. All appointments are made according to the cadre strength. The Director may on the request of Commissioner and based on any resolution by the council, by an order permit the council to make appointment in variation to the cadre strength. The council may, with the prior approval of the Government, appoint any person on a contract basis for particular purpose and for a particular period.

Municipal Service

The Government may constitute common municipal services and frame rules for the employees of the municipalities, namely:

(a) all Municipal Corporations,

(b) all Municipalities, and

(c) all Town Panchayats.

The Government have power to transfer any officer or servant of the municipality to any other municipality and to issue general or special direction for the purpose of giving due effect to any transfer.

Municipal Fund

All moneys received by a municipality are kept in a fund called Municipal Fund. All grants, loans, advances or contributions made by the Government are kept in the fund.

Any expenditure from the municipal fund is made only for the purpose and services within the municipal area.

The council may with the previous sanction of the Government and in pursuance of any resolution passed at a special meeting borrow money by way of debentures by raising loans or by way of raising loans from the public.

Sinking Fund

The municipality maintains sinking fund for the repayment of money borrowed or debentures issued. Sufficient sum is paid in quarterly instalments for making payments. All moneys paid into the sinking fund are invested and applied by the Commissioner.

Budget

The Commissioner, in consultation with the Chairperson and Wards Committees and in accordance with the guidelines issued by the Government, prepares in prescribed form on or before the first day of January every year a budget estimate of income and expenditure of the municipality for the next financial year. Such an estimate is placed before the council with the approval of the Standing Committee on or before the 20th day of January each year. The Commissioner may append with the Budget Estimate a report indicating whether water supply and disposal of swerage, scavenging, transporting and disposal of wastes and street lighting are being provided in a subsidised manner and if so, the extent of the subsidy, the source from which the subsidy was met and the sections or category of local population who were the beneficiaries of such subsidy. The council in a special meeting to be convened for the purpose considers the proposal contained in the budget estimates and approves the same with or without modifications on or before the end of February of each year. A copy of the approved budget estimate is forwarded to the Director.

If the Commissioner is of the opinion that the budget estimate as approved by the council contravenes any provision of the Act or any order passed by the Government, he can refer the budget estimate to the Director. The Director directs the council to rectify the defects in the budget estimate. When the council fails to rectify the defects as pointed by the Director, the Commissioner gives effect to the budget estimate as suggested by the Director.

The Commissioner makes arrangements to publish in one prominent local Tamil newspaper the important features of the budget and the details of the work programmes not later than 31st day of July of that financial year.

The council may pass a supplemented budget estimate for the purpose of meeting any special or unforeseen expenditure arising during the financial year.

Audit

The Government appoint auditors for auditing the accounts of receipts and expenditure of the municipal fund. The Government may for any special reason cause the accounts to be audited by qualified auditors for one or more years. A copy of the audit report is placed before the council every year and a copy of such report is also sent to the Director within the prescribed limit.

Property and Works

The council may accept any sum of money from individuals or trusts on issuing a report by the Commissioner. The council may acquire any land or building, the value of which does not exceed the amount as notified by the Government.

The Government may, with the consent of the council, transfer to the municipality the management of any institution or the execution of any work.

The council may dispose of any movable property. No sale of any land or any immovable property can be made by the council. The council may grant licence to any person for use and occupation of any land or building for a period not exceeding three years on payment of prescribed fees and such licence can not be extended or renewed after three year period is over. In the case of licence granted for a period not exceeding one year, the licence fee is paid at the time of granting the licence. In the case of licence granted for a period not exceeding two years, the licence fee for the first year is paid at the time of granting and the fee for the second year is equivalent to the fee for the first year with ten per cent of such fee and is paid at the time of granting, the fee for the second year is the fee for the first year with ten per cent of that and is paid at the beginning of the second year. In the case of licence granted for a period not exceeding three years, the fee for the first year is paid at the time of granting, the fee for the second year is the fee for the first year with 10 per cent of that is paid at the beginning of the second year and the fee for the third year is fee for the second year with fifteen per cent thereof and is paid at the beginning of the third year.

The Commissioner has to maintain an assets register which contains particulars regarding lands and buildings together with the persons in whose favour the licence is granted and other details. The up-to-date copy of the list of assets is placed annually before the council and a copy of such list is also kept in the office of the Regional Director and the Director.

Rules, Regulations and Bye-Laws

The Government may make rules for carrying out the municipal administration in the state. All rules made can be reviewed by the Government at least once in every ten years and necessary alterations and modifications be made to meet the prevailing contingencies. All rules are published in the Government Gazette.

The council may with the approval of the Director make bye-laws and regulations. All regulations and bye-laws are published in the prescribed manner in the District Gazette. In case of default by the council to frame adequate regulations or bye-laws, the Government can direct the council to act accordingly and council is obliged to follow guidelines.

Special Officer

The Government may appoint District Collector or a senior officer of the Indian Administrative Service as a Special Officer of a municipality to exercise the powers and perform the functions of any municipality where there is no elected body of a council or where the council is dissolved by the Government or where the new municipality is constituted by amalgamating two or more local bodies. Such a Special Officer can hold office for a period of six months from the date of his appointment or till the newly elected councillors assume office. The Commissioner exercises his powers and perform his functions subject to the control and superintendence of the Special Officer.

Control

The Government may either on their own motion or on an application direct the council or the Commissioner to produce any record, plan, statement, accounts, statistics or any other document or to furnish any information. In any case if it appears to the Government that any such proceeding or decision or order passed by the council should be modified, annulled, reversed or remitted for reconsideration, they may pass orders accordingly. However, before passing any such order, the Government has to give reasonable opportunity to the council to make a representation against the proposed action. The Government may authorise the Director, Regional Director or any other officer to inspect or examine any office or work relating to any municipality.

The District Collector may in any municipality other than Municipal Corporations call for any document, require any councillor or Commissioner to furnish any return, plan, estimate, statement, accounts or statistics. If it appears to the District Collector that the Commissioner of a municipality has made default in carrying out any resolution of the council, the District Collector can direct the Commissioner to implement the resolution in accordance with the rules. On receipt of the reply from the Commissioner, the District Collector sends a report to the Government with a copy of same to the council. The District Collector may in case of emergency in a municipality direct for execution of any work which the council or the Commissioner is empowered to execute and the immediate execution is necessary for safety of the public and may direct that the expenses of executing such works incurred are paid from the municipal fund.

Dissolution of Council

If in the opinion of the Government, the municipality is not competent to perform or persistently makes default in performing duties or the meeting of the council could not be conducted for reasons beyond the control of the Chairperson and the affairs of the municipality could not be carried on in accordance with the Act and a report to that effect has been received from the Chairperson by the Government, the Government may dissolve the municipality from a specified date and direct that the municipality be reconstituted with effect from the date not later than six months from the date of dissolution. Before notifying the dissolution, the Government has to communicate to the council the grounds on which they propose to do so, fix a period not less than thirty days for the council to show cause against the proposal and consider its objections or explanations.

With the dissolution, all the members of the council as well as the Chairperson and the Deputy Chairperson deem to have vacated their offices. All the functions of the council, of the Chairperson and of the Committees except the Taxation Appeals Committee are exercised and performed by the Special Officer. The reconstituted council can continue to the remainder of the term.

II
Wards Committee

The Wards Committees are constituted in municipalities having population of three lakhs or more. Each Wards Committee consists of contiguous wards. It consists of all the councillors elected from the wards. One of the members elected from amongst themselves becomes the Chairman of the Wards Committee. Each committee has a separate office located within the territorial limits of a Wards Committee. The term of the Wards Committee and the Chairman and members is coterminous with the term of the council. The staff for each Wards Committee is fixed in accordance with the norms fixed by the Government.

Finance Commission

There is a provision to constitute the State Finance Commission to review the financial position of the municipalities and make recommendations to the Governor in accordance with the terms of reference mentioned in the constitution.

Appendix-I

Constitution of Municipalities

States	*Transitional Area*	*Smaller Urban Area*	*Larger Urban Area*
Andhra Pradesh	Nagar Panchayat (Population 25,000)	Municipality	Municipal Corporation
Karnataka	Town Panchayat (Population 10,000-20,000)	Municipal Council (20,000 - 3 Lakhs)	Municipal Corporation (More than 3 Lakhs, Population density 3000 sq. km. Revenue Rs. 6 Crore per annum)
Kerala	Town Panchayat (Upto 20,000 popu.)	Municipal Council (20,000 - 1 Lakh)	Municipal Corporation (1 Lakh and above)
Tamil Nadu	Town Panchayat Population - 20,000 Income Rs. 30 Lakh	Municipalities Population 30,000 Income Rs. 50 Lakh	Municipal Corporation Population 5 Lakh Income Rs. 30 Crore.

Appendix-II

Composition of Municipalities

States	*Town Panchayat*	*Municipality*	*Municipal Corporation*
Andhra Pradesh	Elected–Determined by the Government Coopted Experts–1 Ex-officio–MPs, MLAs Coopted–1 Minority	Elected–Determined by the Government Coopted –2-3 Ex-officio–MPs, MLAs Coopted–1 Minority	Elected–Hyderabad–66 Secunderabad–28 Other Cities–determined by Govt. Ex-officio–MPs, MLAs Coopted Experts–5 Minorities–2
Karnataka	Elected–11-20	Elected–23-35 Nominated–Experts, Social Workers–5 Ex-officio–MPs, MLAs	Elected–30-100 Nominated–5(experts, social workers) Ex-officio–MPs, MLAs, MLCs
Kerala	Elected–20 Special Experts–2	Elected–20-50 Experts–2	Elected–50-100 Experts–2
Tamil Nadu	Elected Determined by Government Ex-officio–MPs, MLAs	Elected–Determined by Government Ex-officio–MPs, MLAs	Elected–Determined by Government Ex-officio–MPs, MLAs

Appendix-III

Chairman

States	Nagar Panchayat			Municipality			Municipal Corporation		
	Name	*Election*	*Term*	*Name*	*Election*	*Term*	*Name*	*Election*	*Term*
Andhra Pradesh	Chairperson	Direct	Co-terminus	As in Nagar	Panchayat		Mayor	Indirect	Co-terminus
Karnataka	President	Indirect	2.5 Yrs.	President	Indirect	2.5 Yrs.	Mayor	Indirect	1 Year
Kerala	Chairman	Indirect	Co-terminus	Chairman	Indirect	Co-terminus	Mayor	Indirect	Co-terminus
Tamil Nadu	Chairman	Direct	5 Yrs.	Chairman	Direct	5 Yrs.	Mayor	Direct	5 Yrs.

Appendix-IV

Number of Functions

States	*Mandatory*		*Optional*		*Functions of Schedule XII*	
	Muncipality	*Corporation*	*Municipality*	*Corporation*	*Municipality*	*Corporation*
Andhra Pradesh	08	25	—	40	Not Clearly Mentioned	
Karnataka	26	33	38	27	Not Clearly Mentioned	
Kerala	30	30	14	14	Not Clearly Mentioned	
Tamil Nadu	24	24	11	11	All the 11 optional functions are drawn from the Schedule.	

Appendix-V

Functions

Code/States	*Andhra Pradesh*		*Karnataka*		*Kerala*	*Tamil Nadu*
	MC	*M*	*MC*	*M*		
1.	M	M	M	M	M	M
2.	M	M	M		M	M
3.	M	M	M	M	M	
4.	M	M	M	M	M	M
5.	M	M	M			M
6.	M	M	M	M	M	M
7.	M	M	M	M	M	M
8.	M		M	M		
9.	M		M		M	M
10.	M		M	M	M	M
11.	M		M	M	M	M
12.	M		M			
13.	M		M	M	M	M
14.	M		M		M	
15.	D		M	M	M	M
16.	M				M	
17.	M		M	D		M
18.	M		D	D		
19.	D		D	D		
20.	D		D	D		
21.	D		D	M		
22.	D		M	M		
23.	D		D	D	M	M
24.	D		M	D		
25.	D			D		
26.	D			D		
27.	D		M	M		
28.	D			M	M	D
29.	D		M	M		M
30.	D			D		
31.			D	D		
32.			D	D		D
33.			D	D		D
34.			D	D		D
35.			D	D		D
36.				D		
37.					M	M
38.					M	M
39.						M
40.					M	D
41.					M	D
42.					M	D
43.						D
44.						D
45.						D

M—Mandatory D—Discretionary

Kerala—The Municipalities are entrusted many special and sectoral functions.

Functional Codes

1. Street Lighting.
2. Drainage and sewerage system.
3. Sweeping, watering of roads and public places.
4. Maintenance of roads, bridges, drains etc.
5. Naming of streets and numbering of houses.
6. Water supply.
7. Registration of Statistics.
8. Boundary marks.
9. Collection, disposal, treatment of sewage and other offensive matters.
10. Regulation of burial places and disposal of unclaimed corpses.
11. Regulation of markets, slaughter houses, cattle ponds etc.
12. Reclamation of unhealthy localities, securing dangerous buildings.
13. Public vaccination and public health.
14. Preventive of infectious diseases.
15. Regulating trades.
16. Improvement of city.
17. Public parks, gardens, playgrounds, public conveniences.
18. Relief to destitutes, maintenance of asylums etc.
19. Maternity and child welfare centres.
20. Provision of milk dairies.
21. Laboratories for analysis/food adulteration.
22. Planting of trees.
23. Holding fairs, exhibitions, recreation.
24. Ambulance service.
25. Transport facilities.
26. Supply of electricity, gas.
27. Primary education.
28. Extinguishing fire/fire service.
29. Destruction of stray dogs, cattle, birds.
30. Cottage Industries.
31. Veterinary hospitals.
32. Slum improvement and upgradation.
33. Urban forestry.
34. Urban poverty alleviation.
35. Promotion of cultural, educational and aesthetic aspects.
36. Promotion of cooperative societies.
37. Licencing of catering establishments.

38. Mosquito control.
39. Regulation of sale of meat, fish etc.
40. Urban planning including town planning.
41. Regulation of land use and building construction.
42. Regulation of slaughter houses and factories.
43. Planning for economic and social development.
44. Safeguarding the interests of weaker section.
45. Cattle Pounds and Prevention of cruelty to animals.

Appendix-VI

Taxes

Taxes	*Andhra Pradesh*		*Karnataka*		*Kerala*		*Tamil Nadu*	
	Munici.	*Mun. Corp.*	*Munici.*	*Mun. Corp.*	*Munici.*	*Mun. Corp.*	*Munici.*	*Mun. Corp.*
General Purpose Tax	M	M	O	M	O	O	M	M
Water Tax	M	M	O	M	–	–	M	M
Tax on Carriages and Carts	M	–	–	–	–	–	M	M
Tax on Animals	M	M	–	–	O	O	M	M
Tax on Advertisement	O	M	O	M	O	O	M	M
Duty on Transfer of Property	O	M	O	M	O	O	M	M
Drainage Tax	M	M	O	–	–	–	–	–
Lighting Tax	M	M	O	–	–	–	O	O
Scavenging Tax	M	M	O	–	–	–	O	O
Octroi	–	M	–	–	–	–	M	M
Tax on Vehicles	–	M	O	M	O	O	–	–
Tax on Entertainments	–	O	–	–	–	–	–	–
Toll on Vehicles	–	–	O	–	–	–	–	–
Fees of Jatras	–	–	O	–	–	–	–	–
Railway Tax	–	–	–	–	–	–	–	–
Profession Tax	–	–	–	–	O	O	–	–
Tax on Servants	–	–	–	–	–	–	–	–
Pilgrim Tax	–	–	–	–	–	–	–	–
Tax on Timbers	–	–	–	–	O	O	–	–
Tax on Show	–	–	–	–	O	O	–	–
Education Tax	–	–	–	–	O	O	M	M

Appendix-VII

Ward Committees

	Andhra Pradesh	*Karnataka*	*Kerala*	*Tamil Nadu*
Members	Municipality – 5 Wards Corporation – 10 Officers	Ward Members Experts – 5 NGOs – 2 CBOs	Every ward; councillor and 50 persons nominated by Chairman out of heads of educational institutions, presidents of residential associations/area, develop., societies, representatives of industrial (Commercial) establishments/Traders/ trade unions/arts/sports games/cultural organisations doctors.3 important citizens	One or more wards, all ward members,
Chairman	Elected from amongst the members for one year.	From amongst the elected members.	Chairman Ward Councillor	1 from amongst the elected members.
Functions	Prescribed under rules.	Prescribed under rules.	Preparation and encouragement of development schemes, encouraging harmony among various groups, mobilising voluntary labour, assistance in develop., schemes, identification of beneficiaries, ensuring people's participation in voluntary activities, assisting in collection of taxes.	—
Remarks	May be constituted in towns having population less than 3 lakhs	—	Ward Committees are constituted in towns having population of one lakh and more and in towns with less than one lakh population, Ward Sabha is constituted in every ward.	—

Appendix-VIII

District Planning Committee

Andhra Pradesh	*Karnataka*	*Kerala*	*Tamil Nadu*
Not mentioned in Acts.	MPs, MLAs, Adhyaksha of Zila Panchayat, Mayor/ President besides elected members, Chief Executive officer as Secretary, Chairman—elected.	15 members—12 elected, and President of District Panchayat, 1 expert, Distt Collector, MP, MLA, Nominated member of Assembly Chairman—President of Dist. Panchayat Secretary–Collector.	MPs, Chairman of District Panchayat, Mayor or Chairman, MLAs, Elected members, Secretary—appointed by the Government Chairman–Chosen

Appendix-IX

Metropolitan Planning Committee

Andhra Pradesh	Not nominated in the Acts.
Karnataka	30-2/3 elected MPs, MLAs, MLCs, Commissioner of Development Authority—Secretary Chairman—Chosen in prescribed manner.
Kerala	10 members elected, 5 members nominated by the Government (1 Officer not below Secretary, eminent person having experience in public administration. 1 officer not below Senior Town Planner, 1 not below Superintending Engineer of PWD, 1 Officer not below Deputy Secretary, Collector of the District. Officer not below Deputy Secretary—Member Secretary.

Index